Knowledge and Explanation in History

An Introduction to the Philosophy of History

R. F. Atkinson

M

First published 1978 by
THE MACMILLAN PRESS LTD
London and Basingstoke
Associated companies in Delhi Dublin
Hong Kong Johannesburg Lagos Melbourne
New York Singapore and Tokyo

Printed in Hong Kong

British Library Cataloguing in Publication Data

Atkinson, Ronald Field
    Knowledge and explanation in history. –
    (Modern introductions to philosophy).
    1. History – Philosophy 2. History –
    Methodology
    I. Title II. Series
    901   D16

    ISBN 0–333–11208–3
    ISBN 0–333–11215–6 Pbk

Contents

Preface

The present book is a series of discussions of certain central topics, or clusters of topics, in the philosophy of history. It does not, inevitably, cover the whole subject. I have concentrated on topics about which I thought I had something to say, though I have also tried to set my remarks in context by giving an account of recent work, by both historians and philosophers, in the opening chapter.

The *content* of the book is not, except inadvertently, elementary; nor is it intended to be exclusively introductory, though I have tried to write in a way that does not presuppose prior acquaintance with philosophy. No doubt I will be found to have succeeded better in some places than in others. It is to be feared too that the difficulty and disagreeableness which laymen sometimes complain of in philosophical writing is less a matter of technical apparatus, which it is relatively easy to do without, than of direction of interest, conception of relevance, level of abstraction – all of which, being close to the essence of the subject, cannot be avoided. I hope, none the less, that I have succeeded in bringing into view some of the philosophical questions which are asked about history; and even that I have managed to outline reasonable answers to some of them. Any such answers will not be final. Philosophy does not progress by finding definitive answers; it is rather that people (sometimes) progress within it, by improving their understanding of its problems and the ways in which they arise.

I hope too that, despite the high line taken about the autonomy of philosophy at the beginning of chapter I, it will not be thought that I regard philosophising about history as necessarily more worth while than the practice of history itself. My concern is only to emphasise that it is different, and that the questions I address myself to in this book are philosophical, not historical. Obviously, as I emphasise in several places in the text, it is only because history is a distinctive and rich field of intellectual endeavour – because it is clearly valuable in itself – that it is worth philosophising about.

As regards my intellectual debts, I have tried, so far as practicable, to give references to the works I have drawn upon or reacted to. The authors from whom I believe myself to have learnt most, maybe not always the lessons they intended to teach, are Walsh, Dray and Gallie. Beyond this, I became constantly more conscious as I wrote how much of the interest there is in the subject derives from Collingwood. I do not agree with many of his pronouncements, and nobody could agree with them all; but for stimulus and illumination he is unsurpassed.

References.   A complete list of works cited will be found at the end. Where there is only one by an author, it will normally be referred to in the text by author's name and page or chapter numbers. Where there are more than one, the works will be distinguished by date, usually that of first publication in the original language. Dates of editions and translations used will be given in the list at the end, and page references will be to these.

Acknowledgements.   To my colleagues, N. J. H. Dent, R. W. Clayton and Roland Hall, who have each read the bulk of the typescript, I am indebted for many valuable suggestions. I am indebted too to Professor D. J. O'Connor, editor of the series, for his constant encouragement; to the Reader from Cornell University Press; and, not least, to Mr Derick Mirfin of Macmillan for his seemingly inexhaustible patience. Thanks are due too to Mrs Jennifer Denton, who typed a great deal of the book with exemplary accuracy.

R. F. A.

Introduction

It will, I think, be convenient to the reader for me to introduce the book by outlining the main elements in each chapter.

    i. The first section offers a preliminary account of the philosophy of history, distinguishing analytical or critical conceptions of the subject from substantive or speculative ones, but trying also to make clear that the distinction is not so absolute that there can be no interaction across it. Section 2 offers a similarly preliminary account of history, emphasising that it has itself a history, that there are different varieties of it, and that it is by no means always narrative in form. Section 3 consists of a series of brief accounts of some recent writings, by both philosophers and historians, about history. The purpose of this is to fix a few reference points by naming some of the sources of the questions considered in the remainder of the book and, more generally, to give an impression of the scope of the philosophy of history.

    ii. The aim here is to reduce doubts which have been entertained about the possibility of making meaningful and on occasion true statements about the past. Section 2 criticises the 'direct observation paradigm' of knowledge, and argues that statements about the past are not specially dependent upon memory or testimony, but can be securely established on the basis of evidence. Section 3 is devoted to the dissipation of metaphysical doubts about the reality or existence of the past. Section 4 discusses the backward and forward reference of statements apparently about a single point in time; and section 5 the difference between the bases there are for knowledge of the past and future. The chapter concludes with a consideration of whether there are special difficulties or advantages attaching to knowledge about past actions (section 6); and of the distinction between truth and probability in history (section 7).

    iii. Objectivity is the topic here. Section 1 considers the use of the term 'objective' and its opposites, 'subjective' and 'arbitrary'. Section 2 shows how objectivity worries derive from recognition of the inevitability of selection. In 3 a comparison is made between the bases of selection in history and natural science, in which connection the Popperian conception of objectivity relative to a point of view and W. H. Walsh's perspectivism are considered. In 4 suggestions that there might be an absolute basis for selection are discounted, and in 5 an attempt is made to state what the limits of objectivity in history may be.

IV. Explanation in history. The first section distinguishes three main types of account which have been given: the law theory, the rational theory, and the narrative theory; and proceeds to consider the ordinary employment of the word 'explanation', which is claimed to be wide enough to accommodate all three. In 2 there is an extended discussion of the law theory, of which the conclusion is that, although law explanations do occur in history, the emphases and implications of the theory are misleading. Rational explanations are considered in 3, their distinctness from law explanations asserted, and the variety among them emphasised, as is the distinction between rational explanation and justification. The rational theory has little more claim than the law theory to be a general account of explanation in history, though the implications of the former are more consonant with practice in political history at least, even though they are less clearly so in social and economic history. Section 4 considers the thesis that historical writings may be, so to say, explanatory in themselves. Attempts are made to indicate the criteria historical writing must meet for this claim to be plausible, and to disentangle this conception of explanation from the often associated, but much disputed assumption that historical writing is essentially narrative in form.

V. This chapter considers causation, beginning (sections 1 and 2) with a characterisation of the use of 'cause' in history, going on to the questions whether there can be particular causal connections (i.e. causal connections unsupported by universals or covering laws) in section 3, and whether there can be justifications for picking out a certain cause as the true or most fundamental one in section 4. Differences of level among explanations are considered in 5, attention being concentrated on the so-called methodological individualist thesis that the actions of human individuals have primacy as causes, and upon the collectivist, historical materialist contention that in the last analysis economic factors are dominant. Both views are rejected. The chapter concludes (section 6) with a discussion of necessity and chance, constraint and free will.

VI. This, the final chapter, deals with values. After an introductory section, the first question raised (section 2) is in what sense and to what extent history can be regarded as 'value-free'. Section 3 considers the place of moral judgements in history, disputing Lord Acton's contention that pronouncing moral verdicts on the great criminals of the past is central to the office of the historian, but not insisting that moral judgements should be excluded from history altogether. Aesthetic and religious values too are briefly considered at the end of the section. The final section, 4, is concerned not with judgements on individuals but with the feasibility of evaluating the course of history generally, i.e. with doctrines of progress and regress. It is suggested that, whilst in narrow areas over short periods and from particular points of view there could be ground for supposing to have been progress or regress, there is no sense in the notion of evaluating the historical process as a whole – the only possibility is a subjective choice between optimism and pessimism.

Philosophy and History

1. Philosophy of History

(i) It would be absurd to attempt a definitive account of philosophy of history in the first chapter: it is, after all, the subject of the whole book. Very little can be conveyed about philosophy by explicit statements, practically nothing by a few short ones at the outset. As Kant pointed out, the place for definitions is the end not the beginning of philosophy books. Even in their proper place they are rarely intelligible by themselves in isolation from everything that has led up to them. All the same, in spite of such fully justified reservations, there is still a case for some preliminary characterisation of what we shall be concerned with, an account which might fix the starting point and indicate the nature of the expedition even though it cannot fully determine the route to be followed. Everything that can be said at this early stage has to be regarded as open to revision and qualification in the light of what will come later.

Philosophers of history, at least those writing recently in English, have mainly been concerned with the significance and truth of historical statements, the possibility of objectivity, with explanation, causation and values. Their questions correspond closely to those asked in philosophy of science; indeed philosophy of history, whatever may have been the case among its first practitioners, is nowadays most commonly conceived, on the analogy of philosophy of science, as the philosophical study of a distinctive and rich field of intellectual enquiry. The questions of the philosophies of history and science are, moreover, closely related to those considered, usually in more general forms, in epistemology (theory of knowledge) and ethics (moral philosophy, philosophy of value). Nor is this overlapping and interrelatedness accidental: philosophy is one subject. It is an activity, prompted by a distinctive form of curiosity, which may be carried on in relation to a variety of subject matters – morality, art, religion, science, history, etc. – but which remains fundamentally the same activity throughout. Divisions between different 'branches' of philosophy are in the subject matter (partly determined, no doubt, by academic tradition, convenience, division of labour – for nobody can do everything): they are not intrinsic to philosophy. There may be all the difference in the world between morality, science and religion: but the philosophers of them are engaged in fundamentally the same sort of enquiry.

It follows that philosophy of history should not be carried on in isolation from other branches of philosophy. It is not in any sense vain repetition that, say, objectivity and explanation by subsumption under laws should be treated in the philosophies of both history and physics; indeed it is inevitable that they should be. It would be absurd to discuss such topics in any field without awareness of their place in others. Much confusion has arisen in philosophy of history from lack of this awareness. Philosophy needs to be explicitly comparative, otherwise there is the risk of taking as distinctive of one subject a feature common to others, or of dismissing a subject for falling short of an ideal that is nowhere attainable. History, especially in the matters of objectivity and explanation, has suffered a great deal in the latter way – sometimes, be it said, at the hands of historians as well as philosophers. For if, as is being claimed, philosophy really is one subject, practising historians, despite their relevant knowledge, cannot be guaranteed immunity from error in philosophy of history.

Why should history be singled out for philosophical consideration? In principle, no doubt, philosophical questions can be asked about anything: but there are no philosophies of sporting journalism or stamp collecting. The answer, as already suggested, must be that history is a distinctive and rich species of intellectual endeavour. On the face of it, it is an interesting subject for comparison with science, or, more exactly, with the natural and social sciences, for it must not be assumed that they are all the same. Physics, usually classical, Newtonian physics, is too often taken as the model for the natural sciences, and sometimes even for the social sciences too. History seems to resemble the natural sciences in seeking truth and explanation, but to differ from them in that the truths and explanations it seeks (or can get) are different – singular not universal truths – which raises difficulties about verifiability and significance, and, it may be, explanations in terms of purposes not laws. Comparisons and contrasts between history and some of the social sciences are more promising still; for, like history and unlike the natural sciences, they are concerned with human actions, intentions, purposes; but, like the natural sciences and probably unlike history, they seem to be seeking universal truths and explanations in terms of laws.

Somewhat more speculatively, history may be judged philosophically interesting as falling between the sciences and literature. History has on occasion been claimed to be a science – 'no more and no less'; but it has for much longer been regarded as an art, with Clio as one of the Muses. Historians tell stories, at least they all used to and many still do; and these may be valued, as are novels and plays, for the insights they offer into human character and behaviour. But with this similarity there is the enormous difference that the historian's stories, like the conclusions of scientists, purport to be true. History differs from imaginative literature in offering not truth-likeness or truth to life, but truth; not what might or could have happened, but what did.

There is not, of course, very much enlightenment to be gained from comparisons and contrasts in terms as broad as these. But there is considerable interest in attempting to clarify them and to formulate with more precision what the resemblances and differences are. The interest is philosophical, different from and wider than an interest in history as such. It is possible to interest oneself in history without asking philosophical questions about it. Philosophy of history lies outside the professional concerns of historians. But the converse is not true. A philosopher falls short as a philosopher if he refuses in principle to consider history. It is part of the task of philosophy to look at history and try to place it in relation to other fields of enquiry and concern.

(ii) The conception I am outlining of the philosophy of history is often further explicated by saying that, like the rest of philosophy, it is a 'meta-' or 'second order' study. History is the 'first order' study of past actions, events, situations: philosophy of history the study of the study of these topics. Similarly the physicist studies the transactions of atoms or sub-atomic particles; the philosopher of physics studies, not these, but certain rather general features of the way the physicist studies them. Whilst the physicist seeks to establish truths about ultimate particles and to find theoretical explanations for them, the philosopher rather enquires into what counts as evidence or explanation in physics. The same is true of moral philosophy and philosophy of religion, of which the subject matters are not academic subjects in the way physics and history are. The moralist or moral agent makes moral judgements, religious believers used to assert the existence of God and presumably still pray to Him – the philosopher, as such, does none of these things. His interest is in moral judgements and religious assertions and practices, how they could be supported or discredited, how they relate to judgements, assertions, practices of other sorts. He does not, as such, have to participate in the subjects or activities he studies.

The second order character of philosophy is the basis of the defence to the common charge that philosophers presume to meddle in other people's subjects, usually without having done the preliminary hard work – as if scientific truth could be acquired in an armchair instead of a laboratory, virtue without experience of life, salvation without prayer and fasting. Historians have been known to remark ironically that they are content with the humble task of finding out what *did* happen: not for them the more exalted philosophical task of proving that it had to happen. Professor G. R. Elton, in a similar frame of mind, complains of the irrelevance of philosophy to history: 'It [his book] embodies the assumption that the study and writing of history are justified in themselves, and reflects a suspicion that a philosophic concern with such problems as the reality of historical knowledge or the nature of historical thought only hinders the practice of history' (1967, p. *vii*). Compare p. 100, where he writes of 'serious philosophical problems involving the very question whether historical explanation . . . is possible at all. This need not concern us, except to note that what troubles the logician and the philosopher seems least to worry those even among them who have had some experience of what working among the relics of the past means.' (Cf. also J. H. Plumb, 1969, p. 104.) Elton is not simply saying that philosophers make mistakes about history, though he doubtless thinks they do; his point is rather that philosophical concerns are unimportant, if not positively harmful, to the practice of history.

Whether historians are indeed wholly proof against the seductions of philosophical curiosity does not matter. The fundamental rejoinder is rather that philosophers of history are simply not trying to do history at all, and that it is, therefore, of no necessary concern to them that their activities help, hinder or otherwise bear upon the practice of history. Conceivably historians sometimes get entangled in philosophical thickets from which philosophers might extricate them, but even if they never do there is still scope for philosophy of history. Philosophy, whatever may have been the case in the Middle Ages, is not now the handmaid of anything. Philosophers interest themselves in history for their own purposes: the instrumental value, or disvalue, of their investigations to history is wholly accidental.

Thus to assert the autonomy of philosophy is not to dispute the autonomy of history, which is presumably what Elton is mainly anxious to defend. There can be a history of everything, just as there can be a philosophy of everything. The history of philosophy is no more philosophy than the philosophy of history is history. History and philosophy are very much on a footing in respect of their autonomy and, still more, enormous scope. They are equally the outcomes of distinctive sorts of wide-ranging curiosity. Neither, from its point of view, can be placed on the map of human thought and activity: each is a way of drawing the map though, of course, each occupies a definite area on the other's map. The tension that sometimes arises between the two subjects is not, in my view, entirely accidental; it arises from each belonging to the subject matter of the other. They are not indeed the only subjects to make total claims: sociology is another. But it is perhaps surprising that historians are less often perceived as intellectually imperialistic than are philosophers and sociologists. I can only suppose that this is because historians are normally careful to confine themselves to their periods. Collectively historians are concerned with everything in its temporal aspect, but individual historians usually concentrate on very thin slices of time, whereas philosophers and sociologists frequently permit themselves opinions about everything that finds a place on their maps.

(iii) Despite what has been maintained so far it has to be admitted that a great deal of what has gone on under the title 'philosophy of history' has not been the second order study of the work of historians. Often, until recently more often (for example, in relation to the writings of Hegel, Marx, Toynbee), the phrase has referred to a study of the subject matter of history, the historical process itself. Philosophers of history, in this sense, typically aim to arrive at comprehensive views of that process as a whole. They conceive themselves as synthesising or generalising in a grand manner on the basis of detailed data supplied by more workaday historians, to whom they stand in somewhat the same relationship as do biologists, with their theory of evolution, to natural historians.

It is ambitions of this sort that have tended to give philosophy of history a bad name with the not so humble professional historian.

Plainly philosophy of history in this latter sense is very different from the second order study first described. Where the one is content to consider the ways in which historians reach their conclusions, the other uses those conclusions as foundations for new intellectual edifices. Some way of marking the distinction is needful and I will accordingly (following A. C. Danto and probably others) refer to the second order study as *analytical* philosophy of history and to the other, first order study, practised by Hegel, Marx, Toynbee, etc., as *substantive* philosophy of history. There are other terminological possibilities. Professor W. H. Walsh, for instance (1951), favours 'critical', which has overtones of Kant, and 'speculative', which is not a very polite word in philosophical English. What matters, in any event, is the distinction, not the terms used to make it. Among professional philosophers 'philosophy of history' is now most often used in the analytical sense, and this reflects the conception of philosophy generally which is most conspicuous in the English-speaking world: elsewhere the phrase is more commonly used in the substantive sense.

I have been contending that analytical philosophy of history is legitimate, inevitable, and continuous with the rest of philosophy. As such it ought to be quite inoffensive to historians. The position of the substantive variety is, however, less secure. It tends to be condemned both by analytical philosophers and by practising historians, and for much the same reason, namely, that evidential support is lacking for its sweeping generalisations. They go beyond anything that ascertainable historical facts could possibly justify, but are not the sort of assertions that could be established a priori. There is no concealing the fact that substantive philosophy of history is widely regarded with suspicion, though I do not at this stage want in any way to beg the question of its legitimacy.

(iv) The analytic/substantive distinction with regard to philosophy of history is sometimes reinforced by reference to an alleged ambiguity in the word 'history' itself. The word, it is suggested, may stand *either* for what happened or was done in the past (call this 'history$_1$') *or* for the study of it (call this 'history$_2$'). In the former sense history is the historian's subject matter, in the latter it is his study of it. Hitherto I have mainly used the word in the second sense, which is that emphasised in the *Shorter Oxford English Dictionary*, but it is easy to illustrate both senses. It is history$_1$ in such expressions as 'it happened in history', 'history began with the creation of Adam', and 'history consists of class conflicts': it is history$_2$ when we talk of writing the history of the Second World War or of history's place in the secondary school curriculum. In the phrase 'the study of history' the ambiguity remains. For most of us it will have the sense of history$_2$, study will be a matter of reading history books; but for the practising historian it will have the other sense, he is studying history$_1$ with a view to producing an account, history$_2$, of it.

'Historiography' could very conveniently be used in place of history$_2$ were it not for the fact that it has acquired a different sense, being most often used, not as equivalent to history$_2$, but for the (usually non-philosophical) study of it.

The ambiguity of 'history' rarely causes confusion. Its interest from the present point of view is only that, once it has been sorted out, it makes it possible to say that substantive philosophy of history is concerned with history$_1$, with regularities and trends in the events and actions of the past, whilst analytical philosophy of history is concerned with history$_2$. It must, no doubt, be admitted that this rates higher for neatness than as a source of real illumination.

(v) I will conclude this section with a brief consideration of one or two apparent attempts to challenge the analytical/substantive distinction in its present application. They take the form either of a repudiation of the distinction altogether or of a claim that there can be interaction across it.

Professor Michael Oakeshott, for instance, seems to take the former line. Very remarkably he dismisses the possibility of making any distinction between what really happened and our interpretation of it. For him what really happened is simply what the evidence obliges us to believe (1933, pp. 94–100). He is, however, indulging in paradox, and closer reading reveals that his true position is less extreme. In the first place, it appears that a major concern is to associate himself with the idealist repudiation of a fundamental division between idea and object, thought and thing, phenomenon and noumenon. This, though, is a perfectly general standpoint, with no more and no less relevance to history than to any other study. As such it does not compromise the history$_1$/history$_2$ distinction. It leaves room for such a distinction to be drawn with regard to history. All it requires is that it be regarded as a distinction *within* thought or phenomena and not as a distinction *between* thought and thing. Idealism does not in general seek to obliterate the distinctions of ordinary thinking; its aim is rather to put them in their supposed proper place.

The further contention, that what really happened is what the evidence obliges us to believe, is plainly false if taken at its face value. The truth, what really happened, is obviously not at all what any particular piece of evidence leads us to believe: and we may equally well fall into error as a result of making impeccable inferences from all the evidence we are able to collect. The very best we can do need not be good enough. And this remains so even though we cannot at any time do better than believe whatever it is that evidence that we take to be sufficient obliges us to believe, and even though we can never intelligibly contrast the 'truth' and what we believe. The evidence we have does not guarantee us the truth, even though our only access to the truth is via that evidence.

The French philosopher Raymond Aron, especially in the earlier part of his book, is another who seems to question the distinction between the past as it is and as it is thought to be. There is, however, a contention that is at least reasonable buried in the paradox, namely that conceptions of the past *as it really was* are shot through with interpretations not dictated by what actually happened. Once we attempt to go any way beyond the barest record of events we are bound to select and interpret in the light of preconceptions we bring to the events.

I have no doubt that over-simple conceptions of the distinction between what happened and the record or study of it, history$_1$ and history$_2$, sow much confusion in philosophy of history. They encourage both the optimistic illusion that historical truth is easy to obtain and the pessimistic counterpart that it is impossible. And over-reaction to them generates the surely absurd, but not uncommon, view that history has to be something spun out of the historian's head, with no objective reality for it to correspond or fail to correspond to. (See the next chapter.)

Employment of the history$_1$/history$_2$ and analytical/substantive distinctions does not, however, commit one to denying that there can be interaction across them. Sometimes errors of emphasis, or worse, result from this, as when exclusive interest in one area of history$_1$ leads to the thought that methods appropriate to that part of the total subject matter are characteristic of history$_2$ as a whole. Conceptions of historical method founded *either* on the study of medieval history, where evidential materials are commonly scanty, *or* on that of twentieth-century history, where they are superabundant, are equally likely to be inadequate. Other times, however, influences from one side to the other of the analytic/substantive divide are wholly natural and proper. For instance, Marxist views to the effect that a developmental pattern is discernible in the historical process as a whole (i.e. in history$_1$) cannot fail to have implications for the analysis of history$_2$. Marxists may be (I think are) mistaken in their opinions about the historical process, but, granted that they hold such opinions, they would be wrong not to recognise their implications for historical method. To the same extent the would-be purely analytical philosopher of history, anxious to confine himself to the consideration of the methods and intellectual apparatus of the practising historian, cannot avoid taking sides against or for Marxist substantive philosophy of history.

It is further the case that intentionally purely analytical study of the practice of history (history$_2$) cannot be kept totally free from contamination by the sort of general metaphysical belief that often inspires the speculative philosopher of history$_1$. This is the element of truth in P. G. Lucas's over-strong claim (1956) that the distinction between critical and speculative philosophy of history has broken down, with the result that ostensibly analytical controversies are in reality speculative or metaphysical ones transposed into the analytical key. This is liable to happen in philosophy generally. Analytical philosophers, who are not a purely twentieth-century phenomenon, may try to avoid large, vague questions about reality, God, freedom, immortality, and seek to concentrate upon analysing the assertions and arguments of physicists, psychologists, sociologists, historians, moralists, critics, or whoever it might be. But they cannot begin with totally blank minds. They are bound to have preconceptions of what does and does not make sense, what is possible and impossible; and these, though rarely brought fully to consciousness, can often after the event be seen to have shaped and influenced, if not completely determined, the course of analysis. The distinctiveness of the analytical aim does not guarantee an impeccably analytical performance.

As an illustration take the topic of explanation, than which nothing is closer to the analytical philosopher's centre of interest. Is explanation in history in terms of laws, and thus at bottom the same as explanation in the natural sciences? Or is it rather in terms of ends or purposes? Opinions here are, to say the least, liable to be influenced by, and in their turn to influence, positions on the general metaphysical issue of freedom and determinism. One who thinks, for instance, *both* that some form of determinism is true (e.g. that everything which happens comes under strictly universal laws) *and* that determinism is incompatible with free will as commonly understood, will be so much the more reluctant to recognise rational (purposive) explanations in history, or the more insistent that any he cannot avoid recognising are somehow reducible to law explanations after all.

I have made use of the conventional history$_1$/history$_2$ and substantive/analytic distinctions as a convenient way of indicating the line of enquiry to be followed in this book. I think too that it makes for clarity to understand at the outset what the distinctions are supposed to be. But, in philosophy at least, limitations of scope can never be more than provisional; and my emphasis on the distinctions is not intended to suggest that they are absolute or unbridgeable or that their importance lies beyond the possibility of doubt or controversy.

2. History

(i) As with philosophy, so with history, short definitions at the beginning are of limited value. But, once again, there is no avoiding some preliminary characterisation of our subject matter. A philosopher must demonstrate some measure of awareness of its complexities if he is to have any hope of being taken seriously. It is probable that, when philosophers disagree about history, they in fact have different sorts or aspects of it in view. Historians are too often given grounds for feeling that philosophers tend to address themselves to the problems of a subject that never was, nor could be recognised as history.

A possible starting point is the *SOED*, where history is defined as 'A written narrative constituting a continuous methodical record, in order of time, of important or public events, especially those connected with a particular country, people, individual, etc.' I do not wish to suggest that this definition is without merit; it fits the works of Herodotus and A. J. P. Taylor as well as most of those between; but it is nevertheless more instructive for the present purpose to consider ways in which it might be thought to fall short. Three, at least, come to mind. The first is that it fails to emphasise the way in which history has itself developed through time. It does nothing to conciliate those contemporary historians who feel that their subject is relatively new, something like a century younger than natural science, with its greatest achievements more likely to be found in the future than the past. Another shortcoming is its failure to register the variety of history, the way that the subject divides up, not simply by countries, peoples, periods, but into different sorts of history: political and constitutional, economic and social, cultural, intellectual, or whatever it might be. (I am not suggesting, of course, that it would be easy or possible to give a complete, systematic and universally acceptable taxonomy of history.) A third defect in the definition is its stipulation that history be narrative in form when many historians maintain that the most authentic history – pioneering, professional history – is a matter of analysis rather than narration.

I will comment on each of these points in turn.

(ii) *The history of history.*   A serious history of history would be an enormous undertaking. Few historians would be prepared to attempt it and hardly any philosophers have the knowledge and judgement even to begin. The most that can realistically be undertaken here is a brief rehearsal of some of the conventional wisdom on the subject in order to indicate the perspective in which history and its problems are usually seen.

From outside one tends to think of history as continuing from classical times to the present day; but many professional historians seem rather to think that their subject underwent a major change, comparable perhaps to the seventeenth-century revolution in natural science, around the beginning of the nineteenth century. It may even be thought that history 'proper' *began* about that time (cf. H. I. Marrou, p. 29). I am not myself competent to assess the truth or reasonableness of this view. I am conscious that, whereas philosophers are prone to emphasise discontinuities in intellectual history, historians, once they get seriously to work, are more likely to discern anticipations and underlying continuities. This seems to be happening with regard to the seventeenth-century scientific revolution and may well also happen with the nineteenth-century revolution in history. There are indeed indications of this in Professor Herbert Butterfield's *Man on His Past* (1955). But my present contention is only that there is widely thought to have been a great divide, about 1800, before which history was amateur, literary and popular, and after which it could be academic, scientific (at least in the wider, European sense of the term) and professional. The first flowering, if not literally first beginning of professional history is usually seen in the work of Leopold von Ranke, whose *History of the Latin and Teutonic Nations* came out in 1824. Elsewhere in Europe professional history was later. In England the significant date is often taken to be the appointment of William Stubbs to the Oxford chair of Modern History in 1866.

There is some danger of being unduly dismissive about pre-Rankean history. The significance of the before and after contrast is in part a function of one's conception of what matters in history. Anyone who values its literary as supposed to its scientific aspect will inevitably be inclined to rate pre-scientific history higher. More significantly, so will anyone who wants to emphasise vision and intellectual construction in historical writing, 'thought' rather than information. Benedetto Croce's coolness towards the work of Ranke himself is interesting in this connection (1938, part 2 ch. 2); as is, to come nearer home, the contrast between the views of G. R. Elton and G. Leff. The former, with fair contemporary orthodoxy, regards Clarendon, Gibbon, Macaulay as literary figures only (1967, p. 3); for him the great names in English history are F. W. Maitland and Lewis Namier – G. M. Trevelyan and even Lord Acton being dismissed as amateurs (p. 17). G. J. Renier (1950, ch. 6) takes a similar line. Leff, on the other hand (1969, pp. 127–8), feels that an historian's view of the past is in a measure an independent intellectual creation, and as such capable of outlasting the evidential materials from which it was originally fashioned. He would, consequently, still feel able to admire Gibbon and Macaulay as *historians*.

It is also important not to exaggerate the sharpness of the great divide. Unquestionably there was progress in critical standards before Ranke. In Britain, Hume, Robertson, Gibbon, in France, Voltaire, represented high points of pre-scientific history. Their works exhibited literary merit, and were exercises of high intelligence, based upon careful and critical use of printed sources, though, as there was no sustained attempt to go beyond such sources to original documents, these histories cannot be claimed to be based upon research in the modern sense. They hardly could have been for, although beginnings had been made in the collection and arrangement of source materials, a great deal still remained to be done in the nineteenth century. But in addition to, though perhaps connected with, this evidential inadequacy, eighteenth-century history is generally held to betray a defective sense of development through time, and an incapacity to deal with past periods, particularly the dark ages of barbarism and Christianity, in their own terms. This defect is no doubt not peculiar to the eighteenth century. I have seen it complained of Livy that he was incapable of thinking himself back into the life style of early republican Rome, and medieval histories or chronicles are very often held to exhibit the same fault. The historical novels of Walter Scott seem to have had a beneficial influence here, not least upon Ranke himself.

Certainly, after the eighteenth century, making the past live in its own terms became an acknowledged aim of history. It is an aim that can up to a point be realised independently of rooting history firmly in reliable source materials. Carlyle, for instance – post-romantic but pre-scientific – is still often praised for making revolutionary France live, even though his writing is criticised as impressionistic and rather tenuously related to the available evidence. Macaulay is, of course, another pre-scientific historian with a gift for producing vivid narrative. The complaint against him is less that he neglected evidence than that he was unduly partisan and prone to hindsightful judgements. He is, indeed, the archetypal Whig historian, more concerned, in Butterfield's judgement (1931), to enquire *who* was responsible for the good and bad things that have come about than to explain *how* they did so. Acton too is criticised for being readier to condemn than to explain.

The great flowering of historical study in nineteenth-century Germany came from seeds planted at Göttingen in the 1760s, when scholars began to accumulate and arrange documents (cf. Butterfield, 1955). In these early days the feeling was that Germany lagged behind France and England in historical studies, and the ambition was to equal the achievement of Hume. It is in this setting that B. G. Niebuhr, the classical historian, and Ranke himself developed. In Ranke's celebrated formulation the aim was the misleadingly modest-seeming one of presenting the past as it really was, discovering what actually happened on the basis of a systematic and comprehensive survey of existing evidence and of new evidence that could be collected. Past events were to be presented neither as good examples nor as awful warnings. Moral judgements were to be eschewed. This latter self-denying ordinance of the new history was, however, firmly, not to say violently, repudiated by Acton, the inspirer of the *Cambridge Modern History*, who was in so many other respects the leading representative of German historical thoroughness in this country (see chapter VI section 3 below). It is none the less difficult not to see indulgence by the historian in moral judgements, inevitably in accordance with his own standards, on the conduct of men and women of past times, who lived by and offended against different standards, as inconsistent with the ideal of dealing with the past in its own terms.

But this ideal, taken quite literally, is no doubt impossible of realisation. The historian is a man of his own time, writing for others of that time, very likely without cognisance of some of the information, assumptions, values of the past, and most certainly with other information, assumptions, values, that were necessarily inaccessible to the people he is writing about. The Rankean ideal, or exaggerations and misconceptions of it, produced reactions. Croce's has already been noticed. He complains, perhaps not quite fairly, that Ranke sought to write history without problems. Croce insists that the historian's task is not to chronicle what happened, not that it is even possible merely to relate without preconceptions or point of view; his task is rather to *think*, to solve problems, problems set by contemporary concerns.

In England G. M. Trevelyan represents a different sort of reaction against scientific history. His *Clio: A Muse* (1930) was directed against J. B. Bury, Acton's successor in the Cambridge chair and the originator of the celebrated dictum that history is a science, no more and no less. He was further opposed to what might be called the additive conception of historical truth as exemplified in the *Cambridge Modern History*'s parcelling out of topics among several experts. In contrast Trevelyan sought to achieve literary unity, to tell the national story with some of the verve and vividness of Macaulay, though without the latter's prejudice and partisanship. He tried too, like J. R. Green before him (*A History of the English People*, 1878–80), to give due weight to social and cultural factors in national history. There is not, of course, a necessary connection between a scientific conception of history and the idea that it should be exclusively or mainly political and constitutional, rather the reverse. And the influence of sociology and economics is very evident in the work of the true founding fathers of economic and social history in England, namely R. H. Tawney and J. Clapham, of whom the latter was notable for his systematic and careful employment of quantitative methods. There were also major, if not greater, contributions to economic and social history in France where, for instance, the enormously influential journal *Annales d'Histoire Économique et Sociale* was founded by Marc Bloch and Lucien Febvre in 1929.

(iii) *The varieties of history*.   I have been trying in the last few para-graphs to convey some impression of the development of history, though without making any claim to completeness or originality. The present, equally modest, aim is to indicate how the existence of different sorts of history – political, social, economic, etc. – may bear upon questions in the philosophy of history.

Consider, by way of illustration, the matter of objectivity in history. Why do not historians agree with one another? Why is there not steady, accumulative progress in history? Why is the history of a period rewritten every generation or so? There is, of course, the obvious human truth that historians, like other writers, are in business to make their individual voices heard. But the much more fundamental source of the trouble is that, whilst historians have to be selective in what they choose to report, there are no principles of selection clearly dictated by the nature of history itself. To be sure our dictionary definition confined history to important or public events; but there is nothing about history that determines what is important, and anyone who thinks that at any rate he knows what 'public' means should reflect on the impossibility of laying down in general terms which private matters might or might not have a bearing on the explanation and interpretation of the indisputably public. This, as will be argued in more detail in chapter III below, is the situation with regard to history in general; but once one turns to more specialised sorts of history the situation changes and criteria of selection and relevance are more closely specified. The general historian has, as such, no commitment to a view of the relative importance of, say, military and economic considerations – but the economic or military historian necessarily has. He starts work with a decision on this issue already taken; though, of course, it will remain an open question how far a specialised history can really be self-contained. Military history, in the twentieth century if not in earlier periods, presumably cannot be adequately treated without reference to economic factors; and there may reasonably be disagreement on the question how far intellectual history can be considered without reference to general social factors.

The case is much the same with regard to explanation, the most discussed topic in post-war analytical philosophy of history in English. A tidy and economical view of explanation in history is that it is, like all explanation, a matter of subsuming the event to be explained under a 'law'. This attractive doctrine does not, however, fit a good deal of historical writing very well, not least because there appears to be a serious shortage of laws for historians to appeal to even if they would. There are, no doubt, commonsense 'generalisations' about human reactions and behaviour, but even these elude formulation, with the result that their logical status and explanatory force, if any, necessarily remain obscure. But in some sorts of sufficiently specialised history there will be the possibility of employing the laws and theories of an appropriately related science. How far historical events generally can be explained in, say, economic terms is plainly disputable, and many events are considered in general histories under descriptions which do not permit economic theory even to get a grip, but the phenomena of economic history are inevitably presented under descriptions which do. I do not want to beg any of the difficult questions concerning the nature of economic explanation in particular; the point I am trying to illustrate is a perfectly general one. It applies as well to sociological descriptions and explanations, and to psychological ones too. It may, of course, be rare or impossible for a history to be so specialised that its canons of explanation are completely determined by those of the related science; such would very likely be a most unreal case, but its conceivability does at least serve to bring out the way in which the possibilities of explanation are related to and conditioned by the type of history in question.

The variety of history that is in question also has a bearing upon the relative importance of analysis and narrative in history, a topic to which we shall now turn, though not from exactly the same point of view.

(iv) *Narrative and analytical history.* This is a distinction which may not be ignored, although it is not easy to take proper account of it. It appears *both* that historians will protest if it is assumed that all history is a matter of relating events in chronological order *and* that it is at least tempting to philosophers to suppose that what is distinctive of history has some connection with narration. Indeed, as emerged above, the notion of narration may feature in conventional, dictionary definitions of 'history'.

It is not absolutely clear what the narrative/analysis distinction is to be understood to be. A possible starting point, however, might be Acton's celebrated prescription that historians should address themselves to problems rather than periods. The idea presumably is that they should not just mindlessly report what happened when, but should *think*, i.e. interpret and explain. This, though hardly controversial, is, however, plainly insufficient to mark off analytical history from narrative, since on the one hand there can be problems to which the solutions are narratives, whilst on the other even narratives cannot be constructed without the exercise of thought and interpretation, nor followed if nothing in them is explained – it is not as if it were even possible to write down, unselectively, everything which happened between two points in time. The provenance of the distinction we are concerned with is in fact rather complicated. What seems to happen is that a number of different, as it were, local distinctions are allowed to run together into a supposedly global one. The local distinctions include at least the following (the words used to mark them are very various and my choices, though I hope not eccentric, are certainly not inevitable): mere chronicle/finished history; description/interpretation and explanation; accounts of development through time/accounts of what obtains at a time (or, more succinctly, truths of succession and truths of coexistence). Additionally there is the matter of presentation: is it to be chronological or not?, popular or technical? Problems of presentation, although distinct in principle from problems concerning the nature of history, tend nevertheless to get mixed up with them. These different distinctions are then allowed to merge, superficial identifications being made between chronicle, description, truths of succession, chronological presentation, popular history, which amalgam is referred to as *narrative*, and contrasted unfavourably with another amalgam called *analysis*, an equally superficial set of identifications between finished history, interpretations and explanations, truths of coexistence, non-chronological reportage, technical or professional history. It seems to me significant that Elton (1967, ch. 3) protests against the identification of the narrative/analysis distinction with that between mere reportage and explanatory history, and I conclude from his insistence that the identification is quite common.

One thing certain is that the distinction between truths of succession and coexistence will not by itself support the differentiation of two kinds of historical writing, since truths of both sorts will be required in any at all extended account of the past. The aim may be to relate how things were at a time; but since there is no cutting an infinitesimally thin slice of the past, all width and no length, it is impossible to confine an account to how things were literally at an instant – there will always be some succession, some non-contemporaneous events. On the other side, though the prime concern may be with development through time, with the telling of a story, it will be found that this can be done only against a background situation, or at least the scene will have to be set at the beginning; it is impossible to draw a temporal line with no breadth at all. The extremes are impossible, though between them are many intermediate positions: it is , doubtless, legitimate to be more interested in succession than coexistence and vice versa. And, here as elsewhere, differences may reflect the nature of the particular phenomena under consideration as well as the interests of an historian. Social and economic affairs, for instance, may be more stable than, say, political and so the more readily lend themselves to steady state descriptions as opposed to developmental narratives.

But, for every position on the coexistence–succession spectrum, there will be the possibility of differentiating simple telling from selective, interpretative, explanatory telling. There can indeed be chronicles of one damn thing after another, but there can equally well be accounts of one damn thing alongside another. Developmental stories can, but need not, be random chronicles: accounts of a situation can be, but alas are not invariably, selective, interpretative, explanatory. There are here two independent dimensions of variation, not one only.

The writing, the presentation, of history brings in another sort of variation, again independent of the other two. There will always have to be both truths of succession and truths of coexistence, but there are different ways of trying to integrate them. A conventional way, often adopted in general national histories, is to interpolate series of scene setting, 'analytical' chapters at appropriate points in the narrative. An alternative method of presentation recommended and apparently practised by Elton (1967, ch. 3), is to weave in the analytical material, thus producing 'thickened' narrative. One can well imagine that choice of a method of presentation may be influenced as much by the nature of a particular period or what is known about it as by an historian's personal preferences.

Moreover, if there is the possibility of relating narrative and analysis differently in single books, there is also the possibility of separating them between different books. When this is done I have no doubt that the analytical works are more sophisticated than the narrative, though I incline still to insist that they are not thereby necessarily interpretative or explanatory in a higher or more meritorious degree. It seems, from the outside anyway, that a major problem in writing history is organising and keeping track of a great mass of initially not clearly related fact. One way of exercising control over facts is to arrange them in chronological order, another is to bring them under general classifications. The former is the procedure of narrative history, the latter that of analytical history, which to this limited extent follows the practice of the more descriptive reaches of natural science. (Classification is not of itself explanatory, but it is an essential preliminary to general, explanatory scientific theory.) I feel some temptation to maintain that the psychologically simpler or more primitive procedure is the chronological, even though it is difficult to fit everything into a single track narrative. If this were indeed the case, it would be possible to go on to maintain that it is only when we have mastered chronology that we are in a position to pause here and there and look around, make comparisons between different periods, classify and generalise. And this would afford an explanation of what I believe generally to be the case, namely, that analytical works, though largely innocent of chronology themselves, are really only accessible to those who have already acquired some grasp of chronology from other sources. It would explain too why analytical history appeals especially to professionals, who presumably mastered chronology long ago. Unhappily, though, it also seems clear to me that such a doctrine of the psychologically simpler is at best culturally relative, at worst of merely autobiographical significance. Claims for the primacy of narrative history can be relevantly defended only by relating them to the nature and aims of history. Elton, in his spirited defence of arguably old-fashioned political history (1970), seems to be arguing on these lines when he claims that a guiding thread of political narrative is needed to hold other sorts of history together. I am less convinced that the guiding thread must be political than that there must be a chronological guiding thread of some sort – a thought which ties in with the thesis, which will be encountered in the next section, that it is the essence of history (part of what makes history what it is) that it should locate events in space and time. A further point – which also will appear below, especially in the discussions of rational explanation in chapter IV section 3 and of methodological individualism in chapter V section 5 – is that to a significant extent historians consider events under descriptions assessible to those involved in them, as indeed they have to be considered if they are to admit of explanation in terms of the intentions and purposes of agents. I do not assume that history is exclusively concerned with such explanations, and will argue to the contrary below. The present point is simply that, in so far as events are considered under such descriptions, they tend to be resistant to classification and to subsumption under general laws. All the successful sciences have had to depart in greater or less degree from the descriptions and categorisations of common speech and life. Thus, so long as history remains reluctant to take the scientific road to more and more general classification (and it cannot go very far down this road without ceasing to satisfy the sort of curiosity it at present largely derives from), it will be forced to rely on the chronological mode of organisation.*

* In addition to works cited in the course of this section I am indebted to the following: A. Marwick, *The Nature of History* (1970); J. R. Hale, *The Evolution of British Historiography* (1967); D. Thomson, *The Aims of History* (1969).

3. Philosophers and Historians on History

(i) I shall here look at a number of mainly post-war, mainly English writings, not for the sake of producing a comprehensive survey, but rather in order to fix a few reference points. There are various ways of classifying philosophers of history, a convenient one being that of Professor W. H. Walsh (1951), who recognises two broad schools of thought, which he labels *idealist* and *positivist* respectively, though these terms have since ceased to be wholly appropriate. The former group tend to stress the autonomy of history, its distinctness from other studies; the latter to assimilate it to the natural or social sciences. 'Autonomist' and 'assimilationist' might be better terms to the extent that they avoid implying a necessary connection between views about history specifically and general philosophical positions like idealism and positivism.

Michael Oakeshott, Benedetto Croce and R. G. Collingwood, who all wrote before the war, are idealist philosophers taking the autonomist line. Karl Popper and C. J. Hempel will be the prime examples on the other side. The subsequent debate, which is the chief subject of present concern, may be taken to have begun with Hempel's rather extreme expression of the assimilationist position (1942) – for him, so far as I can see, all genuine explanation in history is logically on a par with, though generally in execution inferior to, explanation in applied natural science. It is, or aspires to be, a matter of bringing the event or situation to be explained under a scientific law or regularity, and is accordingly known as the 'covering law' or 'regularity' view of historical explanation. The next writer to be considered is P. Gardiner (1952), who attempts to make concessions to the autonomy of history, though without relinquishing the fundamentals of the assimilationist position. After him will come W. Dray (1957) and W. B. Gallie (1964), who both attack the assimilationist position in principle. I shall glance too at M. White (1965), who comes to the defence of assimilationism, and A. C. Danto (1960) and G. H. von Wright (1971), who try to take an intermediate view; or rather, especially in the case of the latter, to put the disagreement into perspective, giving some credit to both sides.

There is inevitably some distortion in thus tracing one thread through a complicated series of philosophical arguments about history. In one respect, moreover, the situation is very greatly changed since Walsh published his pioneering *Introduction* in 1951 – there is no longer a paucity of writings in English on the subject. Selectivity is consequently all the more necessary.

I shall conclude this chapter by citing some *historians'* writings about history by way of comparison and contrast with those of the philosophers.

(ii) *Idealists.* Oakeshott (1933; but see also 1962) treats history as one among several 'modes of experience' – science and practice are others – all of which, whilst entirely legitimate in their own terms, are arbitrary and abstract from the point of view of philosophy, which is conceived as an attempt to see things concretely and as a whole. The present concern is, however, only with his phenomenology of historical thinking, in which he seeks to emphasise, among other things, the *contrast* between it and science and practice. For him historical explanations are radically different from the law explanations of the sciences: 'the method of the historian is never to explain by means of generalisation but always by means of greater and more complete detail' (p. 143); and 'History accounts *for* change by means of a full account *of* change' (ibid.). As regards the distinction between history and practice his contention is that history studies the past for the sake of the past, not for the sake of the present; that it never seeks to justify present policies by reference to the past nor to read back the concerns of the present into the past. History avoids passing moral judgement on past persons and policies. In his later piece (1962) Oakeshott goes so far as to assert that what very commonly passes for history is more retrospective politics (p. 165) – a complaint which contrasts very sharply with E. A. Freeman's well-known pronouncement: 'History is past politics, and politics present history.'

Croce's opinions about history changed more than once during his life. *History as the Story of Liberty* (1938) is a latish work. In it the emphases are rather different from Oakeshott's. A major one, also prominent in Collingwood, is that history involves *thinking*, that is to say, problem solving, the framing and testing of hypotheses, and is not simply a passive chronicle of events. History cannot be disentangled from 'philosophy', which word, I believe, must here be supposed to refer to systematic thinking generally. At any rate, on this supposition, Croce's otherwise baffling *identification* of philosophy and history makes a sort of sense. His equally mysterious doctrine that history is the story of liberty – why not the story of oppression too?, one wants to ask – seems to include, if not to consist in, the idea that history is exclusively concerned with thoughtful, i.e. purposive and, as such, *free* action. This is in line with his claim that liberty is a principle of explanation in history, not simply a social or political ideal. He appears to be making the same sort of claim as does Collingwood in maintaining that the subject matter of history is actions rather than events.

The problems which the historian tries to solve are set by his present concerns. New questions are consequently continually cropping up and there is no possibility of completing the history of any period, in the way that talk of studying the past for the sake of the past, to use Oakeshott's phrase, might suggest. In spite of this, Croce condemns the passing of moral judgements on historical figures as an unwarrantable intrusion from practical life.

In Collingwood (whose *Idea of History* appeared posthumously in 1946, although it was written in the thirties) are to be found many apparent echoes of Croce, to whom he is manifestly deeply indebted, though still an independent thinker and the most considerable philosopher of history in English. Like Croce, as we have seen, he insists that there must be thought in history, being especially scornful of what he called 'scissors and paste', i.e. the piecing together of a hopefully plausible and consistent narrative by judicious selection from the 'authorities'. History is not simply following, not even critically following authorities: it is a matter of working out the truth directly from primary data by methods of its own. It is hard to resist the appeal of this robust assertion of the autonomy of history, though arguably Collingwood goes too far in his repudiation of authorities. At any rate both Renier (pp. 88–9) and Gallie (p. 18), neither of them by any means an assimilationist, contend that he fails to allow for the way in which an historian's problems typically arise from the works of his predecessors.

We have already noted Collingwood's further contention that the subject matter of history is actions as opposed to events. An action is a happening with an 'inside' or thought side to it, and the thought can in principle be recovered, indeed re-thought, by the historian. History is thus the history of thought – which does not mean what it seems to say, namely that all history is intellectual history and so about philosophy and science etc., but that historians are as such concerned with actions which, in virtue of the thought involved in them, admit of purposive or rational explanations. Scientific explanations, explanations of events by bringing them under laws, are out of place in history proper. They are at most something to fall back on when we cannot see the rationale of actions (cf. Dray, 1957, p. 138). The positivistic ideal of explanation is a poor second best for Collingwood.

In virtue of being the study of actions, history is distinguished by Collingwood from other studies of the past, for instance from geology, which 'presents us with a series of *events*, but history is not history unless it presents us with a series of *acts*' (1946, p. 115). Later on he criticises Eduard Meyer, a German historian, for holding that it is 'by custom' that history is limited to the human past, as if this were no more than an arbitrary classificatory convenience; whereas, since it is essential to history to be concerned with actions, it is necessarily limited to the human past.

It is easy to be blinded by Collingwood's confident authority to the very great implausibility of the claim that history deals only with actions. Much of what goes on in history is significantly influenced, not to say determined, by factors outside human control; by the natural environment, and the non-willed social environment too. Intentional action is but one of the influences upon what comes about. A great deal of human behaviour is, moreover, reactive and irrational or non-rational, rather than rational in the means/end sense.

Collingwood tries to neutralise such protests by conceding that the natural environment comes into history so far, but only so far, as it is reflected in human thought and hence in intentional action. (The same point could be made, but is not by Collingwood, about the given, unwilled social environment.) 'All history is the history of thought; and when an historian says that a man is in a certain situation this is the same as saying that he thinks he is in this situation. The hard facts of the situation, which it is so important for him to face, are the hard facts of the way in which he conceives the situation' (1946, p. 317). It is not the mountain range that divides two peoples, but the thought that it is unclimbable, or that there are devils, not gold, in the hills. Again, in the *Autobiography* (1939, p. 128 note), he maintains that the *effects* of the eruption of Vesuvius in AD 79 are not the concern of history, but only the *actions* the people thus affected thereafter performed.

There is here a curious mixture of exaggeration and refusal to face the obvious. It is, no doubt, all one whether the mountains really are or are only thought to be uncrossable, to the extent anyway that the people concerned cannot distinguish these two possibilities. Necessarily what people think, they think to be true; our beliefs may be false, but having them is holding them as true. And one can see how an historian, concerned to explain why people acted as they did, should be tempted to feel no obligation to distinguish the facts as they saw them from the facts as they are. It is becoming too that he should neither pride himself nor condemn them on account of developments in knowledge which have come about since their time. But it is still not literally the case that the historian can ignore the truth – what *he* takes to be the truth – about the mountains. It must make a difference whether, in the then state of technology, they were or were not unclimbable. There is, at the very least, more to explain, if the beliefs which influenced people's actions were false in ways which could have been detected at the time. And Collingwood presumably cannot have meant to suggest that beliefs that the mountains were climbable, when they were not, would lead to their actually being climbed.

Collingwood's extravagant contention that the subject matter of history is exclusively actions is supposed to help defend the autonomy of history against the natural sciences. (He would have wanted to defend it against the social sciences too, had he thought that a non-historical, 'purely causal', psychology or sociology was possible at all.) 'Historical thought, thought about rational activity, is free from the domination of natural science, and rational activity is free from the domination of nature': these two 'discoveries' might be said to be 'the same thing in different words' (1946, p. 318). History is not science, actions are not events, reasons for actions are not the same as causes of events. Though not in all respects beyond the possibility of dispute, so much is intelligible enough. The methodological moral too is unexceptionable: historians have a job of their own to do, they do not operate by courtesy of the natural and social sciences. They will, moreover, be wise, as Elton suggests (1967, p. 25), to minimise their dependence upon the controversial and rapidly changing conclusions of the social sciences in particular. Even so it is still in the last analysis unreasonable to exclude as historically irrelevant truths concerning nature and society simply because they were not represented in the consciousness of historical individuals.

Collingwood's insistence that actions involve thoughts, which can somehow be re-thought by the historians, has led some to interpret him as crediting historians with a species of intuitive insight into the minds of the dead. It cannot be denied that his phraseology occasionally lends support to this interpretation, but it is none the less beyond doubt that it was not his considered view. Not only does he always take it for granted that historians should continue to go about their business in the way everybody knows they do and must, i.e. by working from documents and other records, he actually insists that history is inferential not intuitive. He firmly repudiates the Baconian contention that history is peculiarly dependent upon memory, let alone any more recondite sort of immediate awareness of the past. Even a crystal ball if we had one, though it would presumably give us knowledge of the past, would not in his view yield *historical* knowledge (1946, p. 252). H. Fain (p. 100) expresses a similar thought when he contends that even the true recollection of an event would count as historical knowledge only if it were also supportable by evidence accessible in principle to *any* historian.

Mention was made in the previous section of another anti-positivistic pre-war work which has exerted a considerable influence, namely Aron's *Introduction to the Philosophy of History* (1938). The argument is too complex for brief description, but is generally critical of attempts to insist that all explanation must be scientific. It is further maintained that historical truth cannot be mechanically derived from the evidence, but needs rather to be constructed. The truth is not adequately characterisable as what the evidence *obliges* us to believe. We are at liberty to interpret the evidence in the light of our present preconceptions, indeed we cannot avoid doing so. The irresolvable controversies of the present are consequently projected onto the past.

Like Collingwood, Aron holds that history is concerned with the 'insides' or thought-sides of events, i.e. with (intentional) actions. From this he infers that history becomes possible only with civilisation, when individual people begin to leave clues to their thoughts. It is sometimes said by people following this line that such clues must take the shape of 'documents', but this cannot be accepted as the literal truth: inscriptions, artefacts, buildings must surely be capable of contributing, though no doubt written remains have a certain primacy. There needs to be some understanding of its language before a society can be studied historically. Without it there may be the possibility of framing some idea of a general style of life, but the characteristic interest of history goes beyond this to *what* was done or suffered by *whom* and *when*. We are interested in individual deeds, located in space and time; and, since deeds are not mere happenings, but happenings informed by thought, there must be access to those thoughts. Hence Aron's remarks that only men, not monkeys, have a history (p. 36); and that prehistoric man cannot be studied historically, but only scientifically.

In the same spirit is E. H. Carr's observation that the *mass* of the people even in medieval times belonged, like prehistoric peoples, to nature rather than history (p. 149) – a dictum which is perhaps a little surprising in view of the scientism and collectivism we shall note when his conception of history is discussed below. Similar too is Gallie's assertion that there is no history of peoples and societies which do not 'speak' to us (pp. 51–2). I cannot, however, see much reason to go along with Gallie's further contention: 'To be studied as history, a set of past human actions must be felt by members of some human group to belong to *its* past, and to be intelligible and worth understanding from the point of view of *its* present interests.' In so far as this goes beyond the tautology that people can take an *historical* interest only in what they can take an *interest* in, it seems to be false. No doubt people often direct their attention to events in the past which seem to have affinity with their present situation. Twentieth-century Germans, embattled on two fronts, turn to the story of Frederick the Great; the Britons of the 1940s to that of the Armada. But it is just not true that historical interests have to be, or are, confined in these ways. It is possible to be interested in societies with no connection with one's own, at least no connection additional to that which the writing and reading of their histories bring about.

(iii) *Positivists.* I take Popper and Hempel as representative positivists. This is possibly unfair to the former, for, although he is indubitably the recent source of the covering law theory of explanation, so vigorously developed by Hempel in relation to history, he is himself of the opinion that there is also a different sort of explanation – in terms of the 'logic of the situation', rational or purposive explanation – which he allows some prominence in history and the social sciences, even though he also insists that these studies are largely concerned with the unforeseen and unintended consequences of intentional actions. Popper's views on explanation in history and the social sciences are to be found in *The Open Society and Its Enemies* (1945), though his foundation doctrine concerning explanation in natural science goes back to *The Logic of Scientific Discovery* (1934).

For Hempel (1942) an explanation – or, to phrase it more conveniently, an explanatory argument – consists of two sorts of premises: first, a law or laws, and, secondly, an initial condition statement or set of such. From the premises a statement reporting the event to be explained can be deduced – if, that is to say, the explanation is complete. Thus the bursting of a car radiator after a frost would be explained by being deduced from premises having the shape of: (*a*) laws concerning the expansion of water as it freezes and the behaviour of metals under pressure; and (*b*) initial condition statements reporting the drop in temperature, the absence of anti-freeze in the radiator water, etc. (It is not insignificant that the premises of even such a simple explanatory argument are difficult to state with completeness, but detailed discussion will be postponed until chapter IV below.) An *explanatory* argument necessarily comes after the event it is supposed to explain. A formally similar argument preceding the event would be a *prediction*. It may consequently be claimed that there is a logical symmetry between explanation and prediction or, more strongly, that explanation is possible afterwards only in cases where prediction would have been possible beforehand – a hard doctrine for those who wish to maintain that this sort of explanation is characteristic of history, of which the events are rarely predicted in fact and not very plausibly to be held predictable in principle.

I have suggested that the Popper–Hempel view tends to assimilate history to science, but it is in fact intended to allow a measure of distinctiveness to history – the idea being that history and the sciences use the same ingredients, but for different purposes. In pure science observations are made with a view to establishing laws, in applied science such laws are used in order to make predictions: in history laws are used to explain 'observations', i.e. singular statements about what was done or happened on some past occasion. Thus what differentiates history from the sciences, including of course the social sciences, is neither subject matter nor method of reasoning, but aim and direction of interest. Whereas the scientist interests himself in the individual for the sake of establishing laws, for the historian interest in the individual is primary, and he employs laws only as a means of discovering and explaining the individual. Science, on this view, may thus be said to be concerned with the universal, history with the individual; or, to employ a grander terminology which derives from W. Windelband (see Collingwood, 1946, p. 166), science is *nomothetic*, history an *idiographic* study. Renier is making the same distinction when he asserts (p. 23) that the sciences are *theorising*, i.e. law-seeking, studies whereas history is concerned with *generalising* only. 'Generalising' is, alas, misleading in this application: it is most naturally, at least by philosophers, taken to mean 'universalising', law seeking; but this is precisely the opposite of what Renier intends. His contention is that history is essentially concerned with the individual; and he is simply trying to defend this thesis by claiming that such apparently universal statements as fall from the lips of historians are really mere generalisations, that is to say, *summaries* of singular statements about a number of individuals. (This sense of 'generalisation' is noted by P. H. Nowell-Smith, 1957.)

Something like the Popper–Hempel account of the distinctive nature of history may thus be acceptable to writers of other philosophical persuasions; but their view of historical explanation in particular invites being interpreted as the setting up of a scientistic ideal, from which the explanations actually provided in history books invariably fall short. They are never complete. Even in the simplest cases, as when a government's loss of popularity is put down to taxation increases, the 'laws' putatively involved are virtually impossible to formulate, let alone justify. Whatever the intentions of its proponents this account of historical explanation is consequently sceptical in tendency, encouraging the idea that history aims, but fails, to supply a type of explanation of which the only really satisfactory examples have to do with natural phenomena. So stern a view, as Hempel himself recognised, could hardly be accepted as the last word on explanation in history. The question is, of course, whether it is possible to modify it sufficiently to save the appearances, without in substance abandoning it altogether. Gardiner's book may be taken as trying to justify an affirmative answer to this question.

(iv) I have to confess that when I read Gardiner's *The Nature of Historical Explanation* (1952) in the year of its publication it seemed to me that it was emphasising the limitations as much as the merits of the Hempelian, covering law theory of historical explanation. Gardiner's position is in fact closer to Popper's than to Hempel's, in that he allows for the possibility of at least two sorts of explanation in history, rational or purposive as well as law explanations. He tries, moreover, to bring out the distinctiveness of the historian's interest in the past, to formulate and conciliate his likely protests against the distortions of covering law dogma. I still find it a little surprising that Gardiner should be regarded as a proponent of the covering law view, though I can see that subsequent contributions to the debate, notably Dray's, tended to emphasise the extent to which Gardiner's modifications and concessions were made within the framework of the view.

Dray, at any rate, in *Laws and Explanation in History* (1957), attacks the view in both detail and principle. He denies that a covering law is a necessary or even a sufficient condition of an historical explanation. A sociological explanation of, say, the French Revolution, in terms of a law connecting revolutions, described in general terms, with a certain sort of antecedent social situation, also generally described, would not count as historical – the detail of the actions of human individuals is essential to history. Dray even denies that causal laws are necessary or sufficient conditions of historical causal explanations. As an alternative to the covering law model of explanation he offers a 'continuous series model', the relating in detail of the antecendents of an event; and gives very great weight to rational or purposive explanations, which he differentiates more sharply than did Gardiner,who also recognised them, from law explanations. There is here a reversion to views similar to those of Oakeshott and Collingwood, but only to the extent that they relate specifically to history. There is no espousal of the general (idealist) philosophical position of these authors. The same is true of Nowell-Smith's long paper (1957).

Gallie, in his *Philosophy and the Historical Understanding* (1964), moves still further away from assimilationist conceptions of history. He welcomes Dray's rational explanation and Popper's situational logic as breaking the covering law monopoly of explanation, but is mainly concerned to argue that previous writers have got the place of explanation in history seriously out of proportion. Narrating is basic to history. Explanation, of whatever sort, is in place only as a means of making it possible to continue, or for the reader to continue to follow, the narrative when 'vision is becoming blurred or one's credulity taxed beyond patience' (p. 105). Though explanation may thus be involved at various points, sympathy is more important than generalising intelligence in following stories. Historical stories, to be sure, differ from fictional ones in being based on evidence and aspiring to be true, but history has affinities with literature as well as science.

Danto (1965) is another who gives narrative a prominent place in history, allowing that there is a sense in which narrating a train of events may be accepted as explanatory – an idea further explored in Fain's *Between Philosophy and History* (1970). Danto does not deny that there may be law explanations for some of the events in which historians interest themselves, but events can be brought under general laws only by first being brought under general descriptions, and, even supposing this done, there always remains the possibility of interesting oneself in the particularities masked by the general categorisation. History, as commonly practised, is in large measure a response to such interest.

There is always danger in highly selective history, not least when its subject matter is philosophy of history. I have picked out a few writings from a great many others because they seemed to make new points, at least in their context, and to that extent advance the discussion. But I do not claim *either* that these advances were necessarily in the direction of the truth, that there was progress in that strong sense, *or* that philosophical opinion generally followed the same line as the works selected. There were all along, and still are, stout defenders of the assimilationist position. One such is White (1965), who offers a sophisticated defence of a somewhat diluted covering law theory, especially attacking the contention that explanation in history is predominantly rational or purposive. And it would be wrong to conclude this section without mentioning von Wright's *Explanation and Understanding* (1971), in which disputes about explanation in history are seen in the context of two philosophical traditions, the Galilean causal and the Aristotelian teleological or purposive – traditions which are perennially opposed, permanent possibilities, neither of which is likely wholly to prevail.

(v) As one would expect, historians have frequently written about their subject. It is impossible to consider many, still less all such works. Reference to a few of them may, however, still be of value as a counterweight to the philosophers just considered. I have tried to select historians who are *both* prepared to make general pronouncements about their subject *and* relatively uncorrupted by philosophy. The second is the more difficult condition. Historians seem often to be inspired, or incited, by philosophical writings, and regularly evince philosophical presuppositions, which they have not always subjected to the same critical analysis as they would the historical pronouncements of their peers.

Historians do not always agree with one another. They disagree, for instance, on the question whether the past should be studied entirely for its own sake or whether present-day concerns may be brought to it. Butterfield's *The Whig Interpretation of History* (1931) is a firm, classic statement of the former view. Butterfield protests against any tendency to pick out elements in the past as responsible for the good or bad things in the present, and recommends, as a specific against this error, telling the whole story in all its details. He claims (p. 72) that such complete stories constitute historical explanations:

In the last resort the historian's explanation of what happened is not a piece of general reasoning at all. He explains the French Rev-olution by describing exactly what it was that occurred; and if at any point we need further elucidation all that he can do is to take us into greater detail, and make us see in still more definite concreteness what really did take place.

We have already encountered, possibly not coincidentally, a similar view in Oakeshott, and again in Dray. Carr, on the other hand, in his *What Is History?* (1961), by contrast emphasises the way in which the questions an historian asks are determined by his present concerns – a view already encountered in Croce. G. Leff, too, in his *History and Social Theory* (1969), puts great stress on history's being a matter of considering events in the light of their outcomes – there is, incidentally, a possible ground here for deeming contemporary history a distinctive field of study inasmuch as it is concerned with events of which the non-immediate outcomes are necessarily unknown.

No doubt historians will continue to divide on this issue, and one may suspect that the opposed positions, at least in their extreme forms, are best understood as reactions to the opposite extremes. Whig history is indeed defective for the reasons Butterfield gave, but it does not follow that it is possible literally to study the past entirely for its own sake and in its own terms. Anachronism, as Bloch remarks (1941, p. 173), is doubtless 'the most unpardonable of sins in a time science' but, as he has himself earlier observed, the historian cannot simply take over the categories of the period he studies. Unavoidably he thinks in those of his own time.

Renier, *History: Its Purpose and Method* (1950), is an historian who emphasises the importance of narrative and anticipates Gallie in insisting that explanation, the detection of causes, is not the main purpose of history, but is rather ancillary to the story-telling task. History is a story, nothing more and nothing less, of the experience of men in civilised society (ch. 2). The story has to be accurate and is told and retold from the ever-changing viewpoints of succeeding generations of historians. There may or may not be laws relating to such phenomena as wars and revolutions, but this is of no concern to the historian, whose interest is always focused on a particular war or revolution.

Carr, who was mentioned two paragraphs back, is also interesting as an exponent of the view that history is less the story of individuals than of social forces. The opposed 'bad King John view' ignores the fact that 'history is to a considerable extent a matter of numbers' (1961, p. 49), which intentionally echoes Lenin's remark that 'politics begins where the masses are'. The scope for rational or purposive interpretation in history is consequently very limited. A great deal of what happens, though it results from the purposive actions of individuals, is not purposed by anyone. (Compare Popper's contention that the main task of the social sciences is the analysis of the unintended social repercussions of intentional human actions: 1945, vol. 2 ch. 14.) There are similar emphases in Leff. Dray, on the other hand, insists that there is still scope for the 'piecemeal' explanation of gross social effects in individual rational/purposive terms.

Carr also maintains *both* that the historian brings his values to history (i.e. in determining what is important or significant) *and* that there is no point in passing moral judgements on historical figures. This latter is a manifestation partly of his anti-individualism, but partly too of a sort of positivism – history is concerned with what people *did*, not what they failed to do; it is to that extent a success story. There seems here to be a fair flavour of Butterfield's 'Whiggism' as well as some failure to take account of the evaluative import of terms like 'failure' and 'success' – but at least it is candid!

Carr, it seems, would like to believe that history is not without affinity to generalising science. Elton, on the other hand, in *The Practice of History* (1967), puts his emphasis on the study of the individual. He argues that history deals with datable events not states of affairs, though he concedes that it may be necessary to give accounts of states of affairs in order to explain the sequence of events. It is curious that states of affairs should be thus formally barred from the subject matter of history, when it is also quite plainly thought that reference to them is in fact unavoidable. Elton's aim is to differentiate history from social science: but it must be doubted whether the event/state of affairs distinction can support so heavy a load. States of affairs are surely themselves datable, with beginnings and ends in time, even if not very sharp ones. If it is datability which is important, there is no reason why states of affairs should not be accounted part of history's subject matter and not simply the setting in which it is to be found. As for sociology, even conceived as a generalising science, the claim can only be, not that it eschews mention of events, but that the events (and states) which it does mention are offered as instances of the universals it aspires to establish. By contrast in history individual events and states are not just instances but the main theme. They are mentioned in and for themselves. Dating – and placing too, of course – is important as individuating them. The idea is that historians are not, as such, interested in how *any* event, state, or whatever *of a type* is related to *any* event, state, etc. *of another type*; but in how *this* event, state, etc. is related to *that*.

Leff, up to a point, follows the same line as Elton in maintaining (1969, pp. 77, 78, 86) that no statement is historical unless it is 'time-specific', that is, unless it locates the events or situations it refers to in time. This, provided that there is due recognition of the importance of placing too, seems to me to convey what is defensible in the thesis that history is concerned solely with events. It is in line with the first of Collingwood's supposed rules of historical 'method', the rule, namely, that historical 'pictures' must be located in space and time (1946, p. 246). The other two rules are that history should be self-consistent and in accordance with the evidence. The rules are in fact clearly constitutive, not regulative as the word 'method' misleadingly suggests. They are not maxims which historians would be well advised to follow, they do not prescribe how historians should conduct their enquires; they rather define, or help to define, what is to count as history. Collingwood actually recognised this himself, when he wrote in his earlier essays on history: 'The so-called rules of the [historical] game are really the definition of what historical thinking is' (1965, p. 98). An author who was not trying to date events, to be consistent, to follow the evidence, would not be functioning as an historian; he would not even be a careless or bad historian, as would one who, for instance, neglected to check digests of documents with the originals, or to enquire whether the author of a purportedly eye-witness account could really have seen the episode he reports. He would be failing to engage in the practice of history in the sort of way that people building with cards or dominoes are failing to play the games in question.

Of the historians Leff is perhaps the most open to philosophical and sociological influences. He maintains both that history is primarily analytical and that it explains by telling in detail rather than by subsuming under generalisations. The apparently universal statements which occur in history books are to be regarded as 'summaries' of sequences of events (cf. Renier and Nowell-Smith above), as also are such apparently causal claims as 'The death of Harold led to the end of Anglo-Saxon resistance'.

Probably partly under the influence of Aron, Leff takes a view rather different from the usual of the relations between history and sociology. As we have noted these are frequently discussed on the supposition that sociology is a generalising science, history being held *either* to be distinct from it on the strength of its concern with the individual *or*, exceptionally, as in Carr, to aspire to become like it. Leff, however, sees sociology as being concerned with the typical rather than the universal, as constructing Weberian ideal types rather than seeking to establish universal laws. On the other side he somewhat qualifies the doctrine that history is concerned exclusively with the individual. Historians, forever faced with the problem of saying much in little space, have to summarise and select, and may accordingly mention individual events and states as representative or typical rather than strictly for their own sakes. They offer imaginative accounts which aim to be both concrete and typical. They aim, compatibly with the evidence, to achieve the sort of universality Aristotle allowed to poetry, though not to history. Leff is in agreement with those who emphasise the importance of 'thought' in history; but for him, as for Gallie, and somewhat differently Croce and Collingwood too, the thought is not of the generalising, 'scientific' sort.

The foregoing survey in section 3 is principally intended to illustrate the sort of views which have been expressed about history by both philosophers and historians. It emerges from it that opinions are too various to be adequately placed by reference to the gross distinction between autonomists and assimilationists with which we began. Finer distinctions which have to be taken into account include, at least, those between: (a) studying the past entirely in its own terms (Oakeshott, Butterfield) or in present day terms (Croce, Carr, Leff); (b) stressing the individual event (Oakeshott, Butterfield, Elton) or the universal law (Carr, though I suspect more a matter of precept than practice); (c) narrating (Renier, Gallie) or subsuming under laws (Hempel most conspicuously); (d) explaining in rational terms (Collingwood, Dray) or causally (Hempel, White). Even these latter distinctions are still pretty rough and insufficiently separate from one another effectively to be dealt with one at a time. They will, however, all receive further consideration below. On (a) will bear the discussion of objectivity in chapter III and of 'true' causes in chapter V, whilst that of values in chapter VI will also be relevant. Historical explanation – is it a matter of covering laws, reason and purpose, or narrating in detail? – will be the topic of chapter IV, reasons and causes that of chapter V. All these matters are universally recognised to be subjects of controversy. But the topic of the next chapter – whether it is possible in principle to make meaningful and on occasion true singular statements about the past – I think is not. Historians tend to take an affirmative answer to this theoretical question for granted, though they often emphasise that the practical difficulty of establishing the truth of certain statements may be very great, and are, if anything, readier than the philosophers to be radically sceptical about the possibility of objectivity in (inevitably selective) extended accounts of the past. The theoretical question is none the less of philosophical interest, and many of the issues involved in it are relevant to the more widely contentious matters considered later in the book.

II

Knowledge of the Past

1. The Problems

The question to be discussed in the present chapter is whether it is right to suppose, as all but a few philosophers unquestioningly do, that historical statements are generally meaningful and not infrequently known to be true. (Historical statements are, of course, only a subset of statements about the past, but many of the problems which concern the former relate to the latter too – our concern is more with puzzles deriving from pastness generally than from historicity specifically.) In what follows I shall discuss, in differing degrees of detail: the 'direct observation paradigm', i.e. the idea that direct observation is the only secure foundation for knowledge; scepticism about the 'existence' of the past and its implications for the practice of history; the similarities and differences between knowledge of the past and knowledge of the future; such special difficulties as there may be in the way of knowing about past actions; truth and probability in history.

For the earlier part of the chapter I shall have principally in mind such singular factual statements about the past as 'Caesar was killed on the steps of the Capitol'. The hope is that this will make it possible to focus on problems concerning meaning and truth which derive entirely from a statement's being about the past. The foundation of this hope is that statements, like the one just given in that they report observable events, but about the present, are widely assumed to be unproblematic, as statements involving explanations or evaluations are not. I am in this way concentrating on only one aspect of the larger question of the possibility of historical knowledge; but an important one since, if there is to be any such knowledge at all, it must *at least* be possible to establish statements like the one about Caesar. It is a necessary, though far from sufficient, condition of historical knowledge. Most historians are, it is true, very ready to take this possibility for granted. Their worries begin only in relation to extended and consequently selective and interpretative accounts of the past, containing explanations and causal analyses, and maybe evaluations too. All the same, the narrower question is undeniably prior to such wider ones, which will be discussed at length in later chapters. It is, moreover, a question about which some philosophers have made very heavy weather indeed.

It may be wondered how there could be difficulties about such familiar types of statement as 'Caesar was killed etc.'; but that there are is beyond dispute. They have pushed some authors into the sceptical position of fearing that there might, for all we know, not have been a past for statements to be about; or that, even if there had been, we lack the access to it needful for their verification. In reaction others have devised more or less fantastic accounts of historical knowledge and its objects as the only alternatives they could see to total scepticism. It has quite commonly been held that statements ostensibly about the past are really about the present (Oakeshott, 1933, p. 108; Elton, 1967, p. 9; Bloch, pp. 54-5) or even about the future in the extreme case of the early A. J. Ayer, who in 1936 failed 'to find anything excessively paradoxical in the view that propositions about the past are rules for the prediction of the "historical experience" which are commonly held to verify them' (1946, p. 102). More impressively, at least two recent authors, J. W. Meiland and L. J. Goldstein, have presented elaborate 'constructionist' or 'constitutionist' theories, which purport to make sense of history without assuming that it is about a past existing independently of it. History is to be conceived not as attempting to *discover* what happened in the past but rather as a matter of *constructing* narrative and analytical accounts in accordance with certain methodological rules, and on the basis of what would ordinarily be called evidence for what happened in the past. Meiland even goes to the length of seriously entertaining the possibility that we have no concept of the past at all.

It might be thought that the proper response to such views would have to take the form of detailed criticism (as may be found, for example, in R. J. Butler; A. C. Danto, especially chs III – VI; P. H. Nowell-Smith, 1971), plus an equally full positive account of how singular factual statements about the past may be established. In fact I shall attempt neither of these things. Not the former, because it is my contention that constructionist views are wrong less in detail than in principle – they are unnecessary, albeit skilfully worked out, solutions to a non-problem. Not the latter, because attempts to generalise about the establishment of statements about the past can hardly rise above banality. There are, it is perfectly true, interesting questions about the differential reliability of various sorts of evidence; but these are the province more of historians than of philosophers, and anyway presuppose rather than demonstrate that knowledge of the past is possible in principle. Instead of attempting these things I shall concentrate on showing: that the reasons which have led to doubt about the possibility of making statements about the past are bad ones; that we are entitled to be wholly confident of the truth of some such statements; and that they are not generally to be contrasted unfavourably with similar statements about the present, which philosophers have in the main proved less prone to doubt.

I realise that so bald a statement of intended procedure must seem pretty high-handed. My defence is: first, that it is only a programme – the time to judge whether it has been successfully carried out is at the chapter's end; second, that the justification for omitting detailed consideration of constructionist or constitutionist views is that they are themselves attempts to grapple with a very general problem. Meiland, so far as I can see, expresses no distinctive view about the ways historians do or should go about their business. Constructionism is just the thesis that *whatever* historians do is to be conceived not as discovering but as constructing the past. Goldstein, by contrast, does have distinctive opinions about historical procedure. He holds that the characteristics of historical thinking are more likely to be discerned when conclusions are being drawn from scanty evidence than when they are being supported by selections from an abundance of it. He also holds that history is not essentially narrative. But such views seem to be independent of his constitutionism, and have on occasion been adopted by writers uncommited to it.

In the third place, as regards a positive account of the establishment of statements about the past, it is the case that I do not dissent (who could?) from the platitude that this has to be on the basis of memory, testimony or 'evidence', i.e. documents or remains deemed to be connected with that for which they are evidence on the strength of general beliefs concerning what is likely to have resulted from what. On particular occasions one sort of foundation may be more important than another; and memory, it will be emphasised below, has the disadvantage of having by far the greater part of the historical past outside its range. But it is to be doubted whether any one sort of foundation can take all the weight alone. Memories admit of being checked by testimony and evidence, but manifestly memory is involved in such checking. Again testimony (second-, third-, fourth-hand, etc. memory) is often denigrated as a specially suspect basis for beliefs about the past; but, although in particular cases testimony can be checked by evidence, so much of what we believe, not just about the past but about everything, is based on testimony that it is scarcely credible that we could get along without it. The general beliefs involved in reaching conclusions from evidence are, moreover, not themselves beyond question – but it is important to recognise that such questioning would not raise doubts about the possibility of *historical* knowledge in particular. I am not in this book taking issue with universal scepticism; only with scepticism which, in so far as it questions the possibility of knowledge of the past, is specific to history. Indeed I shall at times try to counter sceptical arguments intended to be specific to history by contending that, if consistently carried through, they would rule out knowledge of present and future too. I suggested in the first chapter that philosophy of history should be conceived as a comparative enquiry, an attempt to place history in relation to other studies; and from this point of view universal scepticism, scepticism which bears on history only because it bears on everything whatever, because it fails to differentiate history from other studies, is of no concern.

There is a further preliminary matter. I shall begin my campaign against scepticism about knowledge of the past by attacking a certain conception of knowledge – the direct observation paradigm or, in Nowell-Smith's words (1971), the 'confrontation theory of knowledge' – a conception which inevitably contrasts statements about the past unfavourably with those about the present. The precise form taken by this contrast depends, however, on the way in which one conceives what have so far been referred to rather loosely simply as statements about the past. Essentially there are two ways of doing this: one, the more natural, treats statements earlier than, contemporary with and successive to the occasion referred to as different statements; the other, more artificial way involves distinguishing not so much different statements as different sorts of opportunity for verifying the same statement. I will discuss the former approach first.

It amounts to this. A statement is to be taken as a form of words employed on a given occasion (the assertion occasion, occasion$_1$) in order to make an assertion about what happens or is the case on a second occasion (the reference occasion, occasion$_2$), which may or may not be the same as occasion$_1$. When the two occasions are the same, what we have is a statement about the present; when (1) is earlier than (2), a statement about the future; and, when (1) is the later, a statement about the past. In proposing these stipulations I am inevitably *using* the notions of past, present and future in order to explain what is to be meant by statements about past, present and future; but I am not attempting an *analysis* of temporal notions. Conceived as such an analysis, the account I have offered, of temporal notions in terms of temporal notions, would be circular. Whether temporal notions admit of non-circular analysis, i.e. re-expression in non-temporal terms, is at least doubtful (cf. D. Pears; and Danto, chs IV–VI). A more hopeful task would be to show how such notions fit into our conceptual scheme, for example how they relate to action and causation; and how that scheme would be impoverished, if not destroyed, if they were not available. Even this latter enterprise would involve exceeding the scope of the present book.

A trio of past, present and future statements may be about the same thing, event or state of affairs, and they may say the same about it in the sense that if one is true or false the others must be so too. So far it seems to make no difference whether a statement is about past, present or future. But to stop here would be to ignore the significance of tenses, which serve to show, if not explicitly to assert, whether what a statement is about is past, present or future, i.e. to place the reference occasion in time relative to the assertion occasion. And, whilst such relative placing in time does not affect the truth-value of what is said about the reference occasion, it does, so to say, affect one's access to that truth-value. The direct observation paradigm of knowledge implies that we have optimum access to that of the present statement, and no more than inferior or indirect access to that of past and future statements. Statements about the past, if characterised in the way I have been describing, are certainly not the most- and are apt to be thought to be the worst-favoured members of the statement trios to which they belong.

There is, however, the other way of characterising statements still to consider. As we have seen, apart from the placing of occasion$_1$ relative to occasion$_2$, the three statements of a trio make the same assertion. The similarity can be increased by building temporal placing into the statement itself, thus producing an atemporal statement which makes

temporally absolute assertion. An initial trio, for example 'Caesar was/
is being/will be killed on the steps of the Capitol', is thus reduced into
the unity 'Caesar *is* killed . . . in 44 BC' (the month, day, hour can be
specified if desired). The 'is' has to be conceived as tenseless rather than
present. The absence of a genuinely tenseless verb form in English is
part of the reason for judging the unitarian conception of statements
about the past less natural than the trinitarian.

The supposed attraction of the unitarian approach is that it seems to
rule out the possibility of invidious comparisons (in respect of
meaningfulness and/or truth) between past and present and maybe
future statements too. (For this reason it was adopted by Ayer in 1956.)
It appears to me, however, that this makes less difference than its
proponents assume. For it remains the case that the one statement will
be encountered at different times – before, contemporary with or after
the date it contains (the reference occasion date) – and, still presuppos-
ing the direct observation paradigm, the contemporary time will
present itself as optimal for the purpose of verification. This is the basis
for the claim made above that the direct observation paradigm poses
substantially the same problem, whichever way we elect to conceive
statements about the past.

In what follows I shall defend what I have claimed to be the obvious
and correct view concerning statements about the past (namely, that
they are not as such inferior to statements about other times as regards
meaning, truth, verifiability, etc.) by attacking the direct observation
paradigm. But first a word about examples. The one so far given,
concerning the killing of Caesar, is designedly chosen as referring to an
event of a sort which would ordinarily be allowed to be witnessable – at
the right time and place of course. Many of the statements which occur
in history books unquestionably report the occurrence of events of this
kind. Equally unquestionably many do not: for example, statements to
the effect that real wages fell between 1700 and 1750 or that Britain had
passed the peak of its economic power by 1900. I do not wish to suggest
that such statements are not in any way dependent upon observation,
only that they cannot at any point in time and space literally be seen to
be true or false in the way that statements reporting such events as the
killing of Caesar apparently can. The inadequacy of the direct
observation paradigm is shown up very clearly by the occurrence,
elsewhere as well as in history, of non-(direct) observation dependent
statements. I shall, however, forbear to press this point for the time
being, and will conduct the argument as though Caesar-killing type

examples were all that there is any need to deal with. It will appear that the direct observation paradigm is incapable of coping even with such favourable examples as these.

2. Direct Observation, Memory, Testimony

As it is obvious that statements about the past cannot be established by (present) direct observation, the question to be asked is whether they are any the worse for it. One can see why it might be thought that they should be, for they may be in all other respects exactly like statements about the present which are founded in direct observation. Compare, for instance, 'It was raining yesterday' with 'It is raining now', or the above statement about the past killing of Caesar with statements which might have been made by eye-witnesses at the time.

Of course, statements about past events may be supported by evidence or testimony; and in this regard may be felt to be in no worse case than the many statements about the present reporting events or states of affairs which are spatially beyond the range of direct observation. For example, 'It is raining in the hills' (on the basis of black clouds which can be seen in the distance) or 'It is raining in London' (on the basis of a radio news bulletin). Statements about the present are not invariably founded upon direct observation, so that, even if it be thought that observation is invariably more reliable than indirect evidence (which is doubtful), it would not follow that statements about the past are necessarily less credible than those about the present. Against this, however, it may be felt that, with regard to statements about the distant, unobserved present, there is always the possibility of going to have a look, whilst there is no comparable possibility of directly checking statements about the unobservable (not just unobserved) past. This is, indeed, to forget that going to look takes time, so that what is in due course presently seen is different from what the original statement was about, which has become past: but we may nevertheless have here the reason why scepticism about the out of range present – spatial scepticism, as Danto terms it (pp. 81–2) – is less common than scepticism about the past. Hume, interestingly, notices this difference – the 'consequences of a removal in space are much inferior to those of a removal in time' (*Treatise*, book II, part III, vii, p. 429) – and offers a psychological explanation of it. It seems in fact that only philosophers can succeed in doubting whether we can have knowledge concerning what is at present beyond our observation; or are tempted to reinterpret statements about out of range entities as really about the evidence or testimony on the strength of which we make them. But normally quite unsceptical intelligences have entertained such doubts and engaged in such manoeuvres with regard to the past.

Statements about the past may seem, if possible, to be in even worse case than statements about the future. With regard to both we have to rely on evidence; direct observation is ruled out and, in the case of the future, testimony and memory too. (On the possibility of non-inferential knowledge of the future see the note at the end of section 5 below.) But there is nevertheless in principle, and sometimes in fact, the possibility of waiting to see whether a statement about the future is true or not. The picture is that statements about the here and now are in the ideal situation. Statements about the has been and the will be are inevitably worse off; but with the difference that some of the latter will improve with keeping, whilst all of the former can only deteriorate. This is a most misleading picture; if indeed it is not actually incoherent, since the stabilities and uniformities presupposed in the notion that we can establish statements about the distant present and the future by going and looking or waiting and seeing would surely support a like measure of confidence in at least some statements about the past. More generally, they call into question the direct observation paradigm itself, by raising the doubt whether direct observation is necessarily more reliable than indirect evidence, of which the indirectness is largely a matter of its dependence on the same stabilities and uniformities. Anyone who is prepared to confine his credence to statements about the literally presently observable has taken a long step towards an incredible wholesale scepticism; whilst anyone who holds back will be hard put not to allow a high degree of credibility to at least some statements about the past. But, despite the virtual impossibility of consistent adherence to it, the direct observation paradigm of knowledge has a remarkable capacity for maintaining its appeal.

Thus some who want to think better of statements about the past may be so attached to the paradigm as to be tempted to invoke memory, conceived as a species of direct engagement with the past, as a stand-in for direct observation. Such a move is, however, apt to be ineffective as a defence against the sceptic. For he will, on the one hand, readily agree that statements about the past are founded upon memory just because, on the other hand, he is prepared to maintain that memory is radically unreliable. Despite their intitial plausibility, however, both these propositions are mistaken or misleading.

Take the former first, namely that knowledge of the past is somehow specially dependent upon memory. Manifestly everyone constantly makes statements about the past on the basis of his memory. We are also, most of us, tolerant of the idea that we may need to check our recollections by indirect evidence. (This is, incidentally, the opposite of our attitude to direct observation, which we are all too likely to think needs no checking.) All the same we have to rely on our memories; and even when we are minded to check them we have rely on other memories and generally exercise our memories in so doing.

In spite of this it is, however, easy to exaggerate the extent to which our knowledge of the past is dependent on memory. In the first place, the greater part of the past is outside its scope; and in the second it would appear, perhaps paradoxically, that memory has no more to do with most knowledge of the past than with knowledge generally.

On the former point, it is manifest that memory cannot help with the enormous majority of statements about the past which refer to events and states of affairs outside any living person's memory. But this cuts two ways. One might draw the, as I think, correct moral that it would be better not to represent statements about the past as specially dependent upon memory. But the commoner reaction has been to conclude that the reliability of statements about the past depends on whether they fall within, or on how nearly they approach to, living memory.

As regards the second point, the notion that memory has some special importance for knowledge of the past probably gains undeserved credence from failure to distinguish memory's being *involved in* the establishment of a statement and a statement's being made *on the basis of* memory. Memory is involved with all statements about the past; but then it is also involved with all statements whatsoever, whether about past, present or future. Without memory we should be locked in an infinitesimal present, speechless and without thought. But most statements about the past, as well as those about the present and future, are not made on the basis of memory. Some, of course, are. Most of what I could report about what I was doing yesterday, last week, last year, would have to be. But by far the greater number of past events are outside my or anybody else's memory. Since my birth post-dated November 1918 I can remember no event of the First World War, though I can remember certain facts about it that I first accepted on evidence or testimony. Thus I remember *that* the Battle of the Somme was fought in 1916; but it is logically impossible for a man of my age to remember a battle taking place in that year and, though it is possible that I should remember the occasions on which I first heard or read about it, I in fact do not. The expression 'remember that' can be used in connection with virtually any past event which we think we know to have occurred; but it does not at all follow that the event fell within the subject's experience, nor, consequently, that claims about the past prefaced with 'remember that' are necessarily or even usually based on memory. A firm grasp of the non-necessity, not to say the rarity, of a statement about the past being based on memory is a specific against scepticism about the past arising from the notorious fallibility of memory.

So much then on the former of our sceptic's contentions. It is the one which most needs rebuttal. For it is all too easy, if one overestimates the importance of memory in the establishment of statements about the past, to go on to think that even those of them in which we have most confidence are still inferior in point of certainty to statements about the present based on observation. To the extent that we have disposed of the former, the latter sceptical contention loses its *importance*. Not that it is *untrue*. Memory unquestionably is fallible; even though the usage, less honoured in common speech than in philosophical observance, whereby one cannot be said to remember what was not so, may faintly suggest the contrary. We are all constantly driven, by our own doubts and those of others, to check our memories by indirect evidence, and most of us are sometimes forced to allow that perfectly clear and confident recollections are contrary to fact. In rejecting George IV's celebrated false claim to have fought at Waterloo, we need question neither his sincerity nor the clarity and distinctness of his recollection. Countless more scrupulous and less self-deluding people are regularly let down by their memories.

Although the root trouble with scepticism generated by recognition of the fallibility of memory is exaggeration of the role of memory, there is an additional source of error in the supposition that fallibility constitutes an absolute distinction between memory and observation. Linguistically there certainly is a difference. Whatever may be the proper use of 'remember', it is totally incorrect to speak of seeing, hearing, touching what is not there. But it is none the less the fact that we may have to check apparent observations by testimony or indirect evidence, and that on occasion we may have to disbelieve our eyes and ears. I 'see' a particular book on my shelves, I look again in order to make sure, but when I walk over to get it it is not there – there is nowhere it could have gone, nobody moved it, books do not evaporate – I could not have seen it in the first place. This sort of experience is not uncommon.

It would no doubt be wrong to suggest that memory and observation are exactly on a par. Observation may even be generally more reliable than memory; though a better way of putting it is to say of both that their reliability is relative to circumstances and thereby recognise that, contrary to common belief, there are circumstances in which observation is very unreliable, and others in which memory is pretty reliable. My present concern is, however, mainly to emphasise that even observation is not self-certifying, and that the contrary belief is a major reinforcement to scepticism concerning statements about the past. The associated view, of similarly sceptical tendency, that statements can be ordered in a scale of increasing dubiety from bedrock observational fact is equally mistaken; as is the still common assumption that information about the remembered is always superior to that about the unrememberable past, and that the earlier a period the less secure our knowledge of it – an unwarrantable notion, which has a remarkable capacity to coexist with the obviousness of the fact that more is known about some earlier periods, say in the ancient world, than certain later ones, and with the equally obvious fact that knowledge of a period may increase with the passage of time.

Hume (*Treatise*, book I, part III, xiii) cites an argument apparently based on belief in the necessary superiority of knowledge of the more recent past. Statements about the past are claimed necessarily to diminish in credibility as time goes on. First observation, then memory, then first-, second-, third-hand testimony, and so on to the point of complete incredibility. Hume, it is true, attempts a rebuttal of the argument (i.e. that, since every case of passing on testimony is very much like another, the mere multiplication of handings on need not reduce credibility); but the remarkable thing is that he seems not to contemplate the possibility that an assertion about the remote past may be founded with complete security on indirect evidence, and be in no special way dependent upon anybody's memory. In this, Hume, like many both of his own day and since, writes as if he supposed that the sole or principal source of information about the past was testimony, and that assessing the reliability of purported information was mainly a matter of judging the credibility of witnesses as authorities for the truth of their assertions.

Emphasis on memory and emphasis on testimony go hand in hand. In effect, direct observation is taken to be the ideal, living memory the next best thing, with testimony (at best second-hand memory) a poor but indispensable third. This is inevitably sceptical in tendency, and is just another manifestation of the direct observation paradigm of knowledge which, as Collingwood rightly observes (1946, p. 233), makes history impossible. The observation, memory, testimony rank order is itself exceptionable; but I want at this point rather to concentrate on disputing the assumption that history is in some way specially, and hence vulnerably, dependent upon testimony. This assumption doubtless has its origin in the fact that many historians through the ages have thought of themselves as trying to construct hopefully true stories on the basis of testimony. There is, moreover, scope for critical rigour in comparing testimonies and assessing them in the light of conceptions of the probable and possible; and the early examples of, or approaches to, 'scientific history' were mainly on these lines.

The insufficiency of such a characterisation of historical procedure may be partially obscured by the fact that the bulk of the evidence used by historians remains written material, *documents*, in fact, though this word is sometimes given an artificially wide sense (for example, by Croce, p. 114) to cover non-written evidence as well. This usage seems to be intended to draw attention to the possibility of written and non-written source materials being used in very much the same way. This, at any rate, is what the often very long discussions, more by historians than philosophers, of the use of evidence seem designed to bring out. The modern historian's attitude to his *documents* is claimed to differ radically from that of his predecessors to their *authorities*. He is concerned, certainly not solely, and perhaps not primarily, with what the documents *say*; but also with what they *show* about those who wrote and first read them, and about the situations in which they were produced. What is taken for granted in a document may be more important than anything explicitly stated. Questions which nobody at the time would have thought of asking may now be answerable. As Bloch puts it (pp. 63–4), more can be learnt from documents than their authors intended to tell. (There are similar contentions in Croce.) Knowledge of the past is thus not necessarily filtered through a series of other minds, passing with omissions and distortions from each one to its successor (cf. Bloch, p. 53). We can ourselves make direct inferences from surviving source materials, and generally check testimony in the light of non-testimonial evidence. It is thus quite untrue that the best an historian can do is to try to tell a likely story on the basis of testimony that has chanced to come down to him.

3. The 'Existence' of the Past

I have been discussing scepticism concerning statements about the past which arises from the (misleading) perception that such statements cannot be founded on direct observation or from the (largely false) belief that they are compromisingly dependent upon fallible memory. I turn now to consider another, partly independent, source of scepticism: namely the metaphysical idea that the past does not exist or is not real. (The use of 'metaphysical' in this connection is, of course, merely persuasive; and as such no more, though also no less, enlightening than Ayer's use of it (1936, p. 102) to denigrate the opposite conviction that the past is somehow real.) I say this is a 'partly independent' source because one reason why people take the view is their attachment to the direct observation paradigm; but the view can arise in other ways too. The root idea, I suppose, is that anything which actually exists must be present: merely to have existed or occurred is not to be presently existent or actual. However much one may wish to repudiate the security-sapping suspicion that the past does not exist, there seem no words available in which to do so. It is nonsense to say that the past does exist – must it not then follow that it does not?

Metaphysical worry about the reality of the past is as easy to slide into as it is hard to come to grips with. We often talk of time in spatial terms, thinking of it as a line drawn from left to right and divided into days, hours, minutes: but, so far from this leading us to think that we might be able to travel back to a real past, as some authors suggest, it has in my experience anyway the opposite effect of enforcing the thought that we cannot. We cannot, in spite of the science fiction writers, seriously think of the past as a place we could somehow visit. The past has gone forever. It is always today. But during it we encounter things which we have every reason to believe existed yesterday or earlier, or which are the effects of things which so existed. What more, one is tempted to ask, could there be in the way of opportunities for knowledge of the past? What more could be meant by the reality of the past than that are some statements about it which there is every reason to think true? (Just as a sufficient reason for accepting the existence of material objects is that we constantly accept statements about them as true.) It is not easy to improve on this short way with scepticism concerning statements about the past *generally*. There may, on the other hand, be reasonable doubt about the truth, or the possibility of establishing the truth, of particular statements. Such doubts arise from lack of sufficient evidence or the possibility of acquiring it; but perceptions of insufficiency presuppose conceptions of sufficiency, and, in the light of the conceptions with which we all operate in our non-sceptical moments, it can hardly be denied that many statements about the past are sufficiently evidenced.

Doubts concerning the reality of the past are multiply determined, and it is impossible to disentangle all the complexities in a couple of paragraphs. One important factor, I am sure, is over-generalising from the fact just adverted to that there are indeed many particular things we should like to know about the past, but do not and cannot. Another abundant source of scepticism is uncertainty about the placing of the abstract nouns 'past', 'present' and 'future' on the logico-linguistic map. Like St Augustine puzzling over time, we know very well what we mean until we are called upon to say. Then we are all too likely to babble tautologically that the past is not the present, or incoherently that it is (cf. J. Wisdom). Against such confusion the sovereign remedy is firmly to remind oneself that we all, constantly and confidently, accept and reject particular statements about the past; that commonly we can agree with one another in this, or when we cannot could specify the additional evidence that would if available settle our disagreements; that, consequently, we unquestionably know how to operate with the notion of the past even though we may be at a loss to give short, neat answers to such questions as What is the past? and Is it real?

In corroboration of this may be cited the emptiness of the sometimes drastic seeming reactions of those who have taken seriously the supposed (possible) non-existence of the past. In section 1 of this chapter were noted certain authors who have elected to maintain that history is concerned not with the past itself but only with present traces or relics of, or present evidence for, the past. In some cases the authors of such pronouncements may simply be seeking to stress that statements about the past (apart from the insignificant minority established by appeal to memory) need the support of evidence. But typically there will also be a desire to register the indirectness of such evidence, its being connectable with what it is evidence for only on the basis of general beliefs, which are not themselves established by direct observation or indeed living memories, about what leads to or comes from what. (It is forgotten here that, as already noted, most of what we consider ourselves to know about the present is similarly indirect; and that a consistent scepticism about the past would lead on to a virtually total, incredible scepticism.) Other times the motive of those who want to confine history to present evidence is entirely to avoid committing themselves to the real existence of the past. What would normally be called evidence for statements about the (past) subject matter of history, they redescribe as that subject matter itself; what would ordinarily be called the past itself, what happened or was done, they regard as some sort of intellectual construction. But this new way of talking is entirely gratuitous. Not only is it not the way we do talk, it cannot be an improvement upon it, because the view it reflects has no implications – certainly none for the practice of history – different from those of the more usual view. The supposedly shattering thought that the past may not, or does not, exist cannot amount to much, if all that need be done in order to adjust to it is to adopt an unfamiliar way of talking and make no change of practice at all.

A similar emptiness attaches to Collingwood's doctrine that under-standing what someone was doing in the past is a matter of rethinking his thought – not a similar thought, but the very same. The principal charm of this surprising idea is that it purports to furnish the historian with a subject matter – thought – which is somehow present as well as past. It does no other work: as has been remarked of other of Collingwood's doctrines, it does not imply that historians should seek to acquire views about what would ordinarily be called the past in any other than the normal manner of making inferences from evidence. The same sort of methodological emptiness, it was asserted in section I above, also attaches to the constructionist and constitutionist theories of Meiland and Goldstein.

Doubt about the reality of the past is too general to be argued against in a direct way because it extends to any premises from which one might seek to deduce its negation. But, I have been arguing, this very generality makes it insignificant, and reduces it to a pointless recom-mendation to change our normal way of speaking. To be sure, there is nothing sacrosanct about our modes of speech, which often need to change in order to accommodate new discoveries or theoretical understandings – but the alleged unreality of the past is nothing like that. On occasion the insignificance of doubt about the reality of the past is less apparent, because the generality of the doubt is disguised. This is the case with the sceptical conjecture discussed by Bertrand

Russell (1921), that the world came into existence only five minutes ago, despite all of what would in the ordinary way be considered superabundant evidence to the contrary. Perhaps this might be dismissed anyway as merely a philosopher's conceit; but this could not be said of Philip Gosse's evidently perfectly serious fundamentalist belief that the world was much younger than appeared from the fossil record (see Edmund Gosse, 1907). If, from a geological point of view, the world seemed older, it was only that God had, so to say, created a world of a particular age, just as the first man was at a particular stage of maturity when he appeared. (Renier, pp. 124–6, cites a similar speculation in Chateaubriand, 1802.) These aberrant views about the age of the world may be taken in two ways. At face value they are obviously false, as being in conflict with known truths. The present existence of anyone capable of writing or reading this chapter is, given various well established generalisations about human maturation, conclusive evidence that the world is much more than five minutes old. But if we choose to reject this obvious truth, where are we to stop? We have given up any possibility of arguing that the world is even as much as five minutes old. The figure of five is wholly arbitrary: we might just as well set ourselves to disbelieve that anything existed before the present instant. Plainly these sceptical fancies are not to be taken at face value. Their authors cannot have been ignorant of the truths with which they conflict. But they escape falsity at the high price of insignificance. They no longer, interpreted as intended by their authors, make any difference. Since God has obligingly sown the infant rocks with apparently elderly fossils, geology can go on just as if creation had not occurred. But conjectures that make no difference lack empirical, and so historical, significance.

Suppose it be granted that the idea that the past might not or does not exist has been successfully discredited. Is it not still a problem for history that we do not enjoy the sort of present direct access to it which we would need if we were to be able to verify the statements we make about it? Plainly we cannot *now* observe events in the past, even though we could have observed some of them if we had been around in the right place *then*. The statements we make about the past (though not these alone) cannot be established by direct observation, though they may be of the same sort as statements which could have been, and so may be held to have the same sort of meaning. To continue to feel that there is a general problem over the verification of statements about the past is still to be in the grip of the direct observation paradigm. History is indeed very hard to make sense of from this point of view, but the conclusion to be drawn is: so much the worse for the point of view – as Ayer's progression from more to less 'radically empiricist' analyses of statements about the past may illustrate, if not confirm. In the first edition of Ayer's *Language, Truth and Logic* (1936), as already noted, statements about the past were rules for the prediction of the 'historical experiences' which would normally be said to verify them. In the second edition (1946) a 'phenomenalist' analysis was recommended, according to which a statement about the past was a subjunctive conditional to the effect that certain observations would have been made if certain conditions had been fulfilled. Past events cannot be observed by us, but are as observable in principle as events remote in space. We could have been, though we were not, then and there. By 1950–1 Ayer had come to hold that the meaning of a statement about the past is not the evidence that any particular person has for it, but the best evidence that could conceivably be had. Further, he denied that there was properly speaking a set of statements about the past, a point which he repeats in the *Problem of Knowledge* (1956). This is, in effect, to move from the first to the second and less natural of the ways of conceiving statements about the past which were distinguished in the first section of this chapter. As was there argued, it does not eliminate the problems presented for statements about the past by the direct observation paradigm. The present point of interest is, however, that Ayer proved in the event readier to modify his views about meaning and verification than to insist on radical reinterpretations of statements about the past. In this, it is the contention of the present chapter, he was surely right. That there is a past about which true statements can be and often have been made is a datum; something more solid than any theory of speculation that might be thought to conflict with it. It is something that there is no genuine possibility of effectively questioning.

4. *Referring to a Point in Time*

I have written so far in this chapter as though a simple, sharp distinction could be drawn between statements about the past and about the present, assuming that the exemplary statement about the killing of Caesar was entirely about a single point in past time and about an event which was, in the right place, totally observable at that time. Such assumptions are not uncommon in discussions of historical statements, and are important in the generation of sceptical doubts about the possibility of historical knowledge. But, as Danto usefully emphasises (especially ch. VIII), such assumptions are also highly questionable. Descriptions ostensibly of the present may have backward reference, as when we report bruises and scars, booms and slumps, victories and defeats. Some of the backward implications are logical – it is analytic that a wound precedes a scar – others causal – Stonehenge could not have been constructed prior to the development of certain techniques and a social structure capable of supporting them. Similarly, in order for Caesar to be around to be killed, a great number of logical and causal antecedent conditions had to have been fulfilled. Radical scepticism about statements about the past would thus infect a good deal of what is ordinarily thought of as observation-based knowledge of the present, and thus be a long step in the direction of total scepticism. Correspondingly, statements ostensibly about a point in past time may have forward implications. For the maltreatment of Caesar to count as killing it is logically necessary that he did not subsequently engage in sustained spontaneous movement; and, as regards causally necessary consequents, Mark Antony's celebrated oration would not have taken the form it did if Caesar had not died. Even the best placed and most sharp-sighted eye-witness may be unable to distinguish an assassination from an assassination attempt; there may *be* no difference to observe at the point in time. Again, it may be said, for instance, that the fall of the Bastille was the beginning of the French Revolution, the assassination at Sarajevo the occasion of the First World War; but the former statement's truth is contingent upon events subsequent to 1789, the latter's upon events following 1914 – indeed it did not become possible to speak of the First World War until after 1939. Accounts of what happened at a time in the past are thus liable to have built into them elements which became available only at a later time. There seems to be no definite limit to the new elements which can come in as time moves on.

These considerations tell against attempts sharply to distinguish statements about past and present on the ground that the latter can be based on direct observation whilst the former cannot. A great deal of what is reported about what counts as the present is not in full directly observable. The bruise may seem to be, if not the blow; but it would not be a bruise if it had not been for the preceding blow. Much of what is reported of the past could not at the time have been directly observed. To this extent we are not clearly in worse case as regards knowledge acquisition than those alive in the past. There are, indeed, events which, under certain descriptions, could have been witnessed by them but not by us; but we, for our part, may truly apply to events descriptions under which they could not be witnessed by them.

Another implication, also drawn by Danto, is that the whole truth about any period in the past can never be told, that history is essentially incompletable. He has two reasons for this. One, not relevant in the present connection, is that history is concerned only with significant events, which significance is an extra-historical affair. The other reason, which is here relevant, is that there can be no limit to the forward reference of statements about the past. Consequently there will endlessly be the possibility of new truths about any period in the past, truths new in the strong sense that they could not justifiably have been asserted at any earlier time. An impressive example of Danto's is: 'Aristarchus anticipated in 270 BC the theory Copernicus published in AD 1543.' A complete account of the past would presuppose a complete account of the future, which is impossible.

Danto here formulates very neatly one reason why history books may need to be rewritten every generation or so. But care must be taken to avoid exaggeration. The new truths about times past, which continually become available, patently owe their novelty to their not being concerned solely with the times in question. Nothing that has been demonstrated about the incompletability of history excludes the possibility of there being descriptions of events and situations over a short period, if not literally a point in time, under which the whole truth, at some level of generality, can finally be told. Indeed the view I have been considering is essentially a variation on the not unfamiliar theme that only rather 'brute' facts can be definitively established, and that even they are indefinitely open to new comparisons and connections, new interpretations in the light of subsequent events and the changing interests of historians.

Additionally one must be careful not to make too much of the contention that there can be no statements, at least none that are candidates for inclusion in history books, which refer to a single point in time. In particular it is not relatable in a simple way to two, apparently mutually opposed, contentions which are regularly encountered in writings about history. One of these can be expressed as the claim that history is a matter of considering events in the light of their outcomes (Aron, pp. 129–36 and Leff, 1969, p. 3): the other is the claim that history is concerned with the past in and for itself, with the past 'as it really was', from its point of view not ours – in addition to writers cited in chapter 1 section 3 above, see Elton (1967, pp. 48–9), who appears to think that hindsight is actually a disadvantage to an historian. It is tempting, but I think mistaken, *either* to suppose the former claim to be a mere extension of the point that forward reference cannot be excluded from a statement about the past, *or* to suppose the latter to be inconsistent with it. The opposed claims seem in fact to be better regarded not as partial specifications of the nature of history but rather as expressions of different attitudes and directions of interest *within* history – attitudes and interests between which there is bound to be tension, but both of which, except conceivably at the extremes, are perfectly legitimate. (Compare Leff, 1969, ch. 11, part i, who writes of an 'antinomy' in this connection.) The so-called Whig interpretation of history, diagnosed by Butterfield (1931), is one, no doubt unacceptable, extreme. Close to it is the view that contemporary history is impossible because the outcomes of present events are not known. The idea that an historian can and should report events entirely under descriptions that were available to participants in the reference occasion is the other extreme. At particular stages of historical enquiry – or argument (cf. P. Geyl, p. 70) – it can be found enlightening to make a move in the direction of one or other extreme. Namier, as I understand it, moved in one direction; generalising, social-science-minded historians, who include Carr if his practice matches his precepts, want to move the other way. The rights and wrongs of such divergencies are outside the competence of the philosopher of history. His job is to frame a conception of history that leaves room for both.

5. History and Prophecy

Most historical statements rest on evidence rather than memory or testimony; evidence from which inferences are drawn in accordance with generalisations, which themselves may, in principle at least, range from scientific laws and theories at one end of the scale to mere commonsense beliefs and assumptions about what is usually the case in human nature and society at the other. From this it might appear that knowledge of the past is on exactly the same footing as knowledge of the future. In both cases there is inference on the basis of generalisations: in history, backwards; in prophecy, 'futurology', or whatever else we may call it, forwards. I have been trying to dispel illusions that inferential knowledge is somehow defective because of its indirectness. But I would have succeeded too well if the outcome were that there is no difference at all between knowledge of the past and knowledge of the future. What more compelling *reductio ad absurdum* could there be?

It would indeed be absurd to deny that there is any difference at all; but the difference must not be exaggerated either. It is not, for instance, literally true that all our convictions about the future are less securely based than any about the past. The boring, forgettable truth is that we have better grounds for believing some things about the future than many about the past. The *Nautical Almanac* contains a higher proportion of indisputable truths than any history book. All the same, it remains the case that it is impossible to parallel for the future, especially the remoter future, the very detailed knowledge we enjoy of some tracts of the human past. This is a datum, which any account of historical statements has to come to terms with.

One way of trying to avoid the *reductio* is to exploit the distinction some writers have drawn between two sorts of ground there may be for knowledge by suggesting that the grounds are differentially important with regard to knowledge of past and future respectively. Dray, for instance (1957, p. 81), distinguishes between filling in the gaps in historical narratives from 'theory' and from 'evidence' – it is the difference between, for example, supposing that in a period of inflation pensioners *must have* suffered a decline in living standards (because this generally happens as a result of inflation) and concluding from, say, the records of the supplementary benefit offices that pensioners *did* suffer in fact. There is no implication that one sort of ground is necessarily better than the other. Economic theory may be bad and the records good, or vice versa. Danto (p. 125) makes a similar distinction between *documentary* and *conceptual* evidence: I have no wish to accept the rationalistic connotations of *conceptual*, both sorts of ground are empirical, and will therefore use *nomological* (law-based) instead. Such a distinction, if it could be made out, would open up the prospect of holding that, whereas there may be both documentary and nomological evidence about the past, for the future there can be nomological evidence only. The thought is this: we may have, as we often say, general grounds for believing something about the past, for example that the present militancy of a trade union reflects previous bitter struggles, and *additionally* may be able to turn up documentary evidence of actual struggles in old newspapers, court records and the like; but about the future general grounds, for example that present conflict will lead to greater militancy in future, are all it is ever possible to have.

A possible further example is this: It might be held on general meteorological grounds that the Arctic heats up and cools down in a long-term cyclical manner, and further, on the basis of a generalisation to the effect that subsistence communities tend to be found on the margins of the habitable world, that there will have been farming– fishing communities on presently uninhabited stretches of the Green– land coast. This is nomological evidence, and there could be exactly the same sort of grounds for predicting that such communities will settle there again in, say, the twenty-third century. But there could be documentary evidence, records of land transactions, population re– cords, tombstones, traces of buildings, etc. only for the past com– munities, not for the future ones.

Although it is thus not difficult to illustrate the documentary/ nomological distinction with selected examples, the question arises whether it is of the right sort to take the weight it is desired to put upon it. In one respect, at least, examples tend to be reported in question-begging terms – items of documentary evidence are frequently pre– sented under descriptions which analytically preclude their being evidence for future events or situations. Traces necessarily are of the past, as are relics, records and remains. To this extent there manifestly cannot be documentary evidence concerning the future. But to the same extent the documentary/nomological distinction is logically too close to the knowledge of the past/knowledge of the future distinction to afford it independent support in the way hoped. It may be that our question begging, though humanly inevitable usage, simply reflects the fact that there is documentary evidence only for the past: but documentary evidence has yet to be characterised in a way that allows any such fact to be established – established, that is, as a contingent fact.

I can well imagine its being argued that the illustrations given fail to establish any *logical* difference between prediction and retrodiction, assertions about the future and about the past. In either case it is a matter of making inferences from particulars in accordance with generalisations. In each case the 'evidence', if the word can properly be used to cover the whole basis of an inference (normally it would be used for the particulars alone), must include both particulars and general– isations. In retrodiction, particulars (documentary evidence) cannot serve alone: in prediction, generalisations by themselves are insufficient, whatever may be suggested to the contrary by the doctrine that knowledge of the future is entirely nomologically based. If this is correct, there would seem to be no difference in principle between the bases for knowledge of the past and of the future. (See the note at the end of this section.) And it must be correct – so far as it goes. At an appropriate level of generality, a level congenial to many logicians and philosophers of science, there is no difference. Against this one may, however, reflect that, at this level, it is impossible to do justice to the distinctiveness of historical enquiry. Additionally one can report such differences as there in fact are between the bases of our knowledge and belief about the past and about the future, and hope that it will be recognised that the differences add up to a sufficient distinction. The main difference seems in fact to be that using what has been called documentary evidence is a matter of employing commonsense generalisations to make inferences from very particular items of information; whereas using nomological evidence is rather a matter of employing would-be scientific generalisations (purported laws) to make inferences from rather general items of information. The two sorts of inference have characteristically opposite virtues and defects. *On the one hand*, documentary inference will yield detailed conclusions, of which the solidity will be eroded by the imprecision, uncertainty of scope, tolerance of exceptions, exhibited by commonsense generalisations. Though such detailed conclusions will relate mainly to the past, they will not do so exclusively; small-scale, short-term predictions – based on the sort of intentions and projects that are likely to be carried out in certain settings – will be possible too. Nomological inference, *on the other hand*, ought to yield rather general conclusions with a high degree of certainty, subject, no doubt, to a variety of other things remaining equal. That we do not in fact enjoy very much in the way of such knowledge, about either the human past or the human future, presumably reflects the present shortage of well established scientific generalisations about human affairs. I am not sure, however, that this is the whole story. As things are, there is little doubt that historians are more concerned with the detail of what *did* happen or was done than with the outline of what *must have* happened. On the reason for this there may be differences of opinion. One view may be that, realistically, it is all that they can at present hope to get. Another is that the historian's concern for detail reflects a particular direction of interest, which would remain even if the social sciences developed way beyond their present level. My personal inclination is towards the latter view: that there is a permanent place for history, very much as it now is, on the map of human enquiry; that, in short, history is autonomous, neither a precursor to nor a primitive form of social science.

In taking this pessimistic view of the present achievements of the social sciences (and hence of the prospects of nomological 'history', let alone futurology), I do not intend to deny that historians may on occasion employ unquestionably scientific laws, for example in the radio-carbon dating of artefacts, in working out past climatic conditions, the mortality rates in past epidemics, and the like. It is, I am afraid, merely dogmatic to insist, as is sometimes done, that such activity is merely 'ancillary' to history proper, a matter of establishing the framework, chronological, geographical or whatever it might be, within which genuinely historical investigation takes place. Historians, moreover, differ in the extent to which they are prepared to be beholden to the sciences, particularly the social sciences. The situation is complicated; but, among other things, it must reflect different estimates of the achievements of the social sciences, differing degrees of reluctance or willingness to depend on the findings of subjects in which the historian can hardly hope to become expert himself, and no doubt different emphases among historians in their conceptions of the aims of history. Philosophical commentators are unavoidably apt to focus on lines of demarcation between studies; but practitioners are not obliged to follow suit, and, fortunately, not infrequently avoid defensive separatism.

NOTE

Non-inferential knowledge of the future. I have been considering the possibility that there might be no difference of principle between knowledge of the past and knowledge of the future on the ground that both are inferential. I had, however, earlier discussed the claim of memory to be a source of direct awareness of (for each of us a small portion of) the past; and I might be taken, by omission, to be excluding the possibility of non-inferential knowledge of the future. One need not go so far as to allow for clairvoyance and precognition; there is the more humdrum possibility of what is sometimes called 'intentional knowledge' of the future. That is to say, there are occasions when we quite properly make claims about the future, not on the basis of data and generalisations, but on the basis of our immediate knowledge of our own intentions. I do not deny that we may do this, nor that it is linguistically proper to use 'know' in this connection, any more than it is improper to use it on the basis of memory. I would, however, insist, but perhaps no one would want to deny, that in *both* cases sincere and antecedently reasonable knowledge claims may have to be rejected on the basis of inferential knowledge. I 'remember' having marmalade at breakfast, and say I know I did; but I cannot have done if there was no marmalade in the house, and consequently no matter how vivid and compelling my recollections, I cannot know nor strictly remember that I did. Similarly, I may quite properly claim that I will get a letter to the post tomorrow on the basis of my firm intention to do so; but the very obvious fact remains that a great many contingencies may, if they come about, prevent my doing so. And, if they do, it will follow that I did not know after all.

6. Past Actions

At the beginning of the present chapter it was noticed that much of the projected discussion would not be specific to historical statements as opposed to statements about the past generally. It is time now to enquire whether there may be problems specific to at any rate one very common type of historical statement, namely, those about past actions. We have found reason to disagree with the view that history is exclusively about actions; but that they form an important part of its subject matter nobody could deny.

There are philosophical problems about actions and action reports, and solutions adopted may affect the situation with regard to past actions. If, for instance, it were to be thought that very special authority attaches to an agent's avowal of his intention, then there would be a difficulty for history in that explicit avowals are not regularly recorded. Again, there would seem to be a further difficulty for history in the adoption of a radically dualist line about other minds, according to which conclusions about other people's thoughts, feelings, intentions and motives could be reached only by shaky inference from their overt behaviour on the basis of a presumed, but uncorroboratable, analogy between them and us. By contrast, there would be less difficulty in a monistic position, like that of Gilbert Ryle (1949), according to which statements about people's mental states and operations are to be construed not as categorical statements about their supposedly non-physical minds but as dispositional statements about tendencies and capacities manifested or manifestable in their behaviour. The issues here, in the philosophy of mind, are too large to be adequately discussed, let alone settled, in passing in a book about history. It is, all the same, desirable to record their bearing on present concerns; partly as an illustration of the way philosophical problems connect with one another, and partly (though this is not wholly a different point) by way of illustrating the way in which worries apparently specific to history may be aspects of very general philosophical anxieties. It should be

added that it does not follow from the existence of such inter-
relationships that the proper order of enquiry is first to settle the general
question, and then apply the solution to the special case of history, or
whatever it might be. Philosophy cannot be applied in this way. There
is no way of getting the general theory right in advance of considering it
in its various 'applications'. If a general theory makes nonsense of some
general species of human enquiry, which history surely is, so much the
worse for it. Far from concluding from, say, a dualist theory of mind and
body to the impossibility of establishing truths about past actions, we
should do much better to argue the other way, i.e. *from* the possibility of
making true statements about past actions *to* some theory of mind and
body which can accommodate it.

I am arguing, or asserting, that there is no substantial new ground for
doubting the possibility of historical truth in the fact that some
historical statements are about actions. It is necessary also, at this point,
to look at the opposite possibility that there is actually an advantage
here for the historian in that he can imaginatively identify with past
people, sharing their 'thoughts' (intentions), as Collingwood allows, or
even their feelings, which he denies. To this possibility the orthodox
positivistic reaction, exemplified in for instance Hempel (1942), is that
it is of concern to the psychology or phenomenology rather than to the
philosophy of history. It is of no concern to philosophers how an
historian arrives at his conjectures or hypotheses; all that matters is
whether he can verify them, which must of course be in the light of
evidence as assessed by public criteria. Good luck to any historian who
has the knack of hitting upon truths without honest toil; but it still
requires toil to establish that the truths thus hit upon are indeed true,
and it is the routines of verification, not the delights of discovery, that
fall within the province of philosophy.

I am sure that this reaction is essentially correct, even though it may
take an unduly narrow view of philosophy. Nor (as was seen in chapter 1
section 3 above) does Collingwood himself really take a different view.
He could not be further from maintaining that historians should or can
operate by insight as opposed to the·assessment of evidence. His
fundamental contention is only that historians should 'think', i.e. frame
and test hypotheses, pose problems and try to solve them, and not
content themselves with passive chronicle. This no one can gainsay:
but, in view of the way he sometimes expresses himself, it is hardly
surprising that Collingwood has often been misunderstood. Additionally, the idea that imaginative identification and empathy play a

great part in history may gain support from a misunderstanding of the unquestionably correct contention that historians need to be imaginative. Of course they do. But, as Leff very pertinently observes (1969, p. 114), imagination is exercised more significantly in assessing evidence, or in working out what new sorts of evidence might be exploited, than in trying to identify oneself with historical figures. This point in some degree resembles one made earlier about memory. Historians have to exercise both their memories and their imaginations, but not in ways radically different from those required in other studies. History, like all other studies, uses, but is not *specially* dependent upon, memory and imagination.

As was reported in chapter 1 section 3 above, however, there is one recent philosophical writer, Gallie, who does suggest that a special, non-scientific sort of imaginative intelligence is exercised in following historical and other stories. The capacity to switch constantly between an observer's and an agent's point of view is needful; and we have to be able to see the actions in a story as intelligible from our own agent's point of view before we can feel that we understand it. It is, as we have argued, by no means certain that history is exclusively a matter of telling stories; but some of it is, and there is no cause to quarrel with Gallie's claims about telling and understanding stories. Even when all 'how possibly' (necessary condition) and 'why necessarily' (sufficient condition) explanations have been given, we may feel that we still do not understand a story, either because of sheer lack of concrete human detail, or because we are without the relevant human experience to interpret it. It is no doubt in response to such a demand for human intelligibility that some historians make it a major aim to convey how things presented themselves to participants at the time; and that more are given to adorning their narratives with what often seems to be rather randomly selected concrete human detail. Nor is there anything exceptionable in this, provided only that the pictures thus vividly painted are adequately evidenced. It is, however, here that there is some danger in stresssing resemblances between novels and even narrative history, in holding with Dray (1957, ch. 5) that history is logically continuous with literature rather than science. A novelist may aim at human credibility, truth to life, and so fail if he does not attain it: but the more significant failure in an historian would be to supply it in the absence of supporting evidence. He must never attribute to his characters more in the way of motive and intention than the evidence warrants. This must mean that the history of some periods cannot be made intelligible in human (agent) terms. There is room for a concept of *historical* fiction, which differs from fiction generally in conforming to the requirement never to go against, though maybe beyond, what the evidence justifies. The writer of such fiction may draw upon historical scholarship, and no doubt needs the scholarly virtues. But the fact remains that historical fiction, even if conceived in the somewhat austere way laid down, and even though it may be richer and humanly more interesting, is still not history (cf. Fain, p. 173).

7. *Truth and Probability*

The topic of the present chapter has been the significance of statements about the past, mainly singular statements, with universals (laws) and sequences of statements (narratives etc.) left for later. (Narratives will receive some discussion in the next chapter, universals in the one after that.) Before moving on, however, it will be well to consider the distinction between truth and probability. There is a gap here in that significance has so far been contemplated in the shape of aptness for truth or falsity. I have concentrated on arguing for, or disputing objections to, the possibility of establishing statements about the past, of showing that some such statements can be true. To this extent I may seem to have begged the question against any idea that history is pre-eminently the sphere of probability as opposed to truth, of reasonable opinion not knowledge and proof.

There is something in this idea, though it can mislead if pushed too far. There is very much in history that can be no more than probable opinion. But one does not deny this by asking, as has been done in the present chapter, whether truth is achievable in principle. No doubt, as recognised above, many of the statements historians think it worthwhile to assert will be in some degree doubtful; but this does not alter the fact that some can be true. We have, moreover, been dealing with singular statements, reports of 'simple facts'; and, whilst it has frequently been maintained that apparently simple facts may turn out to be complex and dubious (cf. C. L. Becker, 1955), and disputed whether there is a level of absolutely bedrock fact or a sharp distinction between fact and interpretation, there are few writers who will seriously maintain that there are no established facts. The problems concerning objectivity, which are to be discussed in the next chapter, arise after this point has been conceded.

We are then, already committed to holding that a truth/probability distinction can be drawn *within* the class of historical statements, not solely *between* that class and others. Misplacing the distinction will contribute to the remarkably seductive illusion that there is something specially dubious about historical statements as such. But how is it to be shown that the distinction rightly belongs within historical statements? One may reflect that the features which lead people to think that historical statements can never achieve more than probability are features shared with empirical statements generally: i.e. that they are not necessarily true; that, however well evidenced, their falsity is conceivable; that they can always be denied without self-contradiction. It is by no means happy to hold that empirical statements generally can on these accounts never be more than probable, though the notion is central in a long rationalist tradition going back to Plato. But, whatever may be the rights and wrongs of philosophical rationalism, it is disastrous to run together the two ideas that historical statements are capable only of probability on the basis that they are empirical (i.e. in contrast with necessary statements) and that they are merely probable in contrast with some other class of empirical statements, say, statements about the present. In so far as one's concern is with the status of historical statements within the class of empirical statements – with differences among statements about past, present and future, between scientific and historical statements – there is no call to be troubled by any alleged deficiency historical statements share with all empirical statements whatever. The trend of the discussion throughout this chapter has been against suggestions that historical statements need to be sharply distinguished from, and hence perhaps represented as radically more suspicious than, all other empirical statements.

Further support for drawing a truth/probability distinction within history comes from the nature of probability itself. He would be a bold man who undertook to tell the whole story about probability in a couple of paragraphs – its problems are no less contentious than those of history. Some progress can, however, be made if we are allowed two, here unargued, premises. The first is that the probability which may be enjoyed, or suffered, by historical statements is not the probability of the mathematical theory of chances: there is no possibility of putting a numerical value on the probability that Napoleon's illness contributed to his defeat at Waterloo in anything like the way in which one can put a value of one-half on the probability of obtaining a head with any toss of a fair coin. The second, and for present purposes more important, premise is that non-mathematical probability assessments are not merely expressions of subjective confidence but rather to be founded upon evidence. (To couple a subjective view of probability with the notion that history is exclusively a matter of probability is, of course, fatal for history.) Now, to the extent that probability is founded upon evidence, it may be said that it involves having some evidence, but not all the evidence there could be and should be to justify asserting a statement of the type in question as true. (In maintaining this I am focusing on the way probabilities and truths are established, not on the *meaning* of 'probable' and 'true'. In particular I make no claim that truth is to be defined as the upper limit of a probability, nor a probability as a step in the direction of a truth. Going into such questions would involve straying too far afield.) If, then, truth and probability are differentially related to evidence in the way suggested, it follows that they are usefully to be contrasted in relation to statements which admit of the same sort of evidence. Thus such a contrast is fruitful within the field of empirical statements and not between it and, say, necessary statements – for empirical statements are ultimately dependent upon observational evidence, whereas necessary statements are not. This, by itself, does not indeed yield the desired conclusion, which is that there is both truth and probability within history and not simply between historical and other sorts of empirical statement. It needs additionally to be the case that the differences between historical and other empirical statements are not such that the former are inherently less certain than the latter – but this is what the present chapter as a whole has been designed to show. It should perhaps be added that in claiming that a truth/probability distinction is to be drawn within history I am not denying that, say, a statement referring to the future may be more or less probable than one referring to the past. The claim is only that historical statements are not so related to other empirical statements that none of the former can be more than probable whilst some of other sorts of empirical statements can be true.

III

Objectivity

1. The Problems

Many strands are tangled in the problems of objectivity in history. One worry is whether historical statements can be meaningful and sometimes true. This, which we tried to dissipate in the previous chapter, is actually the primary one for Meiland (chs IV and V) and Goldstein (ch. IV) – a judgement which reflects their fear that there may be no accessible past which historical statements can be known to refer to. But, even if it be agreed that statements about the past can be established, this is insufficient to show that sequences of such statements – narratives or other extended pieces of historical writing – are objective too. Manifestly it is impossible to write down all the true statements there are, even about a narrowly defined topic. Selection is inevitable, and with the recognition of this comes the possibility of new sorts of doubt about objectivity. How can selection be other than arbitrary and subjective? This question obtrudes itself at the descriptive let alone the interpretative or explanatory level: there can be no sequence of statements that is both historical and so low down the descriptive–explanatory scale that the necessity for selection does not arise. As one moves up the scale, moreover, new questions about objectivity arise. Notoriously, different historians offer what are apparently irreducibly different interpretations of near enough the same facts; interpretations, that is, between which it seems impossible to choose on so simple a basis as that one is founded on truth and the other on error, from which it is often inferred that any choice must be arbitrary or subjective. Where explanation is concerned a similar view may be taken of judgements to the effect that one type of explanation, or causal factor, is more fundamental than others – explanation in terms of conscious intentions (rational explanation), for example, being often held, and as often denied, to be less fundamental than explanation in terms of class interests. What prospect is there that such disputes might be decisively settled?

Objectivity worries thus arise at different levels and are not all of them of the same sort, in that different considerations bear on them, although a good many have a common source in the idea that selection necessarily compromises objectivity; that selection is inevitably arbitrary, or biased by the historian's personal prejudices, or by his value judgements, which it is presumably taken for granted are wholly subjective and/or arbitrary too. Also involved, whether overtly or covertly, are comparisons and contrasts unfavourable to history with other subjects, usually the physical sciences. So many matters cannot be effectively treated all at once. I will, therefore, postpone discussion of different types of explanation until chapters IV and V, and that of most of the questions concerning value judgements until chapter VI. The principal topic for the present chapter will be objectivity problems connected with selective reporting or interpretation.

A further introductory remark, concerning terminology, will be in place. It will be constantly necessary to use such words as 'objective', 'subjective', 'arbitrary', 'biased', etc. But, in accordance with the policy adopted in chapter I above, I shall not attempt formal definitions of any of them. The worries to be discussed – which are, incidentally, unlike some of those of the last chapter, more often a trouble to practising historians than to philosophers (cf. W. Dray, 1964, p. 23; C. A. Beard and C. L. Becker in R. H. Nash) – are indubitably complicated by ambiguities, inconsistencies and incoherences in the employment of 'objective' and related terms. But premature definitions of them would simply make it harder to formulate some of the worries which need to be discussed, or even beg questions against them. All that is really worthwhile at this stage is to draw attention to two of the main tendencies in the use of 'objective'. According to the first the word means something like: 'related to or correspondent with fact or reality, especially external reality, i.e. things or the world external to the human subject'. The other is more like: 'capable in principle of being settled by any rational person'. The two uses are not unrelated. It may well be felt that it is only because such a statement as 'The book is on the table' is correspondent with reality, i.e. because the book really is on the table, that rational people can, indeed must, agree that it is. But, although thus convergent in some applications of the terms, the uses diverge in others. Mathematical statements would not normally be held to be capable of corresponding with reality in the way that empirical statements do, yet plainly their truth or falsity can in principle be established by rational people. Again, scientific statements of the more general sort, formulations of laws or theories, even though hardly anyone would feel a serious doubt about their objectivity, are much more clearly objective in the latter than the former sense. That is to say, they are objective in virtue of there being a procedure by which a rational person can determine whether they are true or false, for they are too abstract and idealised to be correspondent with reality in any independent sense. Psychological statements, statements about thoughts and feelings, especially when autobiographical (made by a subject of himself), show up very clearly the potential divergence between the two uses of 'objective'. In so far as such statements are about the subject rather than external reality they are non-objective; but in so far as they are capable of determination as true or false, as they sometimes surely are, they are objective. Exaggerated scepticism about psychological statements (the possibility of establishing psychological facts), a scepticism quite common in the British philosophical tradition, is partly the result of failing to recognise the two trends in the use of 'objective'. A more generalised scepticism, extending among other things to value judgements and probability assessments, results if this failure is coupled with a tendency to regard as psychological all statements which are not patently about external reality. This too is prominent in our philosophical tradition. There can be little doubt that it informs at a deep level some of the widespread scepticism there has been about objectivity in history. For, as was noticed in the last chapter, it is apt to be felt that there is no longer an external reality for historical statements to be about.

The two tendencies distinguished in the use of 'objective' very likely do not exhaust the possibilities, but recognition of at least these two will afford some guidance through the ensuing discussion.

What is the opposite of 'objective'? I have used both 'subjective' and 'arbitrary' which, very roughly, make a distinction coinciding with that between the two senses of 'objective'. To the extent that the distinction does so correspond, it follows that the subjective need not be arbitrary, nor vice versa. That these terms are so commonly used interchangeably tends to confirm that the distinction in question is frequently neglected.

How do 'biased' and 'partial', often used in opposition to 'objective', fit in? It happens, I believe, that two different sorts of question are regularly discussed under the heading of objectivity in history. The first is whether objectivity in some shape or form (say, in the second sense, which is the one a number of philosophical writers would defend) is possible in principle – this is a logical or philosophical question. An affirmative answer to it carries no implications of its being easy or difficult, common or rare, to achieve. This philosophical answer at most purports to reveal what constitutes objectivity; not how in practice to attain it. But, obviously, a second, practical sort of question can be asked; and, in the course of answering it, it may well appear that partiality and bias are obstacles to be overcome. It has been remarked (Dray, 1964, p. 22) that practising historians, often with pessimistic relish, tend to address themselves to the second, practical question of eliminating partiality and bias, whilst neglecting or sliding away from the prior logical question of whether objectivity is possible in principle. If, however, it is not achievable in principle, if we cannot even say what it is, the question of how to attain it would not arise.

The logical and practical questions need to be separated, and it is unsurprising that philosophers concentrate on the former, practitioners on the latter. It would, none the less, be altogether unwise to ignore what appear to be attempts to answer the secondary question when trying to answer the primary one. For one thing, terminology is used very variously. Ideally, no doubt, the opposite of 'partiality' should be 'impartiality' not 'objectivity', but alas it often is not. One cannot reliably tell which question is substantially under discussion from the terminology actually employed. More importantly, some views intended to relate to the secondary question may have implications for the primary. For instance, if it be held, as it has been, that bias and partiality are both ubiquitous and unavoidable, it is hard to see what substance could remain in insisting that history is objective in principle.

One term not so far discussed is 'relative', often used, especially by American writers (e.g. M. Mandelbaum, 1938; Danto, 1965; Meiland, 1965), as an opposite to 'objective'. This usage, which makes 'relative' in effect equivalent to either or both of 'subjective' and 'arbitrary', I consider unfortunate, for reasons which will become apparent below. In the usage I shall adopt 'relative' is *compatible* with 'objective', which makes possible, though it does not by itself justify the assertion that the objectivity, such as it may be, of history, as indeed that of morality, depends on its being in a certain sense relative.

NOTE

Beard's much-referred-to-paper, 'That Noble Dream' (Nash, 1969), was cited above as an example of an attack by an historian on the possibility of objectivity in history. Some of Beard's remarks suggest a man bent on intellectual suicide, but his tactics have to be interpreted in relation to his strategy. He appears to be trying to demolish the 'myth' that a received interpretation is objective truth largely in order to open the way for arguing that a new interpretation, stressing economic and social factors, though no less subjective than the old, is also no more.

2. *Never the Whole Truth*

The possibility of making true statements about the past is by general consent insufficient to guarantee objective history, which few are content to conceive as simply a matter of stringing together true statements about a topic. There must, at the very least, also be selection and summary, not to say interpretation. And it is here that the real doubts about objectivity arise. It is feared that in making their selections historians will be expressing their personal and class prejudices, their moral, political or religious attitudes; that what purport to be accounts of the past are shaped less by what happened then than by influences operative in the historian's present. The past cannot change, but history books regularly do, and new ones differ from the old in ways that are not wholly to be accounted for by reference to whatever new information has meantime become available. Historians from one nation, still more from different nations, find it impossible to agree in their accounts of what are in substance the same phenomena. There are Protestant and Catholic, liberal and socialist, even black and white, male and female histories. Among the first tasks of the successful revolutionary is bringing history into line.

Neither the familiarity of this situation, nor a desire to get quickly to grips with the main issue, should be allowed to encourage the illusion that the mere fact of disagreement justifies doubts about objectivity. The simplest way of accounting for disagreement, namely to hold one or more of the parties to be wrong, is wholly compatible with objectivity. No one need fear for the objectivity of mathematics or science just because there are people, even it may be whole cultures, who do not and cannot be got to see such things as that the square on the hypotenuse of a right-angled triangle is equal to the sum of the squares on the other two sides, that bodies free from impressed forces continue in their state of rest or uniform motion in a straight line, or that eliminating anopheles mosquitoes eliminates malaria. Nor does the fact that one gets six different totals when adding a long column of figures support a doubt whether the total is quite objectively whatever it turns out to be. The argument from disagreement to non-objectivity is fallacious. But this, though more than a debating point, does not take us very far. For, of course, non-objectivists are, quite reasonably, simply taking it for granted that no one would want to explain *all* disagreements among historians on the basis that some are wrong. Very likely when historians disagree some untruths will be involved. Sometimes, no doubt, such false statements will be central in generating the disagreement. But, manifestly, it will not always be so.

The same is true of the idea, which reflects the practice of many historians and the precept of some (for example Butterfield, 1931), that disagreements at a higher level of generality can always be settled by going into more detail. This, despite its restricted importance for the present problem, is by no means a superficial idea. It specifies the form often taken by historical discussion. In addition to reporting, historians regularly summarise, interpret, generalise, in the sense of expressing in a few words what they deem to have gone on over longish periods and widish areas – examples commonly cited include Pirenne's thesis that Roman civilisation endured through the barbarian invasions to collapse under the impact of Islam (Marwick, p. 62), various theses about the origins of the English and American civil wars, and even historical materialism itself in such particular applications as to, say, eighteenth-century British politics or those of France 1848–52. Such theses, founded upon the evidence but always going beyond it, seem to have point in suggesting new lines of detailed enquiry and in sparking off enlightening debate. It is thus perfectly true that historical discussion often takes the form of testing relatively general theses against the detailed facts. On the other side, however, it has to be insisted, first, that such theses seem to be valued as much for their organising role in historical investigation and thinking as for their putative truth – so that they are not judged to have been worthless even if finally abandoned in the light of detailed research. And, second, of course, it just seems incredible that *all* disagreement at a given level of generality should be resolvable by, so to say, moving 'down' into greater detail. Ours could be the best of all possible worlds without being arranged primarily for the convenience of naïvely objectivist philosophers of history.

It is, in any event, impossible in principle to report the full, detailed truth. 'Nothing but the truth', by universal consent, fails to secure objectivity. 'The whole truth' is not available; but this, though it has caused despair, would surely justify it only if history were somehow committed to the whole truth. It is hard to see how anybody could suppose it was; though equally hard to explain the great alarm generated by the recognition that selection is inevitable on any other basis.

It may be that the impossibility *in principle* of reporting the whole truth is insufficiently stressed because of the obviousness of the *practical* difficulties – in the shape of life's shortness, costs of publication, patience of readers – which prevent the reporting of very much of it. In fact the notion of 'the whole truth', even about a very narrow topic, is incoherent. It is not a huge totality that is very difficult to encompass; it is not a finite, homogeneous totality at all. Statements are of different sorts, on different levels of generality. Indefinitely many complex ones can be constructed from or in various ways based upon or related to simpler ones; and merely adding them to the simpler ones, or to one another, brings one no nearer to completeness. The whole truth, in the sense of all true statements about a topic, is not an intelligible notion at all.

Of course, witnesses in courts of law swear to tell, among other things, the whole truth. In context this is intelligible, because in a trial there is or should be a question at issue which is sufficiently precise to determine a narrow range of possibly relevant answers. There is here a model of the way in which selection can be compatible with objectivity in history, i.e. that though there cannot be the whole truth there can be a complete answer to a question put. Unhappily there are disanalogies too. There is no law, there are no courts: the historian is legislator, judge, jury, counsel, witnesses, all in one; and there is no purpose external to his practice to shape it and give it point in the way that the maintenance of order is presumably the object of a penal system. These disadvantages, if that is the word, of the historian will have to be enlarged on below. For the present, however, it will pay to consider the way in which statements, *descriptive* statements, occur in history on different levels. This will help to show how the selection problem arises at the level of description and could not be confined to interpretation even if the latter could be firmly distinguished from the former.

Consider first singular statements of the 'Brutus killed Caesar' variety. These, whatever may be the difficulty of verifying them (see the previous chapter), are least problematic from the present point of view. (Problems associated with the employment of 'killed' as opposed to 'murdered' or 'treacherously murdered' will be taken up later.) There is no summary and little interpretation in them, though, obviously, they find their way into history books only because someone considers them important. To this extent they compare favourably with statements like 'most English people welcomed the declaration of war in 1939', which is a summary, or with 'The United Kingdom declared war in 1939', of which the subject is not an individual but a collective.

Presumably no one disputes that historians must summarise, even in the plainest of plain tales. The idea that history is concerned primarily with the individual event, which does in my view express an important truth about the relations between history and science, would have to be rejected if intended to rule out summaries. It is true that historians may not summarise overtly. Instead of reporting the reactions of most English people on 3 September 1939, they may elect instead to report the actions of a few individuals. But this is largely a literary device, designed to secure immediacy and concreteness – the reactions of Mr Smith and Mr Jones earn their place in history only in so far as they can be represented as typical. An historian may even choose to 'describe' the reactions of some fictitious or 'ideal type' of individual – this is a possible way of conveying what generally happened, though I suspect not one very congenial to many historians. In one way or another, though, summarising there will always be, and summarising is a matter of compendiously reporting the content of many lower level statements, statements too numerous to specify or even distinctly to conceive. And summarising involves selecting, for emphasis and representation, some from a vastly greater number of possible statements.

The simple summary, though not usually thought of as a very venturesome intellectual flight, may yet raise doubts about objectivity. Moreover, it is by no means the only sort of higher level, selection dependent statement to be found in history books. There are also statements about collectives – nations, churches, peoples, cultures, civilisations even. These (like statements concerning ideal types) are very far removed from and related in complex non-mechanical ways to statements about individual human beings. The latter contention has, of course, sometimes been resisted. It has been held that statements about collectives are 'reducible' in principle to sets of statements about individuals, in the sense that for any statement about a collective there will be a set of statements about individuals equivalent to it. If such reductions could be carried through there would be no problems peculiar to statements about collectives, but of course they cannot (cf. chapter v section 5 below). The relationship. which there un-questionably is, between statements referring respectively to collectives and the individuals making them up is not mechanical. It resembles rather that between statements concerning an individual's character and temperament (that he is generous, impulsive, moody, and the like) and reports of his particular actions and reactions. In both cases the more general statement, be it about a collective or a character, depends upon less general statements about people or their deeds. It is in virtue of the less general that the more general are assertable, but there is never any precise specifiable set of less general statements that unchal-lengeably justifies or rules out a more general one. In affirming and denying statements about collectives and characters we are un-avoidably exercising selective *judgement*: not calculating, which is determinable by rules, but judging, which is not.

I emphasise this because I believe that there is some danger of resting too much weight on an over-simple distinction between description (facts) and interpretation. It is very widely recognised that historians may disagree in their interpretations when the facts are barely in dispute, indeed it is quite widely felt to be idle to expect agreement at the level of interpretation. It is perhaps not so widely recognised how much selection there must be at the descriptive level. If selection entails subjectivity and arbitrariness then description is compromised too. I say this, of course, not in order to convict description of non-objectivity, but rather to forestall interpretation's being judged guilty by disassociation.

The object of this chapter is to argue that selecting is not incom-patible with objectivity, whilst allowing that different selections may be equally in accordance with the facts. It is, perhaps, worth remarking here, though it will not advance the discussion very much, that different selections do not have to be incompatible. Instead they might be complementary or supplementary (cf. E. Nagel, p. 581). Clearly several accounts of what happened in different parts of a country may simply add up to what happened in the country as a whole. Similarly, accounts of what happened in church, parliament, local government, industry etc. may add up to a composite picture of national life. Some general history books are indeed internally organised on this basis. Even some of the differences between the histories of different nations could be accounted for in this way, although they could not simply be added together, with no changes made in any of them, to make world history.

The histories of France and England, especially during certain periods, will often deal with the same events; but an event which requires detailed treatment in the one history may get only the barest mention in the other. Some events that have to be treated in one may be omitted from the other. The writers of different national histories may not, indeed, really be disagreeing with each other. Each would judge as did the other if their roles were reversed. That different selections can thus be compatible proves that selecting does not rule out objectivity, though, of course, selections can be incompatible too.

It might be thought that there is a shorter route to the conclusion that selecting does not exclude objectivity in history, namely this: As has often been pointed out the price of holding that selection is necessarily subjective and arbitrary is that *no* account of the past, no history, could be otherwise. But this, though the desired result of the sceptic, may be claimed to be self-refuting. For surely the point of applying such terms as 'objective' and 'subjective' to particular histories is to say that they are what *other* histories might not have been. Their point is to make distinctions *within* the class of possible histories, so that there would be no point in asserting a history to be subjective unless there were at least the possibility of a history being objective (cf. C. Blake, 1955). More formally it may be said that to deny the objectivity of history at large is to violate the 'principle of significant contrast', which lays it down that for any assertion to be significant the contradictory assertion must be at least possible. Many sceptical theses fall foul of this principle.

I am sure that the conclusion with regard to objectivity in history is right, but doubt whether it is wise to present it as a direct consequence of a very general principle of significance which has no special relevance to history. Certainly, as things are, we do – most of us – recognise certain histories as objective, or at least more so than others. And reference to the principle may remind us that we do this. But it does not follow that we have to go on doing so. We surely are not obliged to think that every distinction we make is rightly drawn just where it is. Of course we *do* recognise certain histories as objective, but only if we can give the rationale of this are we in a strong position to go on doing so. Appeal to the significant contrast principle does not exempt us from honest toil.

Another way of bringing out the limitations of the principle in its present application is this: So be it that, if it is to make sense to say of history that it is not objective, there has to be the possibility of contrast with something that is objective. But this something need not be a possible history. It might be something quite other, for example a natural science – this is indeed the contrast often intended by those who deny the objectivity of history. To repeat, I personally have no doubt that there is room for an objective/non-objective contrast *within* history: my contention is only that a currently favoured short cut will not take us to that destination.

3. Selection in History and Science

Low views of the possibility of objectivity in history are sometimes reached by comparing history more or less as it is with a quite unrealistic, indeed impossible, notion of natural science. It is, in particular, wholly mistaken to hold that history is selective and science not. In truth the sciences are much more rigorous and explicit in selecting the facts or aspects of fact which concern them than history ever is. There are important differences between history and the sciences, but one of them is not that selection occurs in the one and not in the others. If there is a difference having to do with selection it must, therefore, be that selection is different in the two contexts.

Popper gives clear expression to a view of this kind in *The Open Society and Its Enemies* (1945, ch. 25), maintaining that criteria of selection are firmly determined by the nature of the particular study among the sciences, whereas in history they have, so to say, to be imported from outside. In this regard the developed sciences at least are autonomous in a way history is not. The next few paragraphs will be devoted to expounding and commenting on Popper's discussion.

For Popper neither history nor science is a matter of dredging up facts by the bucketful. A better image is that of a searchlight playing upon areas of reality; the point about the searchlight being, of course, that it is inevitably directed *from* a point of view and that what it illuminates is determined as much by this as by what is there for it to shine upon. So far history and the sciences are the same. The difference is that in physics, for instance, the point of view (criterion of selection) is usually determined by a testable theory. Not so in history. In the generalising or law-seeking sciences individual events are important only in so far as their occurrence or non-occurrence bears upon the acceptability of some putative law or its embodiment in a theory or system of such laws. Consequently, to the extent that we have a theory or the hope of one, we have a criterion for determining which events or aspects of events are relevant. In history, on the other hand, the situation is different. Laws, indeed, are used in order to explain events; but the interest of the events is antecedent to and independent of the possibility of bringing them into relation with laws. Moreover the laws that have to be appealed to in history are heterogeneous, and typically do not cohere together so as to constitute theories. The 'laws' may in fact be mere commonsense generalisations, sometimes trivial or of uncertain logical quantity (i.e. it may be uncertain whether they are strictly universal). There is no articulated body of theory to determine what is relevant in history; it is rather that the historian has to draw on whatever he can find among all sorts of theories and commonsense beliefs, which may be used to explain the events in which he happens to be interested.

It is no part of this general approach to deny the possibility of social theories. Clearly some sociologists and other social scientists aim to establish theories which are logically on all fours with physical theories. In fact no such theory is widely accepted, but even if the case were otherwise it would not affect the distinction between social theory and history. History would still draw upon, without being confined by, the theory in question. Popper in fact allows that criteria of relevance are to an extent determined in histories which are devoted to a rather narrow subject matter, for instance economic relations or mathematics. (It may be recalled that in chapter I above attention was drawn to the possibility of, say, economic history drawing criteria of relevance from economics.) But for Popper this is a minor exception to the general rule that criteria of relevance have to be brought to history from without. He has in mind here very general principles of interpretation or points of view according to which, for instance, it is great men, national character, moral ideas, economic conditions, which are important in history. Such ideas are very far from being testable theories. Alternative interpretations will often be compatible with the same data, and 'crucial experiments' (decisive new data) far to seek. Popper does not indeed think that all interpretations are of equal merit. So far as can be gathered from his rather brief discussion, his view is that an interpretation or point of view is the better in proportion as it approximates to a genuinely testable theory, though he is realistically well aware of the possibility of apparent corroborations being circular.

What Popper has to offer for history may be described as objectivity relative to a point of view (a brief discussion of T. S. Kuhn's suggestion that the Popperian view exaggerates the difference in this regard between history and the sciences will be found in chapter VI section 4 below). Given a point of view, and the more clearly formulated and consciously held the better, certain facts or aspects of facts will be relevant, others not. They will be *objectively* relevant in the sense (the second sense distinguished in the first section of this chapter) that everyone adopting the point of view will, in so far as he is rational and competent, tend to agree in his judgements of relevance, in his selections. Purely personal factors, individual peculiarities of the historian, his prejudices and the like, need not come in; at any rate they will not have an importance different from that they may have in any other objective study. There need be nothing subjective or arbitrary in what an historian reports from his point of view. But there will be no objectivity in the full sense in the selection of points of view. Some may be better than others in the ways indicated, but there is really no ground within history for preferring one to another. It is unfortunate that the examples Popper gives in chapter 25 of *The Open Society* are of such very general points of view – rather bad ones in fact by his own criteria, though his interpretation of Athenian history as a development from a 'closed' to an 'open' society is much better (see op. cit., ch. 10). Notions that great men or national characters are important in history are intolerably vague; they must often be more of the nature of unconscious assumptions, habits or styles of historical activity, rather than properly worked out general interpretations. Economic interpretations are encountered in both uselessly vague and impossibly precise varieties, either failing to have any definite implications for historical practice or achieving testability at the price of falsity. (For a discussion of historical materialism see chapter v section 5 below.) In its Marxist form an economic interpretation is, moreover, specially liable not to be recognised by its upholders as one among other possible points of view.

Walsh, in his useful discussion of objectivity (1951, ch. v), distinguishes three sorts of position which may be adopted in face of disagreement among historians at what he specifies as the interpretative level, although he does not insist upon a sharp distinction between interpretation and description. The three positions are: (*a*) scepticism; (*b*) perspectivism, which is close to Popper's objectivity relative to a point of view; (*c*) objectivism in a stronger, absolute sense. Walsh himself, whilst rejecting the first and showing full awareness of the plausibility of the second, was in 1951 inclined to hold out for the third in the shape of the idea of an 'objective historical consciousness', the 'possibility of developing a point of view which would win universal acceptance' ultimately (p. 109). (By his third edition of 1967, however, he had come to fear that his argument here was 'seriously confused'.)

His original view was maintained despite his clear recognition that it involved formidable difficulties, not least a commitment to the belief that ultimate moral and metaphysical differences among historians are capable of being settled in principle – an optimistic view, raising issues beyond the scope of both his book and this. In its favour it may be allowed that such ultimate beliefs, in so far as they are consciously held, are usually held as true. But, for my own part, whilst I recognise that ultimate beliefs are open to rational criticism and up to a point susceptible of rational defence, I cannot persuade myself that it is impossible or unlikely that there are various ultimate positions, between which there is nothing decisively to determine choice. The prudent course for anyone anxious to promote the idea of an objective historical consciousness would, it appears to me, be to seek as far as possible to represent moral and metaphysical differences as *external* to history, in the way that religious differences are now widely held to be (see section 5 below). (Walsh, in the third edition note referred to, seems rather to stress the fact that moral and metaphysical differences occur in the historian's subject matter; but the first of the additional essays appended to that edition seems to allow for the possibility of ultimate moral and metaphysical differences between historians as well.)

In other respects too the prospects for an objective historical consciousness seem less hopeful than Walsh suggested. On the credit side there may, it is true, be some universality in professional standards among historians (at any rate in societies where history is not wholly enslaved by the regime); standards relating to such matters as respect for truth, the subjection of documents and other evidential material to appropriate tests for authenticity, accurate and full reporting of sources so that other historians can follow the tracks. All this, however, belongs to the technical, fact-gathering side of history, whereas objectivity problems are acute at higher interpretative levels too. But, if it be indeed the case, as practically every writer on the subject affirms, that there is no sharp distinction between fact and interpretation, perhaps this could for once be allowed to count in favour of objectivity. Moreover, where there is mutual respect at the technical level, professional historians, wedded though they may be to very different general interpretative principles, do seem to be able to make allowances for such differences, and to appreciate histories constructed on very different principles as good of their kind.

None of this means, however, that moral, metaphysical, religious divisions are not very deep; nor does it support a realistic hope of there ever being agreement across them on explicit principles of interpretation. Explicitness, though, is not quite certainly the virtue philosophers are professionally prone to take it to be. Historians, particular groups of them anyway, do have notions of what is relevant and important, notions implicit in their practice even when not explicitly formulated. In this regard the expressions 'criteria of relevance' and 'principles of interpretation' can mislead. There is an over-intellectualist flavour about them. There can, as a matter of logic, be firm conceptions of relevance in the absence of explicit formulation; and, as a matter of fact, attempts at formulation may simply crudify, and embroil practitioners in unnecessary disputes. Philosophers are in business to formulate and make explicit; but they too serve truth, and must therefore recognise that successful practice does not necessarily depend upon clearly formulated governing principles. This does not, of course, by itself tell against the possibility of there being irreducible differences over interpretations, nor entail that there is a unitary, objective historical consciousness in the making.

The argument so far in this chapter has moved rather rapidly from a consideration of selection at the descriptive end of the range to interpretative principles of the highest generality. It will be instructive to backtrack a little at this point in order to consider another way of introducing the idea of relative objectivity. Dray, in his discussion of objectivity (1964, p. 29), observes that it is helpful to draw a distinction between selection at the level of questions and at the level of answers. Given this, it may be pointed out that subjectivity and arbitrariness in the choice of questions does not entail that the same will obtain at the level of answers. Questions may not be given, but not everything goes in the way of answers. There may be no choice of answers at all. There can be complete objectivity, relative to questions.

This doctrine has obvious affinities with Walsh's perspectivism and Popper's relative objectivity, with the merit of not being specially related to very general principles of interpretation. The thought is just that, whatever their origin, particular questions may in principle be fully and finally answered. It has the additional advantage of affording some credibility to the view, fairly common among historians, that objectivity problems are less pressing in analytical, problem-oriented history than they are in narrative. Some, indeed, hold 'old-fashioned' narrative history in such contempt that they do not seriously suppose that any degree of objectivity in it is possible at all.

As so far stated, the view seems to be claiming objectivity for answers whilst tolerating the complete absence of it where questions are concerned. This is not, however, inevitable. The view could perfectly well be developed in order to accommodate a non-arbitrary choice of questions. More detailed questions may be held to arise in the course of answering more general ones, and the latter themselves held to be posed by 'the present condition of historical studies' or 'the present state of knowledge'. There would be a good deal in this. Professional historians at a time, and of course within a wider or narrower but never universal reference group, have conceptions of what has been and what remains to be done in various fields. They try to avoid duplicating one another's work, and in a measure parcel out problems amongst themselves. A new method or approach, 'Namierising' for example, developed in relation to one period, may be extended by other historians to other periods (cf. Marwick, p. 92). Another more obvious way in which questions might objectively arise is when new information becomes available, as when, for instance, the victorious Bolsheviks opened the Tsarist archives, or when state papers are periodically released under the thirty-year rule.

I do not want to exaggerate the extent to which questions may thus arise, as it were, of themselves. I am sure that even the most determined upholders of the objectivity of history would be prepared to tolerate some irreducible differences of opinion about the right questions so long as they could feel sure there was complete determinacy about the right answers. Could such confidence be justified?

Not altogether. It must be doubted whether questions can often be so exactly specified as to have completely determinate answers. It is true that very specific questions may be thrown up in a particular line of enquiry, for instance fully and exactly answerable questions about the respective armament, range and reliability of British and German aircraft deployed in the Battle of Britain. But it is only for a history of fighting aircraft that such questions would certainly be centrally relevant. If the object were rather the still pretty narrow one of describing the course of the battle and explaining its outcome, it would be necessary to balance the importance of information related to such technical questions against that related to other still very specific questions concerning pilot training, aircraft manufacture, and so on. And it is very uncertain, even at a mainly descriptive level, whether questions of relative importance often admit of wholly determinate answers. A question is fully determinate only if there can be specified for it a full range of possible answers, so that it has the force of 'Select one from the series a or b or c . . . or n'. But it is rare indeed for it to be possible effectively to specify a finite range of clearly distinguishable alternatives where human affairs are concerned. Of course, questions can always be phrased in such a way that they require 'yes' or 'no' for an answer, as do very often the questions included in opinion polls – but this only increases the proportion of 'don't knows'.

My concern in making these last observations is in no way to dispute the centrality of the notion of relative objectivity for history, I want only to suggest that there is a limit beyond which it cannot be pushed.

4. An Absolute Basis for Selection?

So far I have been discussing the idea that objectivity in history is relative to criteria of selection which are not themselves objectively given except in so far as they are *de facto* recognised by particular groups of historians. For unreflective members within such groups the criteria may present themselves as absolutely objective, but they will not look like that from outside. It is time now to consider the possibility that this is not the whole story, and that in a development of the common idea that history is the study of events in the light of their outcomes might be found an absolute criterion. Aron, as was noted above, gives a good deal of space to this (see especially 1938, pp. 129–36), though he is himself very far from wishing to claim absolute objectivity for history. Of course, as was observed in chapter II section 5 above, there have been a number of writers who have vigorously opposed any suggestion that history should concern itself with outcomes, but this need not stand in the way of enquiring what can be made of the idea in the present connection.

Could it be, then, that certain events are made absolutely important because of their outcomes? Obvious examples include the early days of movements which subsequently changed the world, for example, the activities of the revolutionary exiles in London before the Russian Revolution. Many questions can be raised about the way in which these events are connected with the Revolution and about the explanatory force, if any, of asserting that they were. But these must be put aside in order to concentrate on the implications of the thesis that what makes the activities of Lenin and his fellow conspirators significant is that the Revolution did occur, with its corollary that they would be much less significant, though possibly no less accessible to knowledge, if it had not.

So far, to be sure, we have made no movement beyond relativism. It is only because the Russian Revolution is deemed to be important that its origins become so. But, it may be asked, is not the Revolution objectively important? Are there not some events which by their very nature – usually because of the magnitude of the human suffering and social change involved – cannot fail to be important? Dray, for instance (1964, pp. 31–2), asks rhetorically whether there could be a portrait of Victorian England which did not mention the working-class movement, or a history of Nazi Germany which omitted the killing of the Jews.

Nobody can deny that the Russian Revolution is important, for us and for understanding the world we live in. Its roots go far back and are important because it is important. It is *humanly* important – I would not argue with anyone who claimed it to be absolutely so – and, in so far as history is concerned with human affairs, it is likely to be historically important. But, one must ask, what is supposed to follow from this?

One thing that one must hope does not follow, because it would not be true, is that there could be no history relating to early twentieth-century Europe which did not refer to the goings on of Lenin and his co-conspirators or indeed to the Revolution itself. No doubt political, diplomatic, economic histories of those years would have to mention it; but this is because they are political, diplomatic, economic, not because they are histories. And this is the case also with Dray's Victorian working-class movement and the killing of the Jews. To describe a history as being of Victorian England or of Nazi Germany does indeed suggest perspectives in which the working-class movement and the genocide are important; but these are not the only perspectives in which the places and periods in question can be studied. It is not at all obvious that it would be necessary to refer to the genocide in, say, a history of the German motor-car industry, or to the working classes in a history of the universities or the civil service. It is sometimes said that no one reading a history of British philosophy in this century would ever guess that there had been two world wars. Conceivably this is a reproach to philosophy, but not to its history. There is no reason at all why events of enormous human importance should figure in specialised histories.

I would not deny that the previous sentence is virtually tautological – after all, that entails its truth. Nor would I deny that I have been rehearsing largely uninformed assumptions about what would need to be mentioned in a history of what. Conceivably the genocide had something to do with car manufacture under the Nazis, the Victorian working class with the universities. My claim is only that such conclusions would need to be supported by particular historical enquiries. Even the murder of six million Jews is not made relevant to every enquiry just because of its appalling human significance.

We have not, therefore, it seems to me, found sufficient reason to depart from the relativism of the earlier parts of this chapter. We might all the same conclude this section by considering briefly some of the ways in which knowledge of outcomes may afford principles of selection to historians with appropriate interests or tasks in hand. Inevitably later events which interest us will thereby bestow importance upon earlier events which are judged to be connected with them. Elton, as reported above (chapter II section 5), thinks hindsight a disadvantage to the historian (1967, p. 99), and writes austerely (p. 48), 'the historian studying the past is concerned with the later event only in so far as it throws light on the part of the past he is studying. It is the cardinal error to reverse this process and study the past for the light it throws on the present.' Well – does this authoritative, and not unrepresentative, pronouncement conflict with the view I have been expressing? I hope not. It seems evident that it is the Russian Revolution which makes the early Lenin important; but no doubt Elton's protest is directed against the supposition that, because the Revolution and therefore the early Lenin are important, it follows that Lenin was important *in late Victorian and Edwardian England*. Such a supposition would be, mutatis mutandis, a prime example of Whiggish history. What Elton seems to be insisting on is that a history must always have a major focus and that, if it refers backwards and forwards in time, it must be in the service of that focus and not for extraneous reasons. The danger in hindsight is that it may lead to the distortion of what is intended to be a history of some particular time by encouraging the adoption of judgements of relative importance which make sense only in relation to another time.

It may be added, as has been pointed out by a number of writers (for example Danto, p. 134), that it is a feature of fictional as well as historical stories that events should acquire importance from their outcomes. In the early stages of a conventional novel appear references to apparently trivial incidents, though the experienced reader is all too well aware that they will turn out to have significance as the story develops.

One possible advantage of hindsight is that the historian is in a position to know some things not all of which could have been known by any individual belonging to the time he is studying. In the tritest example, a military historian may well have the battle plans of both sides. He may consequently be able to appreciate the significance of some move in relation to the outcome of the battle in a way that none of the commanders actually engaged could possibly have done. Once again, though, the validity of selection so grounded will depend on the precise task the historian has set himself. If his concern is to describe the course of the battle and perhaps explain the result, hindsight is an obvious advantage. It will, however, be a disadvantage if his aim is rather to portray, say, how it seemed at the time in the British trenches. For many laymen, at least, much of the interest of history lies in the contrast between how it looks now and how it seemed to participants at the time. One may recall in this connection that alternation between an agent's and an observer's viewpoint held by Gallie to be characteristically involved in the following of stories (cf. chapter 1 section 1 above).

5. *The Limits of Objectivity*

To the extent that doubt about objectivity in history arises from the fact of disagreement among historians it will be instructive to compare with it doubt about objectivity in morality founded upon moral disagreement. It is hard indeed not to be impressed by differences in moral outlook and practice between societies and between social classes, educational and occupational groups within a society. Such differences are typically very deeply rooted, often irreconcilable; it is not easy to tolerate them, yet equally hard to believe that those who differ from us are simply wrong. Untravelled, socially sheltered people perhaps tend to think in this way; but they often change when really brought up against moral differences or react with a degree of bluster that betrays a want of inner confidence. Naïve moral objectivism cannot for long withstand the rough winds of diversity. When it withers, the temptation is to rush to the opposite extreme, holding that anything goes in morality, that it is wholly subjective, a matter of arbitrary preference. As in history, so in morality, there is a marked tendency simply to take it for granted that irreconcilable differences cannot be accommodated on any sort of objectivist basis.

In both fields this is an error. In morality there is the intermediate possibility of holding that moral differences are relatable to other, wholly objective, differences between the situations of the people in question. We, having long since nationalised penal procedures, disapprove of private punishments and revenges; but in pre-twentieth-century Sicily, and maybe still, public law enforcement is ineffective and vendetta, with all its disadvantages, makes a savage sense. Again, the middle classes in our own society favour trying to get on in the world, making the best of yourself; the working classes by contrast tend to put the emphasis on solidarity, not differentiating yourself from your comrades, not leaving them behind in the race to the top – a difference which is broadly in line with the differing life situations and opportunities of members of the two classes. There are many more examples less gross than these, but they will serve to make the line of thought clear. Whenever a moral difference can be correlated with a difference in the actual situation it is possible to take account of moral divergence without detriment to objectivity. One can feel that the people whose attitude and behaviour differ in their different situations are still exercising the same moral judgement, and that they would react in the same way in the same situation. Indeed it is *because* they are guided by the same moral judgement that they differ in different situations. It would be taking the same view of situations which differ which really ought to raise doubts about objectivity. That morality should be relative to situation is not merely compatible with objectivity, but a consequence of it.

There is here in morality a relative objectivity not dissimilar to that contemplated earlier for history; an objectivity, that is, relative to point of view or question asked, which makes it possible to explain some of the differences between historians as deriving from their exercising the same historical judgement in the course of different enquiries. Manifestly there are also very many differences between history and morality. The similarity which is relevant here is simply this: that in both cases something that looks initially like a disturbingly irreconcilable *internal* difference can be accommodated, neutralised perhaps, by being represented as related to and derivative from an *external* difference. For such a manoeuvre to succeed it has to be possible *both* to distinguish differences within morality and history from external differences *and* yet to correlate the two. The question therefore must be how far these things are possible.

It must be conceded that it is over-simple to stop at trying to relate moral differences with differences in the *actual* situations of the peoples concerned. Daunting complexities attend any attempt to take account of the *perceived* situation (what they believe that situation to be, which may be different from what it is). For it to be possible to correlate moral views with what may very well be false views about the situation, it is necessary to hold on to a firm distinction between moral judgements on the one hand and (true or false) factual beliefs on the other. This, though not free from difficulty and controversy, can, in my opinion, still be done. The hardest thing, however, is to take into account people's religious and, in the wide sense, 'philosophical' beliefs – 'philosophy' being here taken to cover speculative assessments of the nature of the universe and man's place within it, not the hopefully analytical philosophy of the title page of this book. Such religious and philosophical beliefs, though important influences on moral beliefs, are very difficult fully to disentangle from them, not least because there is no certainty and little agreement on how religious and philosophical beliefs are to be understood. The further one moves away from the basic, utilitarian, ground-rules-for-social-existence area of morality, the harder it becomes to distinguish moral beliefs from, and hence significantly to correlate them with, religious and philosophical positions. The difficulty of carrying through a relativist defence of the objectivity of morality increases as the basic level is left behind.

Objectivity in history has already been considered in relation to precise question asked or clearly articulated point of view. It remains to enquire how far religious and philosophical differences among historians can be treated on the same lines.

By religious differences among historians I mean, of course, differences in personal religious commitment, not simply differences in religious subject matter. (The latter, even though the actions of, say, Henry VIII would be treated very differently in histories of the Anglican and Roman Catholic churches, raise no new fundamental problems.) My belief is that religious faith and affiliation are no longer very important as a source of disagreement among professional historians. It is recognised, but thought not very difficult to allow for the fact, that there will be Catholic and Protestant bias. The situation seems to be much the same as between believing and unbelieving historians. Believers (Butterfield is an example) appear to feel that they can accompany unbelievers as far as the latter want to go. If from that point the believer wishes to go further, he no longer thinks of himself as operating as a professional historian. I am conscious that I may have polled a biased sample of professional historians, but can only record my firm impression that contemporary professional history is effectively secularised. Standards of possibility are taken to be fixed by present-day science. Divine manifestations are not reported as having occurred; but atheists and theists alike will describe, and in much the same terms try to explain, the development of religious movements purportedly having their origins in such events. The rights and wrongs of religious belief itself are, it seems, felt to be something professional historians are not as such required to make up their minds about, something external to history.

The absence, if indeed I am right in supposing it to be absent, of serious disagreement among historians arising from religion is surprising in that religious belief and the lack of it might well have been supposed to be connected with general philosophical positions which, it would seem, could hardly fail to make a difference to the practice of history. How does it come about that religion is effectively neutral with respect to history? I can only suppose that the explanation is to be found in particular features of our Western cultural history over the past few centuries, i.e. that it is to be explained as an aspect of a general secularisation of intellectual life. Conceptions of the autonomy of history, expressing themselves in tendencies to narrow the scope of the subject by avoiding commitment on 'extra-historical' matters, are important too; and may be reinforced by, as well as reinforcing, notions that the past is to be studied, to a great extent, in its own terms.

Collingwood (1946, pp. 134-41), in the course of chiding F. H. Bradley for drawing criteria of possibility from natural science, reveals a more exalted conception of the autonomy of history. He holds that an historian might reach conclusions about what is possible by a process of *historical* thinking: history, as he puts it, being its own criterion. There is a sense in which this is quite unexceptionable. One aspect of being a good historian must be having a sure judgement about what could and could not have happened; and thus provided an historian will more likely reach truth from the evidence than can an amateur, inexperienced in historical enquiries, be his general conceptions of the physically, psychologically, sociologically possible never so clear. But any specifically historical sense of what can and cannot be must still operate within some conception of the possible; and in fact, as Bradley in his *Presuppositions of Critical History* (1874) was very well aware, it does operate within a secular conception of the possible which excludes the event some people believe to have happened on the first Easter Day. There may be reason to question this conception of the possible, though Collingwood gives none; but what I really cannot see is how it could effectively be challenged, as it were, *by* history; unless, of course, one follows Collingwood in his extravagant view that all questions are historical. The interesting query is whether history in a narrow, approximately ordinary sense can generate all its own criteria of possibility – and stretching the meaning of 'history' will not alter the fact that the answer to *this* question is No.

I do not deny that a religious believer may, quite consistently, employ an extended, 'supernaturalist' criterion of the possible: my present point is only that he will have to bring it into history, he will not find it already there. But, as I have already said, my belief is that religiously committed historians typically, when working as historians, employ the same criteria of possibility as their infidel colleagues.

It remains to consider general philosophical – perhaps ideological – differences between historians, say, between Marxists and secularist empiricists or positivists. (This is very far from being a tidy or exhaustive division of philosophical positions, but at worst it picks out two that are currently influential in our own culture.) Is there any reason why there should not be objectivity relative to such positions? The difficulty is that relative objectivity is a matter of the *same* historical judgement being exercised in the service of different questions or points of view. This implies that exercising historical judgement is one thing, asking a particular question or adopting a point of view another. The historical judgement, so to say, stays the same regardless. But it would not seem inevitable that it could stay the same through profound differences of general philosophical view. For such comprehensive views, it may be thought, must have implications for the conceptions of evidence, verification, validity even, in which historical judgement expresses itself. Hegel is commonly credited with having sought to invent a new dialectical logic of the reason which would supersede the barren logic of the understanding, and Marxists have in some measure sought to follow him in this. For my own part, I want *both* to concede the theoretical possibility that a philosophical division might penetrate right down into conceptions of evidence and validity *and* to deny that anyone has yet demonstrated real differences at this level. (The dialectic, in so far as sense can be made of it, is wholly compatible with formal logic – validity is ideologically neutral!) Marxists and positivists cannot really disagree about evidence, verification and validity – this is the foundation for universal professional standards at the technical level (cf. section 3 above). I realise that this judgement may be held simply to reflect my own philosophical perspective, and concede that I cannot jump out of my philosophical skin, but still insist that the possibility of real alternatives at the most basic level has yet to be shown. There is, however, a live possibility of disagreement at the still pretty fundamental level of fact and value, theory and practice, and still more over questions of what is basic or superficial in senses felt to be absolute, not relative to questions a man may have elected to ask or the sort of history he may have chosen to write. There is, no doubt, in fact a good deal of mutual respect across the Marxist/non-Marxist divide; but it has often been my experience in discussion with committed Marxists that they are not willing to concede that there can be legitimate enquiries and true answers in relation to questions they are not minded to ask. Nor have they commonly been grateful for its being conceded that their questions, though different from mine, are perfectly legitimate. The relativistic live-and-let-live contemplated in the present chapter appears to present itself to them as just another facet of a philosophical-cum-political position which they wish totally to reject.

General philosophical positions, then, can and do make a difference to history. Does it follow that history is, 'in the end', not objective, or, as Walsh was reported as having held, that it is objective only in so far as philosophical differences are themselves objectively decidable? I have already declared myself something of a sceptic in metaphysics. There is, however, a further question which can be asked. If general philosophical positions have implications for history could there not also be implications the other way? Need it always be that philosophical differences express themselves in history? Could it not be that historical thinking itself might help decide between philosophical theories? I have reported Collingwood as wanting to give an answer affirmative in form; but the substance of his view is much less clear. He seems either, as already noticed, greatly to extend the meaning of the term 'history' or, as in his *Essay on Metaphysics* (1940), to adopt the philosophically sceptical view that all that is possible in the way of philosophy is writing a history of philosophical views (of fundamental presuppositions, as he called them). For my part, I can see two ways in which history might have implications for philosophy. The *first* is that, if it makes sense at all to think of criteria for assessing a purportedly total philosophical view, which might be conceived as embracing all criteria, then one criterion will presumably be that a view gives some account of history. A view that found no place for history would surely be defective. One would like to go on to say that the account given must be 'adequate'; but I am afraid that little progress could be made in this direction since criteria of adequacy are bound to be internal to philosophical views. The *second* way in which history might have implications for philosophy would be if practising historians themselves developed an idea of what philosophical views made sense in relation to the practice of history. This does I believe happen to some extent. There appears to be a measure of consensus among, say, British academic historians about the extent to which Marxian notions are relevant and helpful. Beyond this, I can only repeat that historians generally are not a united group, and that the professionalism which transcends the divisions among them does not extend beyond the 'technical' level.

IV

Explanation

1. Description, Interpretation, Explanation

A large part of the philosophical attraction of the present topic lies in the possibility, or the hope, of there being in history a sort of explanation not encountered elsewhere. Whatever may turn out to be the truth about this, however, it is as certain as anything can be that there must be more than one sort of explanation in history. The first thing that becomes apparent if one tries to pick out explanatory passages from history books is their great variety. Proponents of every view of historical explanation have managed to cite credible examples. It is, in the first place, by no means difficult to find explanations which can readily be represented as assigning causes or as bringing the event or state of affairs explained under a law or generalisation. At least as common are explanations in rational or purposive terms, or in terms of Popper's logic of the situation, i.e. explanations in which a person's action is accounted for as something which either really was, or was judged by him to be, necessary in order to achieve his aims or purposes or, which comes to much the same, as what would have been expected of a reasonable man who was or thought he was in a situation of a certain sort. If, instead of the law/rational classification, one thinks of explanations as dividing into economic, psychological, sociological, etc. categories, then again it will be easy to find examples of every type in history. Medical explanations, too, for instance in relation to Henry VIII's leg or George

An earlier version of some of this chapter was published under the title 'Explanation in History' in the *Proceedings of the Aristotelian Society*, 1971–2.

III's possible madness, are by no means unknown. There would seem to be no sort of explanation which can be guaranteed not to occur in history – hence the opinion expressed by Lucas that no explanation which is satisfactory in itself can be dismissed as unhistorical.

Questions about historical explanation must accordingly take the form of asking which of many types of explanation predominates in or is characteristic of history. Answers (as was illustrated in chapter I section 3 above) have mostly taken one or other of three forms. Most prominent, since the 1939–45 war at least, has been the 'positivist', regularity or covering law theory of Hempel, Gardiner, White and others: the view that *genuine* explanation in history as elsewhere, in history because *every*where, consists in subsuming under law. Opposed to this are claims that historical explanation is predominantly rational, in terms of intentions, purposes, beliefs, standards – a good many significantly different types of explanation being, it has to be allowed, brought together here under one broad heading. For Collingwood all properly historical explanations are of this type, for Popper some are; and Dray, as reported above, is prepared to follow Collingwood a great part of the way. Thirdly, there are views to the effect that historical writing is, so to say, explanatory in itself (Oakeshott, Nowell-Smith, Danto, Leff) or that specific sorts of explanation, law, rational or whatever it might be, are in place in history only in so far as they contribute to the development and facilitate the following of historical narratives (Renier, Gallie). In support of this latter view may be urged the impression, difficult to escape when reading history, that there is danger of distortion in the project of picking out explanatory passages. In truth there seems to be a continuous gradation from relatively straight reporting or describing, through various levels of interpretation, to explanation. Partly, no doubt, this is a literary effect. Historians always used to, and to an extent still do, aim to present smoothly continuous accounts of their subject matter, with questions asked, problems posed left merely implicit; all scaffolding removed, rough working erased before presentation to the public. Novelists are crass and tiresome if they are forever telling the reader what they are about, why they represent their characters in this or that situation, mention this or that element in their supposed personal and social backgrounds. Their art consists in, so to say, suggesting the questions along with the answers. Historians have often tried to follow suit – not always, be it said, from purely literary ambition; the same effect may be observed in that most austerely workmanlike historical writing which leaves the (selected) facts to speak for themselves.

It should not beg any questions concerning the merits and demerits of the three views to observe at this point that the distinction seen between explanation and interpretation, and between these two and description, will be a function of the view taken about explanation specifically. On the third of the views distinguished above differences of principle are minimal. Narrative, as it were, progresses towards explanatory status to the extent that it is organised, purged of irrelevances, focused on questions left unanswered in earlier narratives or on new questions generated by new information or the changing interests and per-spectives of later generations. On the rational view, as expounded in an extreme form by Collingwood (1946, especially part IV, section 11), there is no real distinction between description, interpretation and explanation. Setting out the facts, by which is meant reporting what happened as *actions* i.e. as being informed by thought or for purposes, is simultaneously understanding and explaining them. For the law view, however, the position is very different. What happened, the story, will be in principle independent of the explanation of it. Possibilities of explanation depend on whether there are available laws or near lawlike generalisations which can be used to connect the events in the story with antecedent events known or knowable to the historian. There will, of course, in so far as explanations are actually achieved, be reason to fit the antecedent events into the story, so that achieved explanations would supply criteria of relevance, principles of interpretation for narratives. The qualification 'achieved' is important, however, because it is characteristic of proponents of the law view that they recognise the very great difficulty of actually obtaining such explanations in history and the unlikelihood of any laws or generalisations which can be pressed into service cohering together to form explanatory theories. The result is that, although in principle explanation might determine interpretation, in practice interpretation is conceived as an inferior substitute for genuine explanation, something brought into history from the outside.

It is hard, in view of the variety of explanations actually present in history books, to credit that any one of the three main views should be claimed to be the whole truth about historical explanation. Adherents of the rational and narrative views do not generally deny that other types of explanation are possible. Notoriously, however, it has been maintained that all genuine explanations must conform, or aspire, to the law type; apparently different sorts, notably rational explanations, being either assimilated or denied to be explanations at all. I shall dispute the possibility of assimilation below. But, manifestly, the main determinant of this view is nothing specific to history, but is rather a monolithic conception of explanation in general. If there is but one sort of explanation then, clearly, it must be this which occurs in history, or none does. On this basis other views of historical explanation would be non-starters. I will, therefore, preface my discussion of the three views of historical explanation with a brief account of explanation in general and a glance at what I take to be the most usual employments of the phrase 'historical explanation'.

If the dictionary is to be believed the ordinary uses of 'explanation' are quite varied and not very close to the model set up by covering law theorists. One sense involves *making known in detail*, as, for instance, when one explains how an internal combustion engine works, and in the course of so doing points out that the carburettor does this or that. One may equally well speak of explaining the taxation or the examination system. Often, where what is explained is a machine, system, organisation, or the operation of such, explaining will involve giving the means/end rationale, i.e. telling what result is aimed at and how it is intended to be achieved – but this is not essential. It is perfectly possible to explain something thought to be pointless or dysfunctional, say, the honours system or the monarchy. For this first sense of the word I do not think that there can be a clear distinction between explaining and describing or reporting. As regards the second sense, *making intelligible*, where it is a meaning that is in question, explaining is mostly a matter of rephrasing in more familiar language – 'familiar' being, of course, a relative term. Words familiar to one person may well not be so to another. To someone who knows what a syllogism is it will be possible to explain an enthymeme as a syllogism of which one proposition is not stated, but not to someone who does not. Again, for most people the phrase 'male sibling', although it is an exact analysis of the concept, fails to convey the meaning of the term 'brother'. Philosophical analyses of concepts may lack explanatory import for many people, as also may scientific explanations, which are not indeed normally of the meanings of expressions, but which may well be in terms less familiar to the layman than those used to describe the phenomenon explained. This relativistic aspect is characteristic of the ordinary use of 'explanation' and the point at which it diverges most sharply from the scientific use. It is a major source of the openness of the ordinary notion. Its tendency is to permit explanations to be as various as the possibilities of human ignorance and incomprehension. *Accounting for* is the third dictionary sense; for instance, accounting for one's conduct. Often this will involve giving what I have been terming a rational explanation, saying what was aimed at and what was believed likely to attain it. Other people's conduct can be explained in the same way. Where one's own conduct is concerned explanation is liable to shade into or overlap with excuse and justification. Usually, to report someone's reasons, without endorsement, is to explain without justifying: to give one's own reasons, which one will necessarily endorse, is to justify, and it may well be from the point of view of somebody else to leave something unexplained. In fact a great deal of what is offered in the way of accounting for human conduct is ambiguous or indeterminate as between explanation and justification.

How does 'scientific' or law explanation fit into this account of common usage? Plainly it is one way of accounting for what goes on. From laws and initial condition statements a statement reporting what is to be explained is deduced. There is here built in a standard of explanatory completeness, namely, valid deduction from true premises, which itself constitutes a justification for the employment of the language of necessity – given the explanation, the event (supposing it be an event which is explained) is shown to have *had* to happen, to have been *necessary*; and its non-occurrence shown to have been *impossible*. Unhappily, especially for studies of human affairs, it is often forgotten that the standard of completeness is so high as to to be rarely attainable in any field. Equally unhappily it is also forgotten that the necessity is conditional upon the laws and initial condition statements. *Given* them, but not otherwise, the conclusions of explanatory arguments follow necessarily. Nevertheless this ideal of completeness and necessity constitutes a profound difference between scientific, law explanations and many 'ordinary', non-technical explanations, which do not aspire so high, but still fall within the dictionary meaning of the word.

The ordinary meaning of 'explanation' is thus wide enough to accommodate all the types of explanation which have been claimed to be characteristic of history. Is not this, one may ask, decisive against the claim of any one view of historical explanation to be the whole truth? Unquestionably it tells against such claims, but not conclusively. In the first place it does not bear upon the question whether other explanations are reducible to or incomplete specimens of the law type – more on that below. Second, common usage is not authoritative in philosophy. It is perfectly possible that a common word, in the present case 'explain', yokes together very different concepts. It could well be that on reflection one might come to feel that a marginally ordinary use of 'explain' picks out something radically different from the other things that go under that word, and that this something (law explanation) does the sort of thing the others do inadequately so superlatively well that it is unreasonable to continue counting them as explanations at all. Of course, in the dictionary sense they will remain explanations. To exclude them would be to change the dictionary sense. But there may be excellent reasons for so doing. Common usage, the dictionary, is an often undervalued assistant, but a very bad master. It may be wrong, and in the end I think it is, for the proponents of the law theory to adopt so high-handed a line with other sorts of explanation. But it cannot be ruled out as wrong in principle. The only way to combat it is to show that some of the other sorts of commonly recognised explanations meet distinctive needs within history; to show that they, as perhaps law explanations *as such* do not, satisfy the sorts of curiosity that lead people to interest themselves in the subject. The task is not eased by the fact that many people, once they have sampled – or imagined – the delights of law explanations, lose all taste for more day-to-day varieties. The loss is theirs, but one can understand their condition. One cannot effectively oppose the law theory without first having felt its great intellectual attraction.

One further word, before leaving the question of explanation in general, on terminology. The most widely used explanation-intro-ducing word is, I suppose, 'because', though the spread of explanations conforming to the dictionary meanings is wider still. Explanations of what something is, or how it works, and narrative explanations, are not heralded by 'because'. Nevertheless the word is very widely used in connection with explanations, but from this it most certainly does not follow that most explanations are in a significant sense causal. 'Because' is as properly associated with rational as with law explanations, even though the former would often, perhaps usually, be said to be in terms of reasons rather than causes. 'Cause', in spite of its narrower range of application than 'because', is not in fact, though it would be convenient if it were, clearly distinguishable in use from 'reason' and it overlaps in application. Someone's reasons or purposes are very often termed causes where human affairs are concerned. Similarly it is unrealistic to suppose causes to be firmly fixed on the near side of the explanation/ justification divide. That someone claims to be engaged in causal analysis in history does not guarantee that he is seeking to assign causes of a sort associated with law rather than rational explanations. More will be said about the use of 'cause' in historical contexts in the next chapter. My present aim is simply to emphasise the fluidity of terminology and the consequent impossibility of grounding firm conclusions about the sort of explanations characteristic of history upon it.

I will conclude this section with a glance at the common use of 'historical explanation' and related phrases. My impression is that the most prominent use, as found for instance in the expression 'can only explain it historically', is to *contrast* an account of how something came about with a rational explanation of it and, more doubtfully, sometimes with a law explanation too. On the former point it appears to me that one most often hears talk of explaining historically from someone who has despaired of giving the rationale of an institution or procedure and consequently falls back on telling how it came into being or to be adopted. It could, of course, be accepted that common usage is as stated without conceding that it supports a contrast between historical explanation on the one hand and rational explanation as such on the other. For historical explanation, in the shape of a detailed account of how something came about, will itself be partly in rational terms, in terms of purposive actions and their often unintended results, which may indeed themselves be explicable in terms of laws. Common usage, though often interesting in its suggestions, is never decisive.

I grant that 'historical explanation' is less often used to point a contrast with law explanations, but suspect that this is because the possibility of law explanations in historical and social contexts is not widely recognised. Nevertheless it might well be said by someone who felt unable, say, to explain the phenomenon of simultaneous inflation and unemployment in economic terms, that he could only explain historically how it had come about. I intend no suggestion that economic explanations are necessarily of the law type. Some would appear to be rational, as when an individual's distribution of his expenditure among a variety of commodities is explained as tending to maximise his satisfaction. The sort of economic explanations contemplated here are, however, rather in terms of laws connecting such statistical aggregates as national income and expenditure, total investment, level of employment, etc. – 'quasi-laws' would, no doubt, be more accurate, since they would presumably be confined in their application to specific sorts of socio-economic systems.

The ordinary use of 'historical explanation' does not support very much, but for what it is worth it tends to diminish the plausibility of the otherwise attractive view (Lucas) that all types of explanation are equally historical. It supports rather the idea that a characteristically historical explanation is a matter of telling in detail how things happened.

In the next two sections I shall discuss law and rational explanations respectively. With regard to the former my claim will be that, although law explanations indubitably occur in history, and although laws and generalisations have to be appealed to or presupposed in constructing narratives and relating them to evidence, undue concentration on this type of explanation seriously misrepresents the characteristic interests of historians. The view that historical explanation is rational is much better in this respect, but in another it too is seriously misleading as tending to diminish the importance of the very great deal that there is in history which neither was nor could have been the object of anybody's rational endeavour. I shall conclude the chapter by considering the narrative view of explanation.

2. Law Explanations

(i) As already remarked, examples apparently of law explanations are not hard to come by. One given by Gardiner is: 'Louis XIV died unpopular . . . having caused France to lose . . . the incomparable position she had gained by the policy of the cardinals' (1952, p. 65). Here that which is to be explained, the *explicandum*, is Louis XIV's unpopularity. The, admittedly pretty rough or approximate, generalisation is stated to be: 'Rulers . . . who pursue policies detrimental to the countries over which they rule become unpopular' (p. 96). The initial condition statement reports Louis's having been such a ruler. It may be noted, as evidence that explanatory passages do not bear their correct interpretations on their faces, and hence as an indication of how everyone finds the examples he wants in history books, that Dray claims that this example can be interpreted in rational terms (1957, p. 134). His allegation is that it presents itself as an explanation only because everyone can see that policies such as Louis's are reported to have been frustrate typically human hopes and objectives. Law explanations, the implication is, which do not thus admit of rational interpretation, would not be felt to explain. This, in my opinion, goes too far. I can see that, for instance, an explanation, couched in terms of specifically twentieth-century economic theory, of some medieval phenomenon might be felt to be defective as involving concepts not reflected in the consciousness of the people it relates to. This does not, however, demonstrate that law explanations can never be sufficient in history. The moral might equally well be just that a particular law explanation was not sufficient in that it left some particular matters, which happened to interest us, unexplained.

Another example of a law explanation, this time from Hempel, is: 'Dust bowl farmers migrate to California "because" continual drought and sandstorms render their existence increasingly precarious, and because California seems to them to offer so much better living conditions.' This is backed by the generalisation: 'Populations will tend to migrate to regions which offer better living conditions' (1942, pp. 349–50).

These are philosophers' examples, with the generalisations involved clearly specified. This is by no means always the case with apparent examples of law explanations. Take another example of Gardiner's, again from a history of France: 'The conditions were favourable to a revolution. The government had no military forces at hand. The working class was passing through an acute stage of unemployment . . .' (1952, p. 66). Here it is pretty clear that the author had in mind some generalisation about the genesis of revolutions, but it is not clear from the passage quoted what the generalisation is. Such uncertainties present themselves even in good history books. A further example, from A. J. P. Taylor's *English History, 1914–1945*, which might well be taken as aspiring to the law model on the strength of its reference to *forces*, is even more indeterminate in this regard: 'The rejection by Labour of Mosley's programme was a decisive, though negative, event in British history: the moment when the British people resolved unwittingly to stand on the ancient ways. The very forces which made Great Britain peaceful and stable prevented her from becoming the country of the New Deal' (p. 286).

Renier refers (p. 47) to the fact that early in the fifteenth century a change in the direction of the Gulf Stream brought fish nearer to the shores of the Low Countries, thus producing a boom in fishing. This, perhaps, reads like an intended sufficient explanation, the increased supply of fish bringing about, being a sufficient condition for, a great increase in the activity of fishermen. Brief reflection, however, makes it clear that, in absolute terms, one has here at most a necessary condition. Without fish, manifestly, there can be no fishing: but fish are not enough. Boats are needful, and nets too; as is a social system with division of labour, in which it can be contemplated that men should go to sea, and which can support a requisite level of technology. This will normally be the case with law explanations in history. Although the language used may often suggest the opposite there will be no absolutely sufficient explanations. For obvious reasons. Indeed, in all contexts, the only way to secure application for the expression 'sufficient condition' (and hence 'cause' if causes be identified as sufficient conditions) is to suppose a background of standing conditions. A sufficient condition (relative to the background) can then be understood to be a factor such that, when it is introduced into the situation, the event of which it is the (relatively) sufficient condition occurs. A necessary condition is correspondingly a factor such that, when it is subtracted from the situation, the event in question does not occur. (The same event, say, the increased supply of fish, may be necessary relative to a certain set of background conditions, and sufficient relative to an enlarged set.) Given these conventions the laws respectively involved in sufficient and necessary condition explanations can be distinguished as follows: In a sufficient condition explanation the law will be in the form 'Whenever (given background conditions) sc then e' whereas with a necessary condition explanation it will have the form 'Whenever (. . .) e then nc'. Alternatively, here ignoring background conditions, the difference could be expressed thus: that, for sufficient condition explanations, the law has the form 'If sc then e', whereas, for necessary condition explanations, it has the form 'If e then nc', which is equivalent to 'Only if nc then e'.

There are considerable differences between sufficient and necessary condition explanations. The former may be said to show that an event was necessary, had to happen, the latter to show that it was possible, could have happened. (Obviously an event which did happen must have been possible, but one may still wonder how, in virtue of what, it was possible.) There is, consequently, a tendency for anti-determinists, upholders of free will who think it compromised by sufficient explanations of human actions, to prefer to think of historical explanations as being in terms of necessary conditions. In this they are very likely forgetting that absolutely sufficient conditions are out of the question anyway, and that the background situations relative to which sufficient and necessary conditions can alone be recognised will often include factors plainly subject to human control. There may be good reasons for holding that explanation in history is normally in terms of necessary conditions, but a desire to safeguard free will is not one of them.

Further, if causes are not to be identified as sufficient conditions, necessary condition explanations will have to be said to be in terms of partial or contributory, or perhaps facilitating causes. Some upholders of the law theory, for example White, seem mainly to have necessary condition explanations in mind.

I do not want in any way to play down the importance of the differences between necessary and sufficient explanations, but for the most part in the present section I shall not insist on them. To do so would often merely introduce irrelevant repetition and complication.

For the same reason I shall not as a rule distinguish strictly universal (deterministic) laws and genaralisations from proportional or statistical ones. It is frequently supposed that laws relating to human affairs will be more likely to be proportional than universal. I believe that this opinion often rests on a failure to distinguish generalisations universal in content but of low probability (i.e. not very likely to be true) from generalisations proportional in content (for example concerning suicides per 100,000 deaths) which may be highly probable or even certain. There may be some disagreement over which of these models better fits the laws or generalisations associated with putative law explanations in history – the one thing certain being the lamentable shortage of highly probable or certain generalisations with universal content (i.e. laws proper, though the expression 'statistical law' is used). Gardiner's law about rulers becoming unpopular is expressed universally, but stated to be rough and approximate, and Hempel's law about migrating populations is qualified by the word 'tend'. In these two cases we seem closer to the universal content, low probability model, and this I suspect to be the usual case over those wide areas of history dealing with events which, very crudely speaking, occur rather infrequently and never in exactly the same forms. Generalisations with proportional content, statistical generalisations proper, are more at home in cases where, again very crudely, virtually identical events occur in very large numbers – there are lots of births and deaths and smaller, but still large, numbers of illegitimate births and suicides, and the proportions of the smaller to the larger numbers exhibit a considerable degree of stability within populations. In some specialised histories such generalisations are important, and may come to be made more general use of, but as yet they would seem exceptional in history rather than the rule.

Thus my belief is that statistical generalisations are so far less important in history than purportedly universal laws. It is anyway the case that most of the observations I wish to make about law explanations would only be irrelevantly complicated by treating universal and statistical law explanations separately, though some law theorists have done so. It should, however, be noted that the law theory of explanation loses much of its necessitarian charm if demoted to the merely statistical level. On the other hand, though, statistical explanations are less threatening for anti-deterministic defenders of free will.

(ii) Two questions for the law theory are whether historical explanations so conceived can ever be complete and whether there are available for history laws, regularities or generalisations of the appropriate types.

On the former it seems to be admitted, even by supporters of the law theory, that law explanations found in history are never deductively watertight. Insufficient is supplied in the way of initial condition statements and laws for the explicandum (the statement describing what it is that is supposed to be explained) actually to be deduced. It is, moreover, rarely or never possible to discover from the explanatory passages themselves how they would have to be filled out in order to be brought nearer to deductive completeness. It is not simply that matters of common knowledge or things the reader could work out for himself are left unsaid. By the standards of the law theory itself, it looks less like incomplete statement than disastrous inadequacy.

It may, however, be urged in defence that it is unreasonable to expect more of explanatory deductive arguments than that their conclusions should follow, 'other things being equal'. This might seem at first sight to be a promising manoeuvre, for the same is true even in the applied science cases – cracked car radiators, overloaded electrical systems short-circuiting – where the law model works best. The cracked radiator is explained by the fact that the temperature fell below freezing and the generalisation that at $4°C$ water expands as it cools and turns to ice. But a great deal more is required before the cracking of the radiator actually follows. How much will depend on people's interests in a particular case, though in practice they will always be content with less than the full amount. There will remain things which, if not equal, will upset the explanation. Does this mean, then, that the incompleteness of historical (law) explanations is no different in principle from that of applied science explanations? If so it is victory for the law theory, for applied science examples are its paradigms. But to concede this would be to allow formal similarities to obscure substantial differences. In the applied science cases we have a much clearer notion of the sorts of things that might or might not be equal and, more importantly, often know that or how to find out whether they are. In the historical cases, by contrast, there may be no clear idea of what is lacking and hence little idea of how to set about supplying it.

There are two ways of interpreting this result. One is that it shows that the law theory does not fit history very well. The other, founded in the assumption that it does and must fit since it is the only possible theory of explanation, is that the explanations up to now provided in history are radically defective (compare White, 1965, p. 28). In support of the latter it may be held that it is unreasonable to assume in advance of all enquiry that most explanations offered in history are acceptable just as they are. On the other side, though, it would seem equally unreasonable to suppose that none are, and even more so to suppose that none is better than any other. There is, consequently, some ground, even from the viewpoint of the law theory, for relaxing its standards enough to allow some historical explanations to pass, if not to achieve honours.

One way is to allege that the explanation requirements we are concerned to satisfy may be for something less than full-scale law explanations. Sometimes, because it is felt that the law or generalisation is obvious, an initial condition statement only may be supplied: other times, since the initial conditions are known, it will be the law which is needed. Arguably the former is the typical case in history. (This would at any rate explain why there is so often uncertainty about the formulation of the laws presupposed in the kinds of examples quoted, and be in line with the suggestion of chapter II section 5 above that history is a matter of arguing from documentary evidence, i.e. from rather particular matters of fact, in accordance with vague, low-level commonsense generalisations, rather than from nomological evidence, i.e. from rather general matters of fact in accordance with putative laws.) If explanation requirements are thus regarded as problem relative, it would follow that even in history they could be fully satisfied, despite the fact that deductively complete explanations were not to be had. Neither the historian nor his public need consequently be embarrassed by the difficulty of producing properly formulated laws.

An argument on these lines, which connects the practice of historians in the area of explanation with interests characteristic of historians, and which accordingly does not have to represent their practice as falling short in relation to some external standard, seems to me to be the most promising defence of the law theory. Hempel's doctrine of the 'explanation sketch' (1942) and White's 'existential regularism' (1965), though similarly intended, appear to be less satisfactory in this regard.

Hempel, who is perhaps the most unbending proponent of the law theory, is nevertheless prepared to allow that explanations are rarely presented in full in either history or science. Often, however, in science the incompleteness is inessential, but in history *and* sociology (a possibly significant conjunction since sociology is regarded as a generalising science) it may be impossible to remedy it. For two reasons: since the generalisations required to complete the explanations are supposed to be common knowledge, they tend not to be given; and they, and the various other supplements requisite in order to render the explanations complete, are difficult to formulate both precisely and in accordance with the relevant evidence. One might feel that there is here *either* a damaging admission of the inappropriateness of the law theory to history *or* a harsh exposure of the standards of explanatory cogency observed in the subject. Hempel, one feels, inclines to the second response, whilst introducing the idea of the explanation sketch in order to soften the blow.

He concedes, therefore, that in history, and for that matter psychoanalysis, all that can in practice be achieved is an explanation sketch, an outline of what a complete law explanation would be like if only it could be found. Explanation sketches require filling out and, crucially, are better or worse in proportion as they indicate where the filling-out statements are to be found. Sometimes it will turn out that they cannot be found.

Whatever Hempel's intentions one cannot but feel that the best he can bring himself to say about explanation in history is not very flattering.

White's existential regularism – 'regularism' being his name for the law theory – treats of contributory causes, i.e. necessary or facilitating causes (see above in the present section), but there is no reason why a view of this type should not as well fit any other type of law explanation. He writes (1965, p. 60): 'A statement of the form, "A is a contributory cause of C", is true if and only if there is an explanatory deductive argument containing "A" as its premise and "C" as its conclusion.' An explanatory deductive argument would be one in which 'C' is validly deduced from 'A' *together with* laws and other assumptions. The attraction of the view is that, on the one hand, it makes the acceptability of historical explanations stand or fall with the *existence* of (complete) explanatory deductive arguments, and that, on the other, it does not require that the arguments actually be produced, as they usually could not be. It may be said that the view is that explanatory statements in history imply that *there are* explanatory arguments and law, but *without* implying determinate laws. In particular White denies that explanatory statements in history imply their associated superficial generalisations – the latter for an explanation in the form 'c because A' would be 'Whenever (or if) A then C', if A is offered as a sufficient condition, and 'Only if A then C', if A is a necessary condition. I am sure that one reason why many historians are unhappy with the law theory is their reluctance to be pinned down to the superficial generalisations associated with their explanations. They want to be able to maintain such things as that Louis XIV became unpopular because his policies were thought to be detrimental to his country, without being committed to holding that such policies always make rulers unpopular, which doubtless would not be true. White's theory, though still stipulating that generalisations are relevant at a certain stage, is at least conciliatory on this sensitive point.

It remains to explain how, as is required by White's view, it can be known that there is an explanatory deductive argument, without its being known what that argument is. Plainly something short of the actual production of the argument must suffice. White's suggestion is that we might have inductive evidence for supposing that there is an argument. The idea is that, given 'c because A', we might first consider an argument based on the generalisation 'Whenever A then C', which is in fact the associated superficial generalisation. If this fails, i.e. if the generalisation is false, we try the generalisation 'Whenever A^1 and A^2 then c'. That failing too, we try 'Whenever A^1, A^2, A^3 . . . then c' – that is to say we move along a series of more and more complex generalisations, the claim being that, in the course of thus proceeding, we may at some stage reasonably become convinced that there *is* a satisfactory explanatory deductive argument even though we have not yet reached it and could not formulate it completely. I have no quarrel with this suggestion, and indeed think that the possibility of having inductive evidence for the existence of an explanatory deductive argument might be developed in other ways too, for example by arguing that there will be an explanatory argument in a given case because it resembles other cases in which we are already satisfied that there is one.

White's view has the great merit of suggesting that some historical explanations might be judged acceptable just as they are, though there remains, to my mind, the impression that they are being accepted as second best, and that historians should at least to a considerable extent concern themselves with trying to bring them up to the law standard proper. And this historians appear to feel little obligation to do. They do not seem to recognise the law standard as authoritative, though hard or impossible fully to satisfy. It is rather that they do not recognise it as authoritative at all.

(iii) Consider now the second, overlapping question whether there are available for history laws or generalisations of appropriate types. These would have to bear upon phenomena ranging from wars and revolutions, changes in economic systems, the rise and decline of religions, at one end of the scale, to the reactions of individual rulers, religious leaders, moulders of opinion, perhaps even men and women in the street, at the other. They would have to cover all phenomena studied in the social sciences, including among them individual psychology, though they would not necessarily be laws recognised in or readily assignable to any particular social science, inasmuch as historians typically report and seek to explain events under 'ordinary' i.e. non-theoretical descriptions. Our question, then, concerns the availability of social laws for the historian. It differs from the question whether, among social laws generally, it is possible to distinguish a subclass of specifically *historical* ones. A number of writers have addressed themselves to this latter question. Popper's answer (1945, ch. 25) is firmly negative; Hempel (1942, p. 355) professes neutrality, though writing as if he inclined to the negative view; and White (1943), at the end of a paper devoted to exploring what is peculiar to historical terms, and so laws too, concludes that they cannot be effectively distinguished from sociological ones. It is indeed difficult, from the point of view of our present concern with particular historical explanations, to see what a specifically historical law – if it is not simply a non-theoretical generalisation – could be. Laws, if that is the word, or developmental patterns in large-scale phenomena, of the sort purveyed by Hegel, Marx, Toynbee and others, are a possibly different matter, but not the present concern.

Examples of laws of the relevant sort have already been culled from Gardiner and Hempel who, as we have noted, freely admit that they are pretty rough and ready. Other times, as by Popper *à propos* of 'If of two armies which are about equally well armed and led, one has a tremendous superiority in men, then the other never wins' (1945, p. 264), it is conceded that they are trivial. Opponents of the law theory regularly allege that putative laws turn out on examination to be either false, trivial or non-universal. The really striking thing here is the *similarity* of the points made by critics and defenders of the law theory. There seems to be less disagreement over what the laws figuring in apparent historical law explanations actually are like, than over the question whether the explanations themselves are properly characterisable as rather remote approximations to a scientific ideal.

Responses to the latter question are determined as much by considerations relating to law and explanation generally as by anything specific to history. Anyone who takes the term 'law' fully seriously, accepting its implications of strict universality and theoretical precision, will rarely encounter laws in historical contexts. The alternative terms, 'regularity' and 'generalisation', which I have been constantly associating with the term 'law', have these implications in much lower degree. There is the less reason to doubt their applicability in history, but they may provoke different doubt, founded upon a rigorist notion of explanation, whether mere regularities or generalisations could explain. Similar doubts are aroused by suggestions, not of course usually made in *support* of the law theory, that historians' generalisations are better conceived as 'summaries' than universals proper (Oakeshott, 1933, p. 161; Walsh, 1951, pp. 39–40; Gardiner, 1952, p. 90; Nowell-Smith, 1957, pp. 123–7; Leff, 1969, p. 95). Oakeshott's example is: 'All the Reformation parliaments were packed,' which, he contends, is not a universal claim about members of an open class, but is rather about a temporally and geographically limited list of items referred to by a certain phrase. I have no doubt that this is a possible sense of 'generalisation', and that it reflects the attitude often taken by historians to the apparently universal statements which occasionally escape even the most self-denying among them. With some apparent law explanations we have, accordingly, to face the choice whether to deny that they are genuinely explanatory at all or to allow that non-law lawlike generalisations, even mere summaries, can figure in explanations.

Why should not a summary explain? Clearly it will not meet the standard laid down by the law theory, but why should that be decisive? One's surprise at the idea that a particular Reformation parliament was packed is undeniably diminished by the discovery that they all were; the individual case is accounted for by being presented as one of a number of similar cases. This, so far as it goes, is surely explanation within the ordinary meaning of the term.

Reluctance to be content with the width of application left open by the ordinary meaning could, however, have a source different from question-begging adherence to the law theory. There is a feeling, which deserves respect even though it can lead to error, that there must be something universal about any explanation. It may be described as the recognition of the 'universalisability' of 'because'. (It will be remembered that not all explanations are introduced by 'because', so that the following remarks must be taken as referring only to those which are, though all explanations make some reference beyond the individual case.) Wherever there is an explanation in the form 'B because A' in one case, a similar explanation can be repudiated in another, only if there is a relevant difference between them. For instance, anyone who explains the outcome of a battle by reference to the larger forces on the winning side runs the risk of being called upon to find a relevant difference between his battle and any of the very many others in which the numerically greater force lost.

It is essential to be clear what the universalisability of 'because' does and does not involve. It does not, in the first place, entail that 'B because A' cannot be maintained in a particular case unless one can justifiably assert 'Whenever A then B' or 'Only if A then B', i.e. the associated superficial generalisations. This is the error of the crudest version of the law theory. Nor does it entail that one has to envisage every one of the possibly relevant cases before offering an explanation in any – on this basis there could be no achieved explanations in any field, whether historical or scientific. What is entailed is only that 'because' always has a reference beyond the individual case in virtue of the generality of the descriptions under which the phenomena in question are explained.

It will be instructive here to consider the partly parallel case of the word 'good', to which the thesis of universalisability also applies, but where its scope and limits are probably more widely understood than they are in relation to 'because'. Objects are judged good as falling under general descriptions, i.e. they are good *so-and-so*s – cars, hammers, paintings, novels, people, actions, or whatever or whoever it might be – whence it follows that there cannot be two objects differing in the sole respect that one is good and the other not. Consequently, anyone who judges an object good and an apparently similar one not so is committed to finding a relevant difference between them. Judgements of goodness thus have a reference beyond the individual case, but it does not follow that, whenever we hold that an x which is A is good, we are committed to the general principle that all *x*s which are A are good. (This is the analogue of the error of the crudest form of law theory.) In some simple cases, to be sure, it may seem so. We may hold a knife to be good because it is sharp, because it takes and retains a cutting edge, and be inclined to generalise to the principle that all sharp knives are good. It is, in fact, doubtful whether this is wise: sharpness is not a sufficient condition of goodness in knives, since there might be offsetting defects such as loose handles; nor a necessary condition in, say, a knife selected for scraping or puttying rather than cutting. But there is no need to press these objections since, in complex cases, generalisation is obviously not possible. Attention may well be drawn to certain features of characterisation and construction in support of the judgement that a novel is good, but no one is likely to want to maintain that all books with similar features are good, or that no book lacking them can be. Comparisons with other novels will, however, be in place. Sometimes, though they possess the features which led us to deem the first book good, we shall nevertheless find them not good because of other particular features. Other times they will seem just too different in aim and execution for there to be much point in balancing their merits and demerits against those of the work we were primarily concerned with. At no point do we seriously expect to finish up with general principles. It is rather that universalisability commits one to a certain pattern of enquiry and discussion, of which the point is more the deepening of our appreciation of the individual work (though, of course, on the basis of comparison and contrast) than establishing general principles of evaluation.

The same moral could often be drawn with regard to explanation in history, namely that, although there is always reference beyond the individual case to relevant comparisons and contrasts, the object of the exercise is the enlarging of one's understanding of the individual case and not its assimilation to other cases by subsuming it with them under a law. It is this that the law theory, even in its more sophisticated forms, fails sufficiently to bring out. It can allow that the superficial generalisations associated with apparent law explanations in history neither are nor are supposed by historians to be laws proper, but it fails to repudiate the implication that what is wanted are simply better, more complex and refined, laws. And this misrepresents the interests of at least many historians in many areas of history. For them the point of the comparisons and contrasts, which the generality of explanation (the universalisability of 'because') lets them in for, is not the discovery or application of genuine laws. Their focus of interest is the particular case.

I do not want to exaggerate and deny that there are *any* examples of straightforward law explanations in history. I am sure that many such occur in the course of narratives and other pieces of historical writing. But I do believe that, when an historian pauses to concentrate on a matter which he feels calls for explanation, his concern is likely to be different from what the law theory suggests it should be.

I have noted suggestions that apparently general laws applied in history are better conceived as summaries. Another, in some respects illuminating, way to characterise them is on the analogy of aesthetic standards or canons of taste. Throughout the long history of criticism there have been recurrent attempts to formulate canons of taste – the golden section, the optimum proportions for the human figure, the unities of time, place and action (as they were conceived in relation to the classical French theatre, if not by Aristotle himself), rules of harmony in music, and the like. The perennial hope has been that such canons might determine which works were good, that they could be appealed to in support of critical judgements, most strongly that they might even constitute guidelines for practitioners in the arts. That the hope is always disappointed does not prevent its being constantly reborn. Canons of taste, however, exhibit all the vices complained of in historical generalisations; falsity (admittedly good works which violate them, bad ones which conform); particularity (they at best fit a particular set of works, not all works conforming to a general description, i.e. they are 'summaries', not genuine universals); vacuity (often, as with such conceptions as 'unity amid variety', 'purposiveness without purpose', 'significant form', there is no way of telling that the canon is satisfied *independently* of judging a work good). In fact it is widely recognised that such canons, if more than crutches for beginners or material for misguided textbook producers, are defensible only to the extent that they encourage one to see through them to the exemplary works, the subjects of comparison and contrast, which are the bases upon which they arise. They are not prescriptive rules, against which works are to be judged – how could such rules be established independently of judgements on the works themselves? Nor are they simply summary records of past judgements on individual works. They both reflect past judgements and point, but not precisely, towards possible future ones; they cannot be so far detached from actual and possible judgements as to have an independent life of their own.

The error of the law theory of historical explanation resembles that of an aesthetic theory which construes aesthetic standards as authoritative over judgements in particular cases. In reality the dependence is much more the other way. Perhaps at the outset the canons guide judgement, but in the end it is the judgements which must prevail. So it is in history – typically, at least. Generalisations both suggest and reflect what has to be said of particular cases, but they do not govern it. The canon of taste analogy may help to bring this out, though like all analogies it has its limitations. The point is that in both fields there is the exercise of judgement in individual cases, an exercise which cannot be adequately represented as a matter of applying independently established generalities – and this is the only point. I certainly have no wish to suggest that historians are evaluating (making value judgements) in the way that critics do – though, of course, the word 'evaluating' is sometimes used virtually synonymously with 'judging'. It is vital to maintain a distinction between describing and explaining on the one hand and evaluating and justifying on the other. Those who dispute the necessity of this distinction sometimes forget that it is still needful for it to be significant to maintain, as they often want also to do, that description and explanation are at times compromised by evaluative and justificatory interests.

3. Rational Explanations

(i) I use 'rational explanation' to refer mainly to the central area of a spectrum running from simple dispositional explanations at one extreme, through those in terms of the purposes and intentions of agents in particular circumstances, to justifications or specimens of direct as opposed to reported practical reasoning at the other.

'Simple dispositional explanation' covers, for instance, accounting for Lloyd George's conduct by reference to his bold deviousness, Asquith's and Churchill's by reference to their indecisiveness and combativeness – examples abound in Taylor's *English History, 1914–1945* and in most political histories. It has been suggested – for example by White (1965, pp. 47–52) – that such explanations closely approximate to the law pattern; and it is implied, if not asserted, by Gardiner (1952, especially part IV), that all rational explanations are like dispositional ones. If both positions could be established the law theory really would begin to look like a general account of explanation in history.

On the former point it is perfectly fair to regard a dispositional explanation as bringing an event under a generalisation. The force of saying that Asquith was indecisive or Churchill combative is that they tended to act, or usually acted, in certain characteristic ways in certain circumstances. Statements to this effect are quite properly called generalisations; though, of course, law theorists are likely to feel that they fall short of full explanation certifying, prediction supporting, status, because, in the first place, they fail to assert that actions of the type in question are performed on *every* occasion of a specific kind, and, second, they are about the actions of named individuals rather than *anyone* satisfying a general description – in short because they are felt not to be genuine laws. I have already made clear my attitude to claims like these, which arise from rather than support the law theory. Another reason why reference to dispositions may be dismissed as non-explanatory is that it leaves a good deal unexplained. We may well be more interested in having explained Churchill's combativeness, or why unlike lesser mortals he had so much scope to indulge it, or such things as the conservatism of the English, the thoroughness of the Germans, than in having other things explained in terms of them. But it does not follow that nothing can be so explained. It is surely an error to suppose that a putative explanation, which leaves something unexplained, explains nothing at all: that in order to explain anything one has to explain everything. The error is not by any means confined to supporters of the law theory. It is also an important determinant of the view that de facto regularities, non-lawlike universals, commonsense generalisations do not explain. The truth would seem to be that they do explain something, though perhaps not much, and perhaps not what we are most interested in. 'All ruminants divide the hoof' affords a rather dull explanation of why some particular creature, which is a ruminant, does so; and this is quite unaffected by the fact that it constitutes no answer at all to the more interesting question why they all do. It is impossible to understand explanation without recognising that explanation requests differ widely in content, and that in consequence purported explanations can be judged only in relation to what it is they are supposed to explain. The most, not the least, that can be required of any explanation is that it should fully answer the particular question which evokes it.

The classical way of assimilating dispositional explanations to the law model is to represent dispositions as the causes of their manifestations. Thus a set of actions like giving painfully large sums to charities, waiving claims to an inheritance because the needs of one's co-heirs are greater, paying more than the legal minimum, etc., might be explained as the effects of generosity. It is because of his generosity that a man does such things. But, one may ask, is this really a law explanation of the causal sort? For it to be such, statements to the effect that generous people tend to perform actions of the sort illustrated would have to be contingent or empirical, that is to say, true (supposing them to be indeed true) in virtue of the facts, of the way experience reveals people do behave, *not* simply in virtue of the meanings of the words employed. But is it contingently or empirically true that generous people give without stint, waive their rights, etc.? They could not fail to; they would not be generous if they did. This is not something one has to learn from experience, it comes from understanding the meaning of the word 'generous'. The same is true of the statements that combative people tend to fight and indecisive ones to dither. Indeed it is virtually obviously so with the simple dispositions so far considered. With more complex ones it is less clear. Ambition, for instance, manifests itself in a considerable variety of ways. There are no acts so logically close to ambition as taking less than one's share is to generosity. But even here the acts performed by ambitious men will be *constitutive* of their ambition; not simply the sorts of acts which men, independently ascertained to be ambitious, have been found by experience to perform. We determine whether a man acted from ambition by reflecting on his deeds in the light of our conception of ambition. We deem him ambitious if we discern in them, despite whatever other differences there may be among them, a common tendency. We explain a particular act as ambitious by pointing out that it shares this tendency.

The argument, then, against the assimilation of dispositional explanations to the law model is that, if it were feasible, the connection between a disposition and its manifestations in action would be empirical, whereas in fact it is logical. The reason why this is not always appreciated is that with more complex dispositions (those manifested in a wide variety of ways) the relationship between the disposition and any particular manifestation is distant and so mistakable for a merely empirical association. It is not denied that, underlying the logical connection between disposition and manifestations, there may be genuine empirical laws. It might, for instance, be the case (though reality is doubtless more complicated) that people with a certain, objectively ascertainable type of family history, involving perhaps loss of the parent of the same sex in infancy, tend to become indecisive. If so, then, although their indecisiveness will not be acceptable as a causal or law explanation of their ditherings, their family history might be, because the connection between the type of family history in question and dithering would be empirical not logical. The position here argued for is simply that dispositional explanations *as presented* are not causal or of the law type. No claim is made, either positive or negative, about the possibility of phenomena explained dispositionally being also explicable in causal or law terms.

My contention, then, is that reference to dispositions is explanatory, a particular action being explained as of a piece with others collected under the disposition, but not explanatory according to the law pattern. Before leaving this topic, however, I should mention two sorts of criticism I have encountered. The former is to the effect that dispositional explanations as here understood are very inappropriately labelled rational. Combativeness and indecisiveness may very well lead people into actions which are irrational, not merely as offending against public norms of reasonable behaviour, but also as frustrating the agent's own more important wants and needs. Plainly this is true. It was indeed with this in mind that I stipulated above that 'rational' applied to the *central* area of a spectrum with dispositionl explanations at one extreme. Some dispositional explanations hardly fall within the scope of the rational because of the relative unimportance of 'mental' factors, notably beliefs and conscious purposes, in relation to them. Combativeness, indecisiveness, irritability manifest themselves in their characteristic ways in greater independence of the subject's particular beliefs and purposes than does, say, ambition. In order to recognise ambition it is necessary to know in what direction the subject wishes to get on, what he and others would count as getting on, what he believes, truly or falsely, will advance him in his chosen path. There are, it is true, typical objects of ambition in the shape of wealth and power: but it would be very superficial to deem a man unambitious simply because he did not bend his efforts to the attainment of these ends. There are many hierarchies to climb, many kinds of fame to spur men on. The range covered by dispositional explanations as conceived in this chapter is wide, and the term 'rational' is less unsuitable at the upper than at the lower edge.

The second criticism is that dispositional explanations are not as such historical. They occur in history books, certainly, as do medical explanations; but, like them, only because the people they refer to are important historically on other grounds. It is because of the positions occupied by Churchill and Asquith that their dispositions rate a mention in the explanation of events which are the concern of the historian. History is not concerned with events, actions, agents, as such, but only with those of some social import-ance – a feature which tends to distinguish history from biogra-phy, though there can hardly be a sharp distinction here. Even in biography, however, individuals are selected for treatment because of their more than individual importance. Still more is this true in history. 'Great men', unquestionably, loom quite large in political history, but it is not to be inferred that history is mainly concerned with their actions and reactions as individuals. The dogmatic insistence that great men make no difference, that if Napoleon or Hitler had never been born some other man would have done the same – a doctrine that seems incredible if taken literally – no doubt feeds on a confused recognition that the evil great men are held to be accountable for is not to be explained solely by reference to what they individually do. Hitler lost an army before Stalingrad, but other factors were involved than just his insane desire to hold on to territory at any cost – the character of the army, the social background of its officer class, the role played by that army in Hitler's rise to power, and many others too. All of this is true, and certainly not intended to be questioned in my claim that dispositional explanation has a place in history. There is indeed a very great deal that cannot be explained in these terms nor in terms of rational explanations generally. This concession does not, however, entail that nothing at all can be so explained.

(ii) The second question, whether all rational explanations are like the dispositional ones so far discussed, loses much of its point if the latter fail to conform to the law pattern themselves. Moreover attempts to force rational explanations into the law framework by invoking such allegedly empirical laws as that people tend to do what (they think) will realise their purposes (see, for example, Hospers, 1967, p. 246) fail for the same reason as attempts to represent dispositional explanations as causal – the reason, namely, that having a purpose is logically too close to doing what (one thinks) will realise it for the connection to be empirical. This is not a connection which can be discovered only by experience. Having a purpose logically entails that, other things being equal – for example, provided it be possible, that it would not frustrate the realisation of more important purposes – one will do what is thought necessary to accomplish it. Should this not be done there is ground for doubting whether one genuinely has the purpose. Here, in the logical rather than empirical connection between purpose and performance, is

the point of resemblance between purposive and dispositional explanation. Where they differ, and it is this that makes the epithet 'rational'
appropriate to purposive explanations (although, as noted, dispositional explanations are not homogeneous in this regard), is in the
much higher degree of complication exhibited by many purposive
examples. Some or all of at least the following elements may be
involved: the subject's wants and characteristics, his situation either as
it is or as he thinks it is, his objectives, his beliefs about what has to be
done in order to get what, conceptions of what is appropriate or
reasonable entertained by him or current in his day, the reciprocal
influences between his actions and those of other people. These elements
are, of course, not wholly independent of one another. A person's
objective, in the sense of a relatively precisely formulated aim, reflects
his wants and his estimate of the situation he is in. Beliefs about what has
to be done in order to get what will not be wholly disentanglable from
norms of appropriateness or reasonableness – there will be ways of
getting what is wanted which are not effectively open to members of
certain societies. They may be judged wicked or shameful. They may
even be literally unthinkable. Attachment to conceptions of national
sovereignty may, for instance, prevent a government even contemplating making the arrangements with other governments which are
necessary to realise their joint aims, with the result that ineffectual or
apparently self-defeating behaviour may nevertheless be explicable as
purposive within the narrow confines of the possible as taken for granted
by the agent and his contemporaries. To speak of rational explanations,
as I, following Dray, have mainly done, is to emphasise certain elements
at the expense of others. Popper's phrase 'situational logic' gives a
different emphasis. In particular explanations one element may be
more prominent than others. Sometimes we may know well enough
what an agent was after but not what his situation was, other times the
reverse, and still other times what is mostly needed in order to render an
action intelligible is an account of the relevant conceptions of
reasonable behaviour. One of Gardiner's examples illustrates the latter
point: 'Oddly enough, when he came to the revolt he emphasised first
his own personal wrongs . . . in order to show that he had fought only
for what was his own. This again was sound feudal theory' (1952, p. 66).
Dray produces a number of examples in which the object seems mainly
to have been to reconstruct the agent's calculation (1957, for example
p. 122, where there is a reference to Louis XIV's easing of military
pressure on Holland in 1688). In the much explained affair of Caesar's

invasions of Britain the problem seems to concern his objective – was it reconnaissance or full-scale invasion and occupation – the scale of his preparations being usually explained by attributing to him the larger aim, which he is held not to have avowed because he failed to realise it.

A conviction of the importance of intentional and normative factors in historical explanation is an important determinant of Dray's emphasis on the rational model and of his feeling that Gardiner fails to do justice to it. Such an emphasis runs the risk of blurring the distinction between *explaining* an agent's conduct in terms of his *acceptance* of the norms and beliefs of his day and *justifying* it by, so to say, direct reference to those norms and beliefs themselves – the distinction between reported and directed practical reasoning, the thinking of the historian and that of the historical agent, more generally the distinction between fact and value. A desire to preserve these distinctions is at any rate a major reason why White (1965) tries so far as possible to keep apparent examples of rational explanations within the framework of the law theory (see also Hempel, 1963). I have argued that this cannot be done, but still need to show that the distinctions in question are not thereby compromised.

(iii) What has to be done is to show how principles accepted by an historical figure, which for him function in justificatory discourse, can be employed without endorsement by an historian in explanatory discourse. But where, it may be asked, is the difficulty? Surely justification is a matter of applying principles one accepts whereas rational explanation is reporting the application by somebody else of the principles *he* accepts. It may seem clear enough, but that problems and confusions can arise may be illustrated by reference to what commonly passes for the history of philosophy – not that philosophy is *practical* reasoning, but one would hope to be able to draw with regard to it a distinction between reported and direct reasoning corresponding to that between rational explanation and justification.

In fact the distinction is often not clearly drawn. Much so-called history of philosophy, it is to be feared, is not genuinely history because the would-be historian fails to maintain a sufficient distance between his own philosophy and that of the authors he studies. Often the concern is exclusively with trying to set out the writers' arguments, not considering at all the influences upon them, their biases or prejudices, their intellectual heritage, or at most considering them only at points where the argument is found to be invalid or unintelligible. Major philosophers tend to be represented as arguing with one another – Hume with Locke, Kant with Hume and Leibniz are familiar examples – regardless of what they in fact knew of one another's works. Indeed the 'historian' argues with them himself. 'History' of philosophy practised in this manner is really simply philosophy – philosophy starting off from certain texts. The main interest is whether or not an argument is cogent, not how somebody came to find it so. A genuine history of philosophy would not, of course, entirely ignore questions of cogency – on the face of it a good rational explanation of why somebody reached a certain conclusion is that it follows validly from premises there is evidence that he accepted – but it would have to take into account many other factors too. Some of these, by their sheer particularity, not to say the labour involved in discovering what they were, would no doubt be deeply uncongenial to the type of mind which characteristically concerns itself with philosophy.

Philosophers, it is clear, are not necessarily qualified to be historians of philosophy. This, so far as it goes, reinforces the desired distinction between direct and reported reasoning. But, on the other side, it has to be allowed that it is impossible to be an effective historian of philosophy without being something of a philosopher. In the first place, anyone whose head does not lie for philosophy, who cannot appreciate the relevance and force of the considerations adduced for and against a position, nor feel the temptation to take a particular route out of a difficulty or the charm of some distinction or generalisation, is in poor shape to gauge what a philosopher drew from the books he read, the contemporaries he talked to, or to see which problems were solved and which left for others, to see indeed what the problems were. The historian of philosophy must be able to understand his subjects, to see things as they saw them, if he is to understand their works. He must be a potential participant in the activity he is studying, even though his specific task as historian is to report not take part. In the second place, philosophy, as an almost purely intellectual activity with little point or purpose outside itself, can hardly be characterised, let alone explained, in other than its own terms. There have, indeed, been attempted sociological (E. Gellner, 1959, ch. IX) and psychoanalytical (J. O. Wisdom) accounts of philosophy; but, whatever their merits as sociology or psychoanalysis, it must be doubted whether they engage sufficiently closely with the detailed content of the philosophical works they deal with to be explanatory of it. If they explain it at all, they do not explain it as philosophy.

It is hard for the historian of philosophy to find the mean: too much participation and it is no longer history; too little and it ceases to be philosophy.

Such problems of participation are most acute in intellectual history, where it is usually impossible to treat the subject matter in other than its own terms. But they arise whenever there are attempts to learn non-historical lessons from history. Thus soldiers at staff college have extra-historical reasons for refighting the campaigns of yesteryear, as have would-be statesmen for studying the politics and diplomacy of the past. Before the development of professionalism, it would appear that history was mostly studied in this way; and I am sure that much casual reading of history is still informed by this same practical attitude. Of course, war and politics, unlike philosophy, do have purposes outside themselves and can in greater measure be understood from outside. Even so it is not unknown for professional historians to find it illuminating to hear the views of a relatively ill-informed and historically amateurish soldier on military history or those of a politician on politics (see M. Ashley). Involved here, no doubt, is a feeling that the problems of war and politics do not change, or that there remain similarities of form through vast changes of technique, scale, social organisation; and the faith or hope that present-day practitioners, with their unconceptualised and so inexpressible know-how, may see things which professional scholars are apt to miss, be they never so intelligent and well-informed. Needless to say anything that the practitioners succeed in 'seeing' must be established by the ordinary canons of historical evidence to be really there. Moreover, the less the history in question is specialised, in the sense of being related to a present-day occupation or profession, the less scope it offers for the exercise of insider know-how. Political history is in the relevant respect much less specialised than military, and the advantages stemming from participant experience correspondingly less.

In certain narrow fields of history there is, then, the possibility of sharing the standards of past agents and of learning from them, and the consequent danger of explanation shading into justification (and, of course, condemnation), fact into value, reportage into participation in a common activity. But this is not generally so. Over the greater part of the subject hopes of learning from history diminish as we become more historically minded, as we become more aware how situations change, even that people change too. Renier (pp. 192–3) remarks that in practice historians assume that human nature does not change, but I cannot believe that historians entertain so simplistic a conception of the sort of rational explanation available in their subject. No doubt it is natural to approach questions of explanation by supposing oneself in an historical situation and thinking in means/end terms. But we soon find it necessary to recognise that past agents are at one with their situations, their ends very different from ours, and their ideas of what is possible or allowable in the way of means no less so. Aims and standards alike are slaves of time. The people of the past did what they thought they had to do, succeeded or failed, according to their own lights, not ours.

Acton, though in other respects a proponent of scientific history, notoriously was unwilling to accept such relativism where *moral* standards were concerned. The historian's task was to understand, but he was not thereby absolved from the moral duty of condemning the great crimes and denouncing the great sinners of the past. The balance of opinion, among both historians and philosophers of history, has, however, swung the other way. Oakeshott (1933, p. 158; 1962, p. 164) and Croce (pp. 47–9) speak for many others when they repudiate the exercise of moral judgement as an inappropriate intrusion of practical attitudes into history. Decision in this matter depends as much on conceptions of morality as on those of history – and the two interact. If morality is thought of as an essentially this-worldly, practical affair, concerned with influencing behaviour (i.e. intending to make it different from what it would otherwise have been), then the scope for moral judgement in history is inevitably very limited, being confined to the rather small range of cases which sufficiently resemble those we and our contemporaries could conceivably be called upon to face. Morality conceived as practical is not indeed exclusively forward looking – an agent pronouncing upon present or future conduct commits himself to adopting the same stance with regard to *all* relevantly similar conduct and situations, and hence sometimes to *past* conduct and situations; but the extent of the backward reference is unlikely to be very great, being mostly though not entirely confined to the recent past of one's own society. Morality is not, however, always thought of in this practical way, and was not by Acton. There are not the same grounds for restraining the exercise of moral judgement in history for anyone who conceives moral standards as very general rules of conduct, unaffected by time, place and circumstance, perennially applicable regardless of whether there is any possibility of influencing conduct. It must, however, be recognised that the development of historical consciousness has tended to make this conception of morality more difficult to sustain, not indeed by compelling the abandonment of absolutes at the level of general principle, but by highlighting the variety of the circumstances in which through history they have to be applied, and consequently the differences among their implications for conduct in different periods. The growth of anthropological knowledge has had a similar tendency. So has the decline in the effective hold of Christianity – unlike Acton, rather few of us now feel that we share a religion, and hence a morality, with the great sinners of the past. But if a new religion, or quasi-religion, were to take hold in the West, we need not doubt that, as its adherents search the past for antecedents and anticipations, moral judgements will return to history. (For further discussion of moral judgement in history, see chapter VI below.)

It remains to consider the so-called assumption of rationality, about which opinions strangely diverge. Popper, for instance, claims *both* that rationality is not presupposed in the offering of rational explanations but rather consists in acting in accordance with the logic of the situation (1945, p. 97), which presumably means that the historian does not bring his conception of rationality to the situations he studies but rather finds conceptions of it in them; *and* that it is necessary to assume as a first approximation that people behave more or less rationally (p. 265). Elton, too, holds that we must assume, though it is not quite true, that every act is the product of reason (1967, p. 81). An important source of uncertainty and disagreement in this area is, I believe, an ambiguity in the notion of rationality, which can be brought out by reflecting that the rational is opposed to both the *a*rational and the *ir*rational. Sticks, stones, very young children, some defectives and the insane, most if not all animals, are arational. They are not capable of being influenced by rational considerations, they do not think; their behaviour may exhibit regularities, but they do not act in accordance with rules (i.e. *conceptions* of regularities, as Kant expressed it). Irrationality is different. It is rather a matter of someone who is capable of thought, open to rational considerations, not paying heed to them in particular cases or not being guided by them. Irrationality is possible only in somebody who could be rational: you have to be rational, in the sense opposed to arational, in order *not* to be rational, in the sense opposed to irrational. The appearance of paradox is entirely superficial. The ambiguity of 'rational' is easily elucidated, and resembles, for instance, the familiar ambiguity of 'moral' as between senses opposed to '*a*moral' and '*im*moral' respectively.

With regard to the assumption or presupposition of rationality it must be supposed that the contrast here is with the arational. Rational explanation, in that it involves holding that people are taking what they think to be effective and allowable means to the realisation of their purposes, is in place only in respect of the non-arational. In so far as we offer such explanations we commit ourselves to holding our subjects to be rational in this sense. Is this realistic? Plainly there are people who, for a variety of familiar causes, are not capable of being rational: but equally plainly most people normally are so capable. Some, of course, have seen fit to doubt whether any person is so, on the basis of some general view to the effect that all human actions, or apparent actions, are determined by factors outside human control. I will not here attempt to argue against this, on the face of it self-defeating, view beyond remarking that it leaves quite unexplained how we have managed to acquire the notion of rational behaviour which it purports to show to lack application. There may, however, seem to be more particular reasons for doubting whether historical figures, though possibly capable of appreciating rational considerations, are capable of responding to them because of the 'pressures' upon them. Political action may regularly be seen as reactive rather than purposive. This seems to me both misguided and misleading. It is perfectly true that the options effectively open to a statesman or general are normally very limited; but these limitations are invariably mediated by the individual's appreciation (or *mis*appreciation – it makes no difference when it is rationality as opposed to *a*rationality which is in question) of his situation. He thinks of himself as under pressure, but he is not under it in the same way as a man who is physically pushed. If he had sized up the situation differently, he would have reacted differently. Even when a statesman's judgement is thought to have been distorted by physical illness, which might be thought of as coming close to a case of physical pressure, it is still hard to see how his conduct, though certainly irrational, can really be held to be arational. Sir Anthony Eden's illness in 1956 caused him to have a fever; but it did not in the same mechanical, arational fashion cause him to see President Nasser as a second Hitler and in other respects misjudge the situation. The sorts of action statesmen are characteristically reported as engaging in simply cannot fail to involve the exercise, or misexercise, of the rational faculties, and cannot therefore be arational.

There is, then, a sense in which it may be presupposed that people, the sort of people historians are commonly interested in anyway, are rational i.e. not arational. It is, however, not required that we presuppose them rational in the sense of not irrational. It would be absurd to do so, for they plainly very often are irrational. Even so it is quite natural to *begin* by assuming them rational (non-irrational) in their means/end judgements; but this should be no more than a beginning, and we should in the end be prepared to find that they are not. There are various possibilities. One is that they have false beliefs about what will result in what – such errors not necessarily being marks of irrationality; this depends upon whether they could have been avoided in the particular situation. Other possibilities are that our subjects have very different ends from what we supposed or very different ideas of what is allowable. There can be no certainty that it will be possible always to make sense of apparently irrational behaviour, not even in the minimal sense of being able to locate the respect in which it went wrong. But it is, none the less, probably a sound maxim for some time to persist, even in face of apparent counter evidence, in supposing that the behaviour we are concerned with is non-irrational. In this way discoveries may be made.

I have been trying to suggest how there may be point in attempting the rational explanation of apparently (and really, so long as not too grossly) irrational action. There is, moreover, also point in attempting rational explanation in respect of phenomena which are, so to say, in the large not susceptible of such explanation because they were not purposed by anyone. It may still be possible to show how they came about as the result, the unintended, unforeseen result, of a number of individuals pursuing their various, maybe incompatible, ends in their severally rational or irrational ways. The same is possible for phenomena which by their nature are insusceptible of rational explanation, for instance, hindsightfully described wars, revolutions, etc. which it is logically impossible anyone should have intended to initiate (compare chapter 11 section 4 above). A commitment to rational explanation may thus incline one to represent phenomena, which are for one reason or another rather unpromising subjects for rational explanation, as resultants of the rational activity of individuals. And this direction, towards greater detail, is one in which many historians appear to want to go. The rational model has little more claim than the law model to stand as a general account of explanation in history; but it can at least be said for it that, in this regard, its implications are more consonant with the practice of historians. In asserting this I am not claiming that gross events necessarily can or should be analysed in the way described. I am not defending metaphysical, methodological or any other sort of individualism. My only claim concerns the practice of historians. This practice is, of course, itself influenced by views taken of the possibility of there being large-scale explanation in history and law explanations of social phenomena generally. Carr, who is optimistic in this regard, consequently has comparatively little time for individualistic rational explanation. Practice, and theory too, will, moreover, also reflect the sort of history that is in question. The illustrations given or implied above have mostly been from political history, in which individual agents are readily discernible even though what comes about is also determined by many factors outside their control. But in social and economic history the individual has less obvious prominence, and the scope for rational explanation is correspondingly less.

4. Narrative as Explanatory

It remains to consider the third view that narrative – recounting what happened – is explanatory in itself, regardless of whether the events, actions, situations purportedly explained are connectable with ante-cedent events, etc. by laws or generalisations, or of whether they were the objects of anybody's rational endeavour. It is not denied, as it could not be, that such law and rational explanations occur in history; the claim is rather that it is neither necessary nor sufficient to historical writing's being explanatory that they should, or, more strongly, that they earn their place only to the extent that they help on the story told.

The attractions of the view are plain. It allows that there is something distinctive about explanation in history, which consorts well with, even if it is not entailed by, the conviction expressed at the beginning of this book that history is a distinctive field of intellectual enquiry. Ad-ditionally it permits it to be held that a good deal of historical writing actually succeeds in being explanatory; whereas on the law view most of it does not, and on the rational view could not. But the present concern is with the truth and reasonableness, not the attractiveness, of the view. As regards the former I have already contended that the ordinary use of 'explanation' is hospitable enough to accommodate it, and, further, that the most common use of such phrases as 'explain historically' rather suggests it. But too little turns on ordinary usage for it to be necessary for objectors to dispute my claims for it, and some of them (for example C. B. McCullagh, 1969) are happy enough to concede the word 'expla-nation'. What they question is whether (possibly quite correctly so-called) narrative *explanations* are genuinely explanatory in the sense that matters. Though such doubts are not in principle absurd, it is more difficult than seems always to be recognised to specify the sense which matters without begging the question. It is not good enough to condemn narrative explanations simply and solely because they are not, say, law explanations – a pitfall not altogether avoided by McCullagh.

This sort of rebuttal is also effective against complaints that narrative explanations are defective because they consist entirely in conjunctions of singular statements (reporting that this happened, *and* then that, *and* then the other . . .) and include no universal statements. (It may be conceded for the sake of this argument that there could be such a narrative.) But it is no *argument* against the narrative view to contend that all explanations must contain universals. This is what is at issue. Narratives are, incidentally, unquestionably universal in the different sense (discussed in section 2 (iii) of this chapter in connection with the universalisability of 'because') in which alone it is certainly the case that all explanations must be universal. That is to say, no story can be held to be explanatory of an event or situation without a similar story about a similar event being explanatory too. 'Similar' is an imprecise term, but may be taken to refer to such matters as the degree of detail, how far back the story goes, the range of factors brought in – it is impossible adequately to express in general terms what needs to be illustrated by reference to concrete cases. I cannot, however, believe it to be seriously questionable that, for instance, two narrative accounts of the outbreaks of different wars might be judged similar in a variety of respects, with the effect that it would have to be recognised that neither could be rejected as non-explanatory without the other.

A similar rejoinder can be made to the objection that narratives cannot be explanatory because they do not afford a basis for prediction, i.e. point to antecedently available grounds for holding that the event allegedly explained was likely to occur. One might, however, here forbear to press the charge of begging the question on the grounds that it is untrue, even of law explanations which are here being held up as the ideal, that they have to be predictive. If they are in terms of necessary conditions only, as no one seems to deny they often may be, they do not justify predictions; and they are not generally held to be unacceptable in cases where prediction is impossible in the sense that actually making it could not be guaranteed not to affect the event 'predicted' in a way that would undermine the prediction or, contrariwise, make it true – the so-called Oedipus effect (Popper, 1957, p. 13).

Probably the most neutral way to formulate the issue concerning narrative explanation is on these lines: since it is universally allowed that *mere* narrative (chronicle) can fail to be explanatory, it may be asked what conditions have to be satisfied before it becomes so. Defenders of the narrative theory may be represented as maintaining that the working up of 'mere' into explanatory narrative is not entirely a matter of bringing into it or transforming it into law and/or rational explanations; their critics may be represented as maintaining that it necessarily is.

As thus characterised the narrative view relates to explanation only. It does not include the clearly false contention that narratives can be constructed and founded on evidence without any reliance on matters of general knowledge (laws or generalisations) or means/end purposive or rational interpretations of human behaviour. It is not, therefore, to be disposed of by demonstrating that on occasion its upholders themselves make use of general laws. Nor are they, as here represented, committed to holding that law and rational explanations are altogether out of place in historical writings, but only that they are not necessary for such writings to be judged explanatory as wholes.

There is, unfortunately, another issue entangled with the present one, the issue whether historical writing is, or should be, narrative as opposed to analytical in form (see chapter 1 section 2 above). Renier, Gallie, and to an extent Danto, all *both* suppose or maintain that narrative is characteristic of history *and* insist that historical writing is explanatory without involving the application of scientific generalisations (i.e. they reject the law theory as the whole or even part of the truth about history). Though perhaps most usually thus associated these two positions are nevertheless separable. Leff, for instance, is adamant that history is nowadays mostly analytic, yet agrees that explanation in it is not applying generalisations but giving detailed accounts. For him history is neither (primarily) chronological narrative nor subsumption under laws. Elton, though he has more time for narrative than Leff, agrees with him about the possibility of there being explanatory, non-law-applying analysis. It would be well, therefore, if the conception of historical explanation here under consideration could be purged of any implication that history is entirely narrative, though it may well be difficult to achieve this in so far as the case for the view has normally been founded on the contrary supposition. This is no doubt the reason why some of the intended opposition to it seems really to be directed against the idea that history must be narrative (this, at any rate, is *one* of the things which McCullagh, for instance, is most anxious to dispute). There appears in fact to be an ambiguity in the use of the world 'narrative', which is sometimes employed in opposition to (something like) 'bringing under scientific laws', in which sense it could cover analytical history too, and other times used primarily in opposition to 'analytical'. Not that this is simply a case of ambiguity leading to confusion and cross purposes (though there is plenty of both): it is more that profound, if imperfectly self-conscious, disagreement generates ambiguity. For some the very distinctiveness of history, its capacity to explain, to afford insight of a unique sort, is bound up with the narrative form; whereas for others the history which is explanatory in the highest degree, the most genuine, front-line history, is analytical. Philosophers and historians both are to be found on either side, though I suspect the former is more popular among philosophers. The issue is, however, to a great extent one *within*, not just *about*, history; and consequently one which a philosophical account of explanation in history should try not to prejudge. It will accordingly henceforth be the claim of historical writing generally (whether narrative or analytical) to be explanatory in itself which will be considered – a thesis admittedly more general than the title of the present section might have suggested. I hope that the outcome will not be that explanatory historical writing is represented as more homogeneous than it actually is.

The question is, then, what conditions have to be satisfied before 'mere' narrative (writing about the past) can be counted explanatory. There would, I believe, be common consent that the truth of the individual assertions made is not enough, and that reporting events in chronological order is neither necessary nor sufficient. These are negative points. Positively what is required is some species of coherence – comprehensiveness with unity, nothing relevant omitted, everything irrelevant excluded – a coherence which carries with it intelligiblity and explanatory power. I do not claim to be able fully to articulate this conception; indeed my conviction is that it cannot be done in general terms but needs rather to be illustrated by reference to particular works. Before saying more about this, however, I shall give a little space to truth and chronology, which tend, in my view, to be too much taken for granted.

The truth of particular assertions is regarded as at best a necessary condition for the acceptability of historical writing. It must, of course, be based on evidence. By itself, whether impossibly by clairvoyance or more credibly by (testimony to) uncheckable memory claims, truth is useless. In order to count in history putative truths must be relatable in publicly checkable ways to evidence. Information offered on the basis of memory will not necessarily be inadmissible, but the credentials of the rememberer, even though he be the historian himself, must survive scrutiny (cf. Fain, p. 100). It is, however, something of an exaggeration to require that all assertions made in history books should be individually evidenc*ed*. Many will be uncontroversial and quite properly taken over from other historians. Even so the assumption will be that they are *capable* of being evidenced. This is the effective force of the contention that evidenced truth is a necessary condition of acceptability. All the same there remains some slight overstatement still. Mistakes of detail are inevitable in large works. Minor in-accuracies, even some instances of carelessness and neglect, though always flaws, seem to be thought compatible with a work's being acceptable on the whole; and even with its actually being better than a completely accurate but uninspired piece (compare Elton, 1967, pp. 120–1, and Fain, pp. 244–7). Thus is it intended to be registered that there is more to history than truth and evidence, inasmuch as defects in these particulars are felt to be compensatable by merits elsewhere.

Though I would expect the observations of the previous paragraph to be accepted as mere commonplaces, I cannot help wondering whether they do not underestimate the importance of truth and evidence in the growth of history into a body of *knowledge* and hence into a possible source of explanation. Is not *part* of what leads us to want to call historians' stories explanatory just that they are (felt to have a good claim to be) true, whereas other stories are little more than half-remembered snippets of information eked out by supposition and guesswork? Comparisons between stories in history and theories in science, on the basis that both 'go beyond' the evidence – comparisons not uncongenial even to such anti-assimilationists as Renier, Gallie and Danto – are misleading in this regard. Unlike elementary science, history is not at all a matter of organising rather familiar types of fact under progressively more and more unfamiliar laws and theories: it is much more a matter of reporting successive and coexistent collections of individually possibly unfamiliar facts, which can indeed hardly fail to be instances of familiar types, but which are not considered in that light. (The historian's concern is, typically, what did, not what usually does, happen.) It appears to me that it should follow from this that the evidenced truth of each particular assertion made is a somewhat more important element in history's claim to explanatory capability than is adequately brought out in the conventional doctrine. I am not, of course, suggesting that any collection whatever of evidenced truths constitutes explanatory history.

My inclination is to make a similarly slightly enlarged claim for chronological ordering. A consistent chronology, which often proves unexpectedly hard to establish at the detailed level, is, it seems to me, a considerable step in the direction of explanation, though doubtless it will leave a great deal unexplained. A clear conception of the temporal ordering of happenings is often the greater part of what is lacking when we are puzzled by what has come about. It does not follow from this that events have to be *reported* in chronological (narrative) order.

Still, truth and chronology are patently not the whole story, and it remains to consider further the conception of coherence adverted to above. It is notable how suggestions made about this, usually in relation to history conceived as narrative in the narrow sense, are, if not generally inadequate, at best insufficiently general. Take, for instance, the requirement that history be intelligible in human terms. Unquestionably in writing narratives historians will try to provide this, and the attempt to do so will suggest enquiries that need to be undertaken. There is the obvious danger that requisite information may not be there, in which case it is necessary to resist the temptation to imitate the historical novelist. Could a true account of what went on be rejected as history because it was not humanly intelligible? There can hardly be a simple general answer. Intelligibility in human terms admits of degree, and a low level of means/end understanding of behaviour – even without a clear grasp of either ends or beliefs about means, one may still be able to see it as end-directed – is fairly easy to achieve. But sometimes this will not be enough to require, at other times too much, for a great deal of what interests us in history (renaissances, industrial revolutions, etc.) cannot in the gross be made intelligible in human terms.

Another frequently made suggestion is that what makes an historical study hang together is its being about an appropriately unified subject matter, an 'entity' such as a nation, class, religion (see the critical discussion in Fain, ch. xv). Given this it might be thought that particular occurrences could be explained by being presented as episodes in the development of the entity in question. Something of the scope of a history and of the criteria of relevance employed within it may be conveyed by saying that it is of, say, the English people (contrast the force of the Churchillian variant, the *English-Speaking Peoples*), the Roman Catholic church or the Russian peasantry. These are groups enjoying a reality partly or wholly independent of an historian's concern with them. With regard to such entities, however, as Fain points out, the thesis that narratives may derive their unity from being of them is not strictly true. For every such entity there is the possibility of a coherent historical account, which deals with it in some measure, but also includes events not connected with it while excluding some which are. This is inevitable when an entity, the historian's subject matter, is specified independently of his point of view and the questions he is minded to ask. Other 'entities' are, it is true, not thus independent, but internal to the historian's direction of interest. Among such may be included the Renaissance, the Enlightenment, the Industrial Revolution – at least as first introduced; now that they have caught on they have a measure of objective existence independently of any particular historian. It is not their unity which confers unity upon historical treatments of them. It is rather that, in coming to see them as unities, we register our recognition of the coherence of the histories of which they are, so to say, the *internal* subject matter – internal in somewhat the sense in which, say, curtsies and grimaces are whilst boats and plum puddings are not internal objects of 'making'. Of entities conceived in this way the thesis is insignificant rather than false.

A further common suggestion is that events in a coherent narrative have to be causally related. 'Cause', as already noted, is a slippery term – more on that in the next chapter. It may, however, be remarked here that the suggestion is false if 'cause' is employed narrowly, insignificant if widely. It may not be too great an exaggeration to maintain that every event in any historical story – every mention of anything in any sort of coherent historical account – has to have a bearing on everything else if it is to earn its place by contributing to the whole. But there are many ways of having a bearing upon which do not amount to being the cause or the effect of; unless, that is, 'cause' is used so widely as to cover them all, in which case it ceases to mean anything very much. I am quite sure that there is no conception of causation which could serve as the foundation of a true, general account of coherence in history.

This confidence derives from the conviction that coherence and so explanatory capability must be question relative. This is a corollary of the inevitability of selection discussed in the previous chapter. The defects of 'must be of an entity' and 'must be causally connected' rest upon the impossibility of determining what is coherent and relevant out of relation to the point of view of an historian and the questions he has in mind. The variety of possible points of view and questions is so great that general accounts of coherence and relevance can achieve truth only at the expense of significance. Though cases can be found to which general accounts apply, none can be made to fit everywhere without extension to vacuity.

The relativity of coherence to questions asked is, however, only part of the truth about coherence in history. Reference has additionally to be made to the discussion of the previous chapter about the context in which historical questions arise. There it was suggested that, for a group of historians at a time, there will be a conception of the state of historical studies, of what has been and what is still to be done or redone. Some questions are thus self-generated from within history and it is on this account that their answers – the writings produced in the course of answering them – are felt to be specially explanatory. In corroboration of this may be urged the reflection that it is only after having obtained some acquaintance with a field of study that one becomes able to see problems and difficulties. (This is not peculiar to history.) Much as individual students grow in sophistication, some proving able to go deeper than others, so are historical writings themselves distinguishable as more or less sophisticated, as coherent and explanatory in higher or lower degrees. But a degree of sophistication can be specified only in relation to what has gone before, not absolutely; and development is not along one line only, but along an indefinite number of different ones.

To leave the matter here would be to overstate the extent to which historical questions are self-generated. Some have their origin at least partly outside history, in new possibilities of enquiry and explanation opened up by developments in psychology, sociology, statistics, climatology, textual criticism, or whatever it might be. The variety of kinds of possibility is important. Restrictive conceptions of explanation in history are encouraged by over-emphasising one possibility at the expense of others. Yet further new questions will be suggested, new directions of interest, points of view, perspectives inspired by conditions of life in the historian's own time. Answers to questions arising in this way may well be felt to be highly illuminating, but can only be *historically* explanatory if they, and the questions which prompt them, can be felt to be in some way continuous with existing history. Sharp discontinuities provoke conceptual worries, which should not be confused with the fear of unemployment they may also produce among conservatively minded practitioners. Old dogs are notoriously reluctant to take on new tricks, but they have a point when the tricks appear to belong to games utterly different from any which their contemporaries and predecessors have been accustomed to play. Thus the sociology or Keynesian economics of past periods are not as such history. They need to be domesticated by being shown, among other things, to yield answers to questions not all of which are utterly unlike those historians have been accustomed to ask, to clarify and explain not simply in *a*historical senses but in ways overlapping with the establishedly historical. It is not at all that the limits of history cannot be enlarged, or extended in some directions, pulled back in others – plainly they have been. It is only that new developments, which are necessarily *from* origins as well as *to* termini, must connect at some point(s) with that multi-faceted thing that history at any time is. The offence of one-sided theories of historical explanation is that they omit to take due account of history as it is.

The question-relativity of explanatory capability serves to highlight both the strengths and the weaknesses of the not uncommon belief that analytical history is explanatory in a higher degree then narrative. On the *pro* side is the fact that questions are likely to be conspicuous in analysis. On the *con* side, however, it needs to be said that too great a virtue can be made out of mere explicitness (compare chapter III section 3 above); and the truth surely is that some questions require narrative, others analytic answers. Whether answers are explanatory depends less on which sort they are than on whether or not they are indeed true and complete answers to questions which are themselves, in the sorts of way just indicated, worth asking.

My answer, then, to the question how historical writing can become explanatory without necessarily being brought closer to the law or rational model is, in summary, that it is by having its assertions properly evidenced, its questions clearly conceived (even if especially in narrative history, not always explicitly formulated) and related to conceptions of the present state of historical studies or internally or externally inspired developments of it. I have doubtless done enough to make plain my support for the view that narrative, in a sense wide enough to include analysis, can be explanatory in itself. But have I *shown* this? ('Shown' is a strong word, less often justifiable in philosophy than frequent talk of validity and invalidity might suggest.) What I have done is to point out that the word 'explanation', in its ordinary sense, can be used of narratives; I have drawn attention to some of the factors which lead to narrative being considered explanatory; I have maintained that it is merely question begging to set up a narrow concept of explanation which excludes narrative, for, obviously, the legitimacy of the narrow concept is as much in question as whether narrative can be considered explanatory – the answer to either question having implications for the other. I have further tried to distinguish the thesis that historical writing is explanatory in itself from other implausible theses often confused or associated with it, in particular from any notion that narratives can be constructed and related to evidence without recourse to general knowledge, that law and rational explanations have no place in history, and that history is essentially narrative as opposed to analytical. No doubt more of the same could be done, and maybe done better, but probably it would not have any stronger appeal to doubters. This is the normal case in philosophy, where agreement is always at a discount, not just because of perverse contentiousness, but because controversy genuinely tends to be the shorter route to the conceptual understanding aimed at. All the same, I have to confess in the present case to some unease about the side I have chosen, the case I have tried to make – I think mostly because ideally it should have the support of detailed comparisons and contrasts between pieces of historical writing judged explanatory and others judged not. Availability of space apart, there must be doubt where I have the historical expertise, not to say freedom from philosophical *parti pris*, adequately to carry out such exercises. But I can at least place on record my recognition that my case stands or falls with the outcome of them.

Throughout the present chapter a foggy, commonplace conception of explanation, which doubtless fits history well enough, has been opposed to clearer conceptions, which may be less good for history, though they plainly deserve a place in the cognitive repertoire. In appearance, in order to accommodate history, a choice has to be made between obscurantism and revisionism. It will help to bring out the misleading nature of this appearance by considering, in very general terms, how the concept of explanation has fared through the argument of this chapter – a story which also affords some indication, though over-simplified and achronological, of the concept's history in modern Western thinking.

We began with the 'ordinary' concept as specified, no doubt imperfectly, by the dictionary. It was vague rather than ambiguous (i.e. more a matter of one fuzzy meaning than several clear ones), oriented towards the situations and concerns of practical life and the sorts of puzzlement which there arise. It did not exclude, but gave no special prominence to, the relatively sharp notion which has been termed law explanation – though it was somewhat more congenial to the older notion of rational explanation, in so far as accounting for conduct is a central element in the original notion of explanation. In this ordinary, undifferentiated notion of explanation there is no reason to deny that history, very much as it is, is sometimes explanatory. But then sharper notions of explanation are marked out. They do not fit history very well, nor do they exhaust the ordinary notion of explanation: but neither, when they are extracted from it, is anything at all precise left to contrast them with. The *residual* of the ordinary idea of explanation could only be a poor, pallid pulp, with no nourishment left in it for history or anything else. No wonder that people incline to spurn it, and turn to what would otherwise be the unpalatable alternatives of holding that history is explanatory in ways in which it pretty plainly is not, or is not wholly, or holding that it is not explanatory at all. (Much the same has happened with the traditional conception of reason in its relation to morality and conduct generally.) It is because it seems to be saddled with this residual of the ordinary concept of explanation that the so-called narrative view is perceived (sometimes one suspects, and I admit, by its supporters) as trying to make much out of very little. What is needed, in order to do justice to history, is somehow to recover the richness of the full ordinary concept, but without obscurantism; without either repudiating the possibility of precise, scientific sorts of explanation, or attempting to confine them to safe areas; and without attaching undue importance to a more old-fashioned sort of history than professionals are nowadays prepared to own. It is no easy task to reunite a concept which has begun to fall apart.

There is no putting back the clock; no sense in pretending that things have not developed in the way they have; and so no avoiding unfavourable comparisons between what we have been calling narrative explanation and the sharper notion of law explanation. But it must be remembered that, if there is a key to the understanding of history and with it historical explanation, it is that it is a study which has achieved the highest level of sophistication and professionalism, *without becoming theoretical*; without to any significant extent developing a technical vocabulary of its own; and without attempting to classify the phenomena with which it deals in the systematic way, which is the only sure path to laws and theories and the sort of explanations offered by the sciences. There is a marked contrast between the precision and subtlety of the content of historical thinking and the somewhat homespun simplicity of its form. The same contrast is evident in much legal thinking. On the lawyers bear obvious social and institutional pressures (not always as strongly as could be wished) not to leave everyday concepts and habits of thought too far behind. (There is more on the analogies and disanalogies between legal and historical thinking in the next chapter.) The obstacles which prevent history soaring off into theory are not the same. In particular, I would not want to contend that social phenomena are inherently insusceptible of scientific study. But, as I assert in several places in this book, it is possible to have an interest (it is only a suspicion of cultural absolutism which prevents my writing 'humanly necessary to have an interest'), a would-be informed, intelligent interest, in just those particularities of social phenomena which tend to be obscured in the development of a science. History, as we have it, is the fruit of some two centuries of systematic, professional cultivation of this interest; an impressive exemplification of what can be achieved by the careful use of very ordinary intellectual tools.

NOTE

Walsh on Colligation.   In *Proceedings of the Aristotelian Society*, 1971–2, I referred to Walsh's suggestion (1951, ch. iii, part iii) that an event may sometimes be explained or interpreted by being shown to fit into a general trend and thus 'colligated' under an 'appropriate conception'. He has in mind such things as the reoccupation of the Rhineland being conceived as an episode in the recovery of Germany or the origins of the Second World War. It seemed to me then, as it still does, that Walsh's account fits a good deal of what is to be found in history books; and I was inclined to see affinities between it and the idea of historical narrative as intrinsically explanatory. My one criticism was that I saw no reason, especially in view of the hindsight often involved in historical descriptions (cf. chapter II section 4 above), why appropriate conceptions should be restricted to ones which could have been entertained by people involved in the events in question. I ought here to make amends for having failed to take account of Walsh's later observations on colligatory concepts (1967). In that place he clearly recognises that appropriate conceptions may be brought to as well as found in history. They must indeed fit the facts, but this means only that they must be truly predicable of them by the historian, with his new knowledge and framework of ideas, not necessarily by the past agents themselves. Further, he has come to hold that colligation has to do with interpretation rather than explanation, and to be more sceptical of the notion of non-law-applying explanations.

V

Causation

1. Historians' Causes

The aim of this chapter is rather like that of the previous one, which was to enquire whether there is anything special about explanation in history. Here the same sort of questions will be asked about causation. Do historians have a special conception of it? Are they more interested in certain sorts of cause than in others? Is there objectivity in their causal assessments? Inevitably there will be some overlap with the earlier discussion but it is, none the less, better to attempt separate treatments. There are, in the first place, some questions specific to *causal* explanations. Second, to begin, as we have done, with a consideration of explanation generally, without commitment to the idea that explanations are inevitably or usually causal, at least avoids begging the question against the possibility of rational and narrative explanations.

In what follows I shall consider the meaning of 'cause', the possibility of particular (unique, individual) causal connections, notions of 'true' and fundamental (ultimate) causes, and at the end give some attention to ideas of determinism, inevitability and free will.

I shall begin by quoting certain passages in which historians have made causal pronouncements. The first, from Thucydides (1, 23, pp. 48–9), is the model for many subsequent ones.

War began when the Athenians and the Peloponnesians broke the Thirty Years' Truce which had been made after the capture of Euboea. As to the reasons why they broke the truce, I propose first to give an account of the causes of complaint which they had against each other and of the specific instances where their interests clashed: this is in order that there should be no doubt in anyone's mind about what led to this great war falling upon the Hellenes. But the real reason for the war is, in my opinion, most likely to be disguised by such an argument. What made war inevitable was the growth of Athenian power and the fear which this caused in Sparta. As for the reasons for breaking the truce and declaring war which were openly expressed by each side, they are as follows.

The next quotation is from David Thomson's *England in the Nineteenth Century* (1950, pp. 217–19):

What, in the light of previous history, was the war of 1914 about? At the time it was said that Britain entered the war in fulfilment of her treaty obligation. . . . Behind this reason, which certainly did much to determine both the unanimity and the timing of Britain's declaration of war, lay the deep-rooted historical tradition of her foreign policy which resisted all attempts by other great powers to dominate the Low Countries and the approaches of the North Sea. . . . We must be careful not to underestimate the actual share of both her Belgian and French commitments in bringing Britain into the war, and to exaggerate her economic and colonial rivalries with Germany.

Behind the decisions of 1914 lay more than a quarter-century of rivalry in power between Britain and the great imperial states of Europe; of periodic war scares and crises; of feverish competition in armaments; of nervous tensions and anxieties. . . . The participation of Britain in the World War, viewed in its longest perspective, was the inevitable consequence of her world-wide supremacy, both economic and naval, during the mid-Victorian era: for that supremacy was something she was losing, but which she would not be likely to bring herself to accept as lost without a struggle to retain it. That is where the naval challenge of Germany became so important.

The final passage is from A. J. P. Taylor's *English History, 1914–1945* (p. 453):

What caused the second World War? There can be many answers: German grievances against the peace settlement of 1919 and the failure to redress them; failure to agree on a system of general controlled disarmament; failure to accept the principles of collective security and to operate them; fear of communism and, on the Soviet side, of capitalism, cutting across ordinary calculations of international policy; German strength, which destroyed the balance of power in Europe, and the resentment of German generals at their previous defeat; American aloofness from European affairs; Hitler's inordinate and unscrupulous ambition – a blanket explanation favoured by some historians; at the end, perhaps, only mutual bluff. The question of its immediate outbreak is easier to answer. The house of commons forced war on a reluctant British government, and that government dragged an ever more reluctant French government in its train.

From passages like these certain features stand out.

(*a*) There is considerable variety in the sorts of factors offered as causes: states of affairs, events and actions, reasons for actions. There would appear to be no restriction of category upon what historians are prepared to cite as a cause. Collingwood is clearly wrong to maintain that in history causes always take the shape of reasons (1946, p. 214), just as he is wrong to hold that the subject matter of history is exclusively actions: but it would be equally wrong to think that reasons cannot be causes.

(*b*) Taylor, at least, is quite willing to contemplate the possibility of a plurality of causes: 'There can be many answers' – I do not think the observation is wholly ironical. Such an attitude, which I think is usual among historians, has implications for the conception of cause involved (for its characterisation in terms, say, of necessary and/or sufficient conditions). The conception has to be such that it allows the possibility of plurality.

(*c*) The particularity of some of the factors referred to should be noticed too – *this* war is claimed to have come about on account of fear in a particular quarter, resentment or aloofness in another. Doubtless these factors are of sorts which usually bring about wars and the like, but generality is not stressed, and it is very rare for the authors of causal pronouncements in history to make clear what, if any, general claims they would be prepared to subscribe to.

(*d*) There is willingness to entertain the idea that some causes are more important than others. Thomson, for instance, is concerned that his readers should not attach undue weight to certain factors, and historical controversy often has the form of debate about the relative importance of causes.

(e) Most conspicuous of all, perhaps, is a tendency to distinguish between longer-term, fundamental causes, which may be said to render the event inevitable, and more immediate, occasioning causes. The causes held to be fundamental are, however, themselves of various types, and by no means obviously rock bottom in a sense that would preclude their being themselves explained – there is scope here for historical materialism and other general theories of historical causation.

The five features mentioned, which are no doubt not equally evident in the quoted passages, are important for different reasons. The first two are because of their implications for the sense or senses the term 'cause' must be taken to bear in history; the next as constituting a possible difficulty for the 'regularity' theory of causation which has dominated much recent discussion; the fourth, that causes may be more or less important, because it may raise questions about the objectivity of causal judgements; the fifth because it may do so too and because it is a point at which general philosophical commitments may influence history.

The next section will be devoted to a consideration of the meaning of 'cause'.

2. The Use of 'Cause'

It is fairly easy to explain the meaning of 'cause' in the sense of constructing phrases not containing the word which can replace phrases which do. Instead of causes we may speak of factors *producing* or *bringing about* an effect, factors given which the event *had to* occur, or without which it *could not*. Just because these and many similar forms or words can so readily replace causal expressions, analysis of the latter in terms of them is not very illuminating. (This is even true of analysis in terms of necessary and sufficient conditions, which is genuinely helpful up to a point.) Puzzlement about causation simply rearises over what it is to bring about an effect or prevent its occurrence. Nevertheless, that there are a number of equivalent forms of words available may serve as a reminder that causal claims do not have to be made by means of the *word* 'cause'. Nor should the way in which cautious historians tend to fight shy of the word mislead anyone into supposing that they thereby avoid causal claims. There is, indeed, no sharp distinction to be drawn between causal and non-causal (say, 'purely descriptive') language (cf.

M. Scriven, from p. 20). If the contrary is its implication, Taine's much quoted maxim, 'After the collection of facts [comes] the search for causes', must be rejected. Causal claims, or assumptions, are embedded in what for many purposes would be accepted as simple description of situations and occurrences. Matches are struck (i.e. caused to ignite by rubbing on high friction surfaces), the rain wets pavements, the sun warms stones; enemies are defeated, territories settled, institutions reshaped. Causal suppositions and presumptions are present in contexts where there is no overt concern with explanation at all. Even in cases where it would be natural to say that there was agreement on facts but dispute over causal connections, there will still be causes in the facts. What from one point of view is pure fact may from another contain a questionable causal claim. Any prospect of finding descriptions wholly free from causal intrusions is as hopeless of accomplishment as that of finding descriptions relating entirely to an instant of time (cf. chapter II section 4). The moral is the same. The content of the present chapter relates primarily to contexts in which historians are consciously concerning themselves with causes and is intended to bear upon, even if it does not give a full account of, their causal claims. It is, however, clear that *general* scepticism about the possibility of justifying causal claims could not be confined to the overtly causal contentions in history books, but would self-defeatingly extend to all descriptive writing whatsoever.

It is, then, possible, but we have suggested not very illuminating, to paraphrase causal statements. But is there no possibility of a more fundamental, non-circular analysis into wholly non-causal terms? Is it not possible to produce radically non-causal expressions, equivalent at least in the sense of having the same truth-values as causal expressions (i.e. being true whenever the statement analysed is true, false when it is false), even if they are not in all respects the same in meaning? This the so-called 'regularity' theory of causation, which derives from Hume's *Treatise* (book I, part III), purports to do. Here the idea is that a cause is a factor of a type temporally antecedent to and regularly associated with a type of effect. Thus being bitten by an infected mosquito (a type of event) would be the cause (sufficient condition) of contracting malaria (another type of event) if it is always the case, when people have been bitten by such a mosquito, that they subsequently develop malaria. We should have a cause in the shape of a necessary condition when there is a type of event (say, combustion) which never occurs unless there is a certain sort of factor (in this case oxygen) antecedently present.

This is the conception of causation, which, by diverging in a measure from 'ordinary' (including historical) employments of the notion, generates some of the problems of the present chapter. One of these is the way in which causal connections are apparently sometimes attributed to unique cases, quite out of relation to generalisations about other cases (see the next section) – there was, of course, a somewhat similar problem for the law theory of explanation. Furthermore, as will soon appear, there may be reluctance to accept as causes what are, in regularity terms, sufficient or necessary conditions; and willingness to accept as causes factors which are neither. It is beyond doubt that uses of the term 'cause', in history and elsewhere, are much more various than the regularity view suggests. (There is an introductory discussion in J. Hospers (1967). An important work is H. L. A. Hart and A. M. Honoré's *Causation in the Law* (1959), though it should not be taken for granted that lawyers use the term in exactly the same way as historians. Another recent thorough discussion may be found in J. L. Mackie's *The Cement of the Universe* (1974), especially chapter v.) There has often been a tendency to dismiss non-regularity, non-Humean uses of 'cause' as merely confused, but I believe that the implication of the more careful recent discussions is that historians and other 'ordinary' speakers have no reason to allow themselves to be brow-beaten in this way. They should not be too ready to abide by restrictions, imposed in the name of Hume, philosophy, even science, on what they are otherwise inclined to say. The possibilities are very much more open than a simplistic understanding of the regularity theory might suggest.

I have reported both that causes in history need not be necessary or sufficient conditions and that necessary and sufficient conditions need not be causes. The causes cited by Taylor in the above passage seem not to be either sufficient or necessary, unless indeed one counts the failures as necessary. In spite of this it will be of interest to consider some of the attractions and disadvantages of attempting to characterise an historical cause in either of these ways.

Take first the idea of a cause as an *antecedent sufficient condition*. This is at first sight promising. It reflects the pragmatic elements un-questionably influential in the common notion of causation – a sufficient condition, if it is subject to human control, represents what can be done in order to obtain a certain result. More generally, for the historian whose concern is with accounting for rather than bringing about results, it would seem to constitute a complete explanation. There are, however, difficulties, both generally and for history in particular.

The general one (cf. chapter IV section 2 above) is that factors offered as causes are never literally sufficient conditions. They hardly could be intended as such when several are put forward, as they are in the passages quoted, for the same event. There would be gross over-determination if they were, but one detects no consciousness of anything of the sort. In any case, even if only a single cause is offered (and what historian would think this adequate to the intricacies of his subject matter?), there will always be other factors thinkable of which the absence would preclude the effect. If causes have to be sufficient conditions they never are, nor could be, fully specified. A possible reaction to this would be to try to represent historians' causes as necessary conditions – this possibility will be explicitly considered shortly, but I am sure some historians' causes are conceived more as factors *tending* to bring about an effect than as factors without which it could not occur. It would seem nearer the mark, therefore, to think of the sort of causes cited as *parts* of sufficient conditions, as elements which would figure in a sufficient condition if it could be fully specified. Some would here prefer to speak in terms of a distinction between partial and complete causes (causes proper). A slight objection to either way of talking is the apparent implication that (partial) causes always admit of being, so to say, additively accumulated until at the limit the complete cause is achieved. In some contexts this implication would be unobjectionable, but allowance must be made for the possibility of contexts in which causes are on different levels – taking the form of the acts and attitudes of people, tendencies in national policy, trends of various sorts, etc. and etc. – and consequently insusceptible of summation.

An approach alternative to that of distinguishing partial from complete causes would be to rely on the difference between standing and variable conditions employed in chapter IV. A cause, as a relatively sufficient condition, would then be a factor such that, when it is present in the situation as defined by the standing conditions, the effect occurs. Causes as relatively sufficient conditions would be easy to specify, and some, at least, of the causes actually encountered in history could be represented as relatively sufficient conditions. Nor is it a difficulty that no absolute decision can be taken whether a given factor belongs with the standing or the variable conditions. Rather the reverse, for this gives scope for the recognition of different points of view, by reference to which different though not necessarily incompatible levels of causal explanations might be distinguished.

There is, however, still a risk of the standing/variable condition distinction proving a misleading guide to the practice of historians. It fits better their notion of relatively superficial precipitating or occasioning causes than that of the more important causes lying, as Thomson puts it, 'behind' them. The sort of factor one may be inclined to light upon as a relatively sufficient condition will often be by historical standards a rather minor element in bringing about the event in question. Such factors as the firing on Fort Sumter, the assassination at Sarajevo, the guarantee to Poland in 1939, though they have their importance, are never the conclusions of historical enquiries. Historians interested in the causes of the American Civil War or of the First and Second World Wars are much more likely to concern themselves with setting out the nature of the situations in which occasioning factors of the sort mentioned could have such far-reaching consequences.

It is not, of course, that historians will never recognise such events as causes, but on the whole their tendency is not to do so, or at any rate to move away from doing so in proportion as the outcomes they are concerned to explain recede from near present politics into history. (This is the process of 'revisionism'.) There may be discerned here a point of contrast between the historical and the ordinary, practical, still more the legal, concern with causation. Practical men and lawyers typically tend to terminate their causal investigations upon human actions. Their concern is to assign responsibility, to identify the point at which a difference in action would have led to a different outcome. Historians, as typically, tend to go further. Though it would no doubt be an exaggeration to contend that they are never interested in responsibility (it will emerge in section 4 below that some disputes ostensibly about causation will reflect disagreements about the location of responsibility), they are practically always interested in more than this. Their being so is an aspect of that virtue of detachment which is notoriously so difficult to retain in contemporary history. A real danger of too closely associating historical and legal conceptions of causation arises from the fact that protests against over-concentration on a supposedly scientific, regularity conception of causation have been most impressively made on behalf of the law (for example by Hart and Honoré).

We may turn next to the possibility of identifying a cause as an *antecedent necessary condition*. I have denied that historical causes invariably or usually are such, but a consideration of the possibility will still help to fill in the background against which historical causes can be seen for what they are.

A necessary condition is that of which the absence precludes the outcome in question. A prominent type of situation in which necessary conditions are likely to be regarded as causes is one in which the concern is to prevent or eliminate something deemed bad rather than to obtain or keep something good. (This is one way in which values infiltrate causal interpretations.) Whilst the cause of full employment, if only we knew it, could well be a relatively sufficient condition, the cause of cancer is more likely to be a necessary condition; and moreover, since our concern with cancer is normally practical, a necessary condition under human control at tolerable cost. It is this sort of practical interest which explains why certain obviously necessary conditions are never offered as causes. Continuing solar heat, a necessary condition of virtually everything of human interest, is never cited as a cause of anything in particular. Nor is possession of a constitution which enabled him to survive pneumonia at twenty-five reckoned among the causes of a man's dying at seventy.

It is not easy to make out how deeply are practical considerations – notions of agency, the thought of causes as levers which can be operated in order to produce or prevent what is liked and disliked – embedded in conceptions of causation. Part of the difficulty is indeterminacy about being subject to human control or influence. Are we to mean actually, foreseeably, potentially or in principle so subject? Only if one is prepared to go the whole way down this road does it begin to seem plausible to maintain that the idea of human agency is dominant. Collingwood (1938, pp. 85–108; 1940, pp. 285–6; cf. Hospers, 1967, pp. 297–300) represents causation in ordinary life, but not history where he thinks causes are reasons or intentions (1946, p. 214), as having its source in the idea of agency, of one person having an influence on another person and, by extension, an effect on a thing. This could, of course, be a true account of the origin and development of the idea of causation, without agency being a predominant element at the present time. My own opinion is that it is at most one element among others, and one not specially important in the sorts of causes recognised by historians. Unquestionably the historian's subject matter is largely human practical affairs, but his interest in it is typically not in the relevant sense practical. His subject matter after all lies in the past, where it is logically proof against alteration by human agency. Nor does he have to confine his interest to types of causes which could be subject, at the appropriate time, to human intervention. Though it is true that he is typically concerned with factors which are in a broad sense human or social, as opposed to 'natural' (i.e. not physical or geographical, for instance), such social factors are not necessarily subject to human control. The social/natural distinction is not the same as that between what is and what is not within the scope of human agency.

I have considered the prospects of identifying causes as sufficient and as necessary conditions. A further possibility is that they might be *necessary and sufficient conditions*, i.e. complex conditions in which every element is individually necessary and the whole lot of them collectively sufficient. Causes so concerned will be very difficult to specify unless either they are relativised to a pretty comprehensive set of standing conditions or causal judgements are subjected to very sweeping 'other things being equal' clauses. Either way causes as necessary and sufficient conditions lose most of their necessitarian potency (see the last section of the present chapter). It is tolerably clear that Taylor's several clauses in the quoted passage neither do, nor are intended to, add up to a necessary and sufficient condition.

The matter of such plurality of causes deserves a second look. Taylor is, I believe, in line with common practice in recognising a number of non-competitive causes. If plurality is to be accommodated there are limits upon the way in which a cause can be conceived. There can, though in different ways, be more than one necessary and more than one sufficient condition; but only one necessary and sufficient condition – at least *at a time*, though there could be a 'chain' of necessary and sufficient conditions stretching back before an outcome.

The several necessary conditions there may be for an outcome in one way will not be alternatives; every one must obtain for the effect to take place. But their plurality may afford alternatives. From a practical point of view there may be alternative ways of preventing the effect if it is disliked. From a theoretical point of view there will be a choice of which to mention in the light of what is taken as granted or assumed to be known. People apparently in disagreement about causes may, consequently, all be right in the sense that they all mention conditions which are really necessary, the differences between them deriving from different lines of enquiry or points of view.

The way in which there can be a plurality of sufficient conditions is rather different. There may be alternative sufficient conditions for a type of effect, i.e. different ways in which it can be brought about. Every sufficient condition must contain all necessary conditions, but there may be different ways in which the necessary conditions can be supplemented in order to constitute a sufficient condition – not all the elements in a sufficient condition need therefore be necessary. But, though there may thus be several sufficient conditions – ways in which the type of event may be brought about – any actual instance of the event will normally be brought about in one way only. At least this is the usual assumption, though there can be difficult cases. Should a man be shot through the heart as he swallows cyanide (each presumably a sufficient condition of death), the natural move would be to identify as the cause whichever happened first. If they were literally simultaneous one would be at a loss. Sometimes no doubt finer analysis of the situation will permit the identification of a single sufficient condition; but I can see no guarantee that such analysis can always be carried through, nor, consequently, how to exclude in principle an irreducible plurality of operative sufficient conditions. All the same, to the extent that plurality is felt not to be the normal case, assignments of different sufficient conditions to the same event would be competitive, and so the fact that historians do not regard their multiple causes as competitive confirms that they are not taking causes to be sufficient conditions.

It is only when a cause has the shape of a necessary and sufficient condition that all plurality of causes is ruled out (except in the sense of successive links in a causal chain). It is guaranteed by logic that a necessary and sufficient condition leaves no room for any other (at the time). It contains all and only necessary elements. Any other necessary and sufficient condition would therefore have to contain them too. It could not, so to say, be smaller than the necessary and sufficient condition we started with. Nor, on the other hand, could it be larger, for then it would have to contain elements which were not necessary. This is guaranteed by logic. What logic fails, however, to guarantee is that there is a necessary and sufficient condition for every event. One could, indeed, vacuously, always choose to regard the elements in respect of which a variety of non-necessary sufficient conditions differ from one another as a single disjunctive necessary condition. (If the sufficient conditions are ABC – D and ABC – E, A, B and C being necessary, [D *or* E] can be said to be necessary too, thus making ABC + [D *or* E] necessary and sufficient.) But, apart from the gross unrealism for many contexts of supposing factors can be distinguished in this way, there is here only a manner of speaking which adds nothing to substantive knowledge. Less trivially there is always the possibility of seeking, by analysis of the elements in respect of which the various sufficient conditions differ, to find among them a common factor, which would be a genuinely additional necessary condition. Sometimes success will attend such efforts, but there is no guarantee that it always will.

The only way in which the notion of the necessary and sufficient condition can be put to much use in human studies is when simplified, abstract 'models' of a subject matter are constructed, as is often done in economics. An economy may be represented by a set of equations expressing the relationships between such factors as national income, level of employment, savings, investment and the like. Within such a model it may well be possible to specify the necessary and sufficient condition for, say, an increase in unemployment. It would follow that one could also give the necessary and sufficient condition for a rise in unemployment in any actual economy *exactly fitted by the model*. But it is notorious that economic models at best fit only where they touch. And it is in any case characteristic of history not to go in for abstract model building. In much the same way as it is dangerously misleading to take the more developed theoretical sciences – physics in some of its branches – as the model for all science, and hence the point of comparison and contrast with other studies, so is it grossly misleading to make the necessary and sufficient condition the model for all causation. To do so has the by now familiar result of making historians' causes seem very poor relations: merely necessary, if that; imperfectly analysed sufficient conditions, with much redundancy in them; mere fragments of sufficient conditions. If sense is to be made of what historians employ causal language to express, it must not be forgotten that theoretical scientists, as they are often represented by philosophers of science, have no monopoly of the concept of causation.

3. Particular Causal Connections

Here the problem arises from apparent conflict between the idea that there may be irreducibly singular causal connections in history and the requirement of the regularity theory that any causal connection between elements in a single case is bound up with those elements being universally associated. For *this* A to be the cause of *this* B it has to be the case that *whenever* A occurs B follows. (This formulation does not cover the fully variety of possible causes, but further elaboration is not necessary for the present discussion.) Historians, there is no doubt, make causal claims which they are unable, or unwilling, to relate to universals. Moreover, of the sort of ostensibly universal causal claim which historians sometimes permit themselves (say 'Famine causes brigandage' or even 'Power corrupts'), it has been contended by some philosophers of history that, so far from their being the foundation of causal assertions in particular cases, they are dependent upon them. The universals are reached by generalisation from a number of individual cases in which famine has been found to cause brigandage or power to corrupt.

The present concern is not to defend or attack the regularity theory, but to consider whether it really does rule out the sort of singular causal assertions apparently to be found in history. Even if it did, it would not follow that it is the practice of history which needs to change, but in fact we shall see that there is no more than the appearance of conflict.

We may begin by illustrating the way in which some regularity theorists have dismissed the possibility of singular causal connections. Mandelbaum, for instance, who was prepared to allow them (1938), provoked the following reply from Hempel (1942, pp. 354–5):

> This is essentially a view whose untenability has been pointed out already by Hume; it is the belief that a careful examination of two specific events alone, without any reference to similar cases and to general regularities, can reveal that one of the events produces or determines the other. This thesis does not only run counter to the scientific meaning of the concept of determination which clearly rests on that of general law, but it even fails to provide any objective criteria which would be indicative of the intended relationship of determination or production. Thus, to speak of empirical determination independently of any reference to general laws means to use a metaphor without cognitive content.

Gardiner (1952, part III, especially section 3) does not take a materially different view, though he expresses himself in a more conciliatory fashion. He can see that there is an intelligible ground for hesitating to agree that causal conections in history are entirely on the regularity pattern in the perfectly correct recognition that historians are normally concerned with a unique war, revolution, death; not wars, revolutions and deaths generally. They are not concerned to establish laws for future use. Nevertheless, he thinks there remains a necessary relation between particular causal judgements and laws, although he will concede to Mandelbaum that this does not require that laws have *first* to be established and *then* applied to the particular case. Discerning causal connections and discovering causal laws are simply two aspects of the selfsame process. Again, Gardiner will concede that it is possible to find causal connections intelligible in familiar human circumstances without the formulation of generalisations. In a word Gardiner, rather characteristically, takes account of the points made by critics of the regularity view by representing them as based on misunderstanding and so as no more than surmountable obstacles in the way of accepting it. Dray, on the other hand (1957, ch. 4), equally characteristically, is readier to give credence to genuinely different possibilities. In other fields, as well as history, there are generalisations like 'Dirt causes disease', 'Infections cause tumours', which are reached by generalisation from causal discoveries in individual cases. And the causal claims made in the individual cases need not reflect theoretical (universal) beliefs, but may be founded upon practical experience of manipulating circumstances in order to obtain or avoid certain outcomes in the individual cases. When a 'law' or universal has been obtained by generalisation from individual cases, to bring the case back under the law will not be additionally explanatory. Dray does, however, make it quite clear that he defends views like Mandelbaum's for only one sort of causal generalisation in history. He does not not deny that 'scientific', regularity causal explanations are also to be found there.

A number of comments may be made. In the first place there would seem to be no objection in principle to the idea of general causal claims being founded on causal judgements made in a number of individual cases. (This does not mean that there is no problem of explaining how causal judgements are justified in the individual cases; they plainly cannot be justified by appeal to general statements based upon them.) Some causal generalisations in history do seem to have the status suggested. Appeal may be made here to the fairly common doctrine noticed above – for example chapter IV section 3 (iii) – that apparent universals in history are often merely 'summaries'. There is no reason why causal generalisations of the kind in question should not happily coexist with causal explanations which fit the regularity model. Reflection on Dray's medical examples tends to confirm this. They may initially have been produced in advance of acceptable regularity explanations being found for the phenomena, but nobody doubts that such explanations are available in principle. There are already well developed sciences in the medical area at least, if not generally in history.

A further ground for allowing the possibility of coexistence may be found in the recognition that the appearance of conflict between the ideas that particular causal judgements involve universals (the regularity view) and that causal generalisations are derived from particular judgements (Mandelbaum) rests on a failure to compare like with like. The universals of the regularity theory are statements of universal *association* ('whenever A then B') – if they could not be expressed without use of the term 'cause' they would not even look like non-circular analysis of causal judgement. But the generalisations derived from particular causal judgements are themselves causal judgements (As *cause* Bs). Such generalisations need not, indeed, be universals at all. The causal judgements passed on individual cases are more likely to support a more cautious generalisation, for example that famine usually or sometimes causes brigandage, than the bolder claim that it always does.

The contention that there is a difference between the associative universals and causal generalisations (even when the latter are universal) may be resisted on the ground that the regularity theory entails that all causal judgements are implicitly universal, so that, if this A *genuinely* causes this B, then *any* A will cause B or *all* As will. In a way this is correct; but it fails to take account of the complexity of actual individual cases and the consequent summary character, from the regularity point of view, of the singular causal judgements made in them. The state of affairs reflected even in such a commonplace singular causal claim as, say, 'His smoking caused his lung cancer', will not be a perfect correlation between the gross phenomena 'smoking' and 'lung cancer', but rather a correlation or set of correlations between pairs of elements in the whole complex. Under certain conditions smoking may lead to tar deposits on the lung, tar deposits of a certain density may be associated with tissue changes, which are again associated with the development of malignancies. Against this sort of background it can be seen how a singular (summarising) causal assertion can be true of the individual case, without a like assertion being true of any, let alone every, other instance of the same gross phenomenon (any, every other case of smoking).

But does it not still follow that the sort of singular causal claim being considered is one formulated with exceptional inexactitude? *His* smoking, it was said, caused *his* lung cancer, but is not the truth rather that some factors x_1, x_2, x_3 etc., involved in his but perhaps not everybody's smoking, perfectly correlate with other factors y_1, y_2, y_3 etc. involved in his but again perhaps not in everybody's lung cancer?

Should not, therefore, the crude summarising 'His smoking caused his lung cancer' be abandoned in favour of a series of precise causal claims, 'x_1 caused y_1', 'x_2 caused y_2', etc., all of which will admit of universal generalisation? It goes without saying that such an heroic course is not often taken. Part of the reason must be ignorance. There is some in cases like that of lung cancer, but in history it may be of a much deeper order. Where established sciences bear, as in the medical example, ignorance presents itself as of a point of relative detail (which may, indeed, be of great practical moment). In history there is often only the hope, or wish, for future sciences. We do not even know what it is we do not know. Another part of the reason is the frequently practical direction of our interests. We concern ourselves with the causation of lung cancer in the hope of avoiding it. Smoking, from the scientific point of view a gross and indefinite complex and not one thing at all, from a practical point of view is one thing, which we can either engage in or not. We can *directly* concern ourselves with smoking, do something about it, in a way we cannot with tar deposits and changes in lung tissue. The 'exact' causal truth lying behind 'His smoking caused his lung cancer', even if we knew it, could not have the practical relevance of the latter. History, to be sure, is not in the same boat as popular preventive medicine. Its concerns are not directly practical and (as was observed in chapter IV section 3 above) few historians now think of themselves as compiling handbooks for statesmen. All the same, the subject matter of history remains largely practical affairs and, to the extent that historians are interested in rational explanation, they will have to employ language/concepts accessible to the agents in question. They cannot afford to be much more scientific than their subjects. Of course, when practical affairs are conducted by people learned in exact social science (the Treasury with its scores of economic advisers and sophisticated model of the economy?), historians will have to become social scientists too if they are to understand what goes on. But as yet there are not very many cases of this sort.

I have been defending the legitimacy of non-universalisable causal claims in individual cases, at least to the extent of denying that regularity conceptions of causation compel their abandonment. But, beyond a report of Dray's remarks about their being founded in practical experience, nothing has been done to show that they may positively be justified. (Regularity theorists are too ready to dismiss them out of hand, but quite right that they should not go without saying.) It is important not to allow phenomenology to usurp the role of logic. An account of how we come to make certain causal judgements may incidentally show that we are justified in so doing: but it need not. It is not self-evidently impossible that we regularly make unjustified claims.

It is a condition of survival that, in the process of growing up, we all learn in some measure how to cope with things and people. Reflection on the capacities we thus acquire could, no doubt, in principle lead on to explicit causal beliefs, but obviously to a great extent it does not. People are inclined to reflection in differing degrees. It is not universally the case that it improves performance; it may impede it – not only in the case of the proverbial centipede. In relation to many basic capacities there are lacking the very concepts required to make effective reflection and explicit causal belief possible. Capacities are acquired insensibly or, as with some practical skills like swimming and bicycle riding, one learns by a mixture of imitating, having a try and (with luck) finding at some stage that one can do it, though it may remain impossible to say (or think) what one has to do to succeed. This is very much the situation with capacities for getting along with other people. Experience of living, even among the more reflective, is only exceptionally stockpiled in explicitly formulated beliefs about what will happen as a result of what, what has to be done in order to get what. Reflection rarely penetrates as deep as our basic capacities.

Such unreflective, preconceptual deposits of life experience inform the judgement we bring to the situations of ordinary life and, up to a point, history too. By exercising this judgement we reach our commonsensical – singular, non-universalisable, summary – causal convictions. In the nature of the case it is impossible to set out the grounds of them, but most of us on occasion find ourselves quite confident of such things as that it was the wife's full-time job, not the children's surpassing the educational level of their parents, which caused family discord; that in one case it was domestic unhappiness, in another illness or financial anxiety which led to loss of grip in the boardroom or, indeed, the Cabinet. Increase in the scale of the situation is not in itself an obstacle to the operation of 'intuitive' causal judgement (this moral is persuasively drawn by C. P. Snow's ever-insightful Lewis Eliot as he climbs the staircase to power), though in larger scale situations there may be more background which can only be the object of discursive knowledge.

What is in question, however, is not how confident we are in our causal beliefs but whether we are entitled to be so. From a purely practical viewpoint the answer very often is that we are, since there is nothing better to go on. It may be supposed too that causal beliefs are more likely to be correct in familiar situations, although, encouragingly, it is not impossible to transcend the bounds of personal experience. On the debit side, however, it is to be feared that the standard of correctness is by no means clear. The supposed test of successful practice is vitiated by a propensity to interpret results in the light of the assumptions of which the credibility is in question. The agreement of others is always cheering, but there cannot be ruled out the possibility of consensus in error. Nevertheless, despite such grounds for doubt, in practical affairs we can only act by the best lights we have and trust those who will so act. To wait upon the development of scientific knowledge, to prefer supposedly scientific conjecture or imperfectly established theory to the judgement of the practically experienced is a sure recipe for disaster, even though the opposite policy carries no guarantee of success.

But all this relates to the practical sphere whilst history, as recognised more than once above, is not subject to the constraints of practice. It is not exclusively concerned with rational explanation, and may employ procedures of causal assessment not available to participants in the events it recounts and seeks to explain. Surely history does not have to rest content with intuitive causal judgements? Certainly nobody has to, but history seems none the less to be a study in which people mainly do – partly, I think, because a certain sort of source material, contemporary documents, has come to be taken as primary; partly too, perhaps, on the basis of a 'division of intellectual labour' principle (or tradition). It is not by any means forbidden for an historian to try to improve upon commonsense causal interpretations of people's behaviour by applying explicit psychological theory. Some have done so, and with results allowed to be occasionally illuminating, but their example has not been generally followed. Why not? One reason is well-grounded doubt whether usable theory is itself securely established. It is sad that psychoanalysis should be at once the apparently most illuminating and least respectable of psychological theories. Another, more fundamental, reason is that evidence tends not to be available in sufficient quantity or appropriate form for the effective application of theory. Too determined an effort to employ explicit theory is thus apt to lead the historian beyond his data, to tempt him away from what he can show *did* happen to what he has extra-historical grounds for supposing *must have* happened. Historians improve on the work of their predecessors, not by exercising a superior capacity for causal judgement (who could be sure that they had it?), but by finding more reliable data to exercise their judgement on. Unquestionably it is intellectually meritorious to bring science into areas hitherto given over to intuition. But there are many meritorious tasks, and the one typically taken up by historians is large enough for them to be in little danger of unemployment.

4. The 'True' Cause

The present topic has its source in the way that historians are rather ready to allow the possibility of an indefinite number of causes for a particular gross event: the outbreak of a war, a religious upheaval, a social revolution. Such tolerance, however, opens up the possibility of disputes over which causes are more important or significant, disputes which may be sharpened by claims that such-and-such is the true or real cause of the event in question. (It is supposed throughout the present section that a type of cause judged important in one situation may be less so in another. Whether one type of cause may be *generally* more important is the topic of the next section.) Disputes over the relative importance of causes may take on a doctrinal character and divide historians into schools or factions. Successive waves of explanation of such major events as the English and American Civil Wars, the French Revolution, the two World Wars tend to be related in this way.

To this situation there are different ways of reacting. One is to hold that it arises from superficial views of what historians ought to be about. Oakeshott, as I understand him, compatibly with his claim that explanation in history is a matter of telling in detail how something came about, would object to any singling out of a cause as specially important; indeed even to think in terms of causes at all is to permit practical attitudes to tear the seamless web which the past studied for its own sake ought to be. There is no doubt that theses about causes can reflect practical concerns – the desire to assign responsibility, to find in the past lessons for the future. On the other hand, though, Oakeshott seems to give too little weight to the inescapable need for selection. The whole story cannot be told. Completeness is meaningless out of relation to a point of view or question asked, which fixes a criterion of relevance and level of generality.

At the opposite extreme to Oakeshott's would be the view that disputes about the relative importance of causes are just further manifestations of the subjectivity and arbitrariness that some, including some historians, find characteristic of history. Between these extremes lies the possibility of setting out the rationale of arguments about the relative importance of causes. Authors differ in the precise lines they take. White, perhaps, comes near the centre in holding the true cause to be the 'abnormal' (contributory) cause, as selected from a point of view not every historian will share – its being recognised that it will not always be possible to establish that one point of view is superior to another (1965, ch. IV). Evidently this is a species of the sort of relative objectivity defended in chapter III above in another connection. White – like Gardiner before him, who takes a generally similar view – is anxious to repudiate any idea that it is some feature intrinsic to a cause which makes it more important than another. Importance is rather determined by the point of view of the historian and the level of generality on which he operates (Gardiner, 1952, p. 104). White is further concerned to insist that, relative to a point of view, it is entirely an empirical matter which is the more important cause. He repudiates suggestions that importance might be determined by such moral considerations as that certain people are to be held culpable for what occurred. Dray, on the other hand, would allow moral factors a legitimate role (1957, ch. 14). Bloch recognises that they do influence the assignment of causes, but finds it unacceptable that they should. 'In history, the fetish of a single cause is all too often only the insidious form of search for the responsible person and hence a value judgment' (p. 193).

The notion of abnormality from a point of view may be illustrated as follows. Take an event like the destruction of a school or hospital by fire. From the point of view of the users of the building generally the cause is likely to be some such event as an unextinguished cigarette end being dropped into a wastepaper basket. This is the abnormality, the deviation from the ordinary course of things, from which all the rest follows. The fire prevention officer, by contrast, may be more impressed by the importance of the fire doors having been wedged open on the particular occasion, perhaps in order to clear the corridors for a delivery of furniture. From his point of view setting light to wastepaper baskets with cigarette ends is all too common; what strikes him is rather that devices intended to prevent fire from spreading were, exceptionally, inoperative. Yet again, from the point of view of the architects, or their disappointed clients and disgruntled insurers, the cause may well be, not the fact that the fire doors were open, but that great reliance had been placed on fittings inherently liable to misuse. Further points of view are conceivable, but it is doubtless already clear enough how differing points of view determine certain factors as given and others as abnormal or variant and so deserving of causal status.

A further type of example, common in the literature, is of the man with a chronic ulcer taken ill after eating fish for supper. He has lived with his ulcer for a long time, but is not much given to fish eating, so he identifies the latter as the cause. His doctor on the other hand, well aware that fried fish is usually eaten without pain, and believing that ulcers can be treated and even cured, will identify the ulcer or postponement of surgery as the cause. Again – to adopt a type of example from Collingwood (1940) – when a car has skidded off the road, the driver, for whom vehicles and roads are given, will perhaps identify the cause as going too fast or maybe water on the road. The car designer is more likely to interest himself in steering geometry, weight distribution, tyre construction; the road engineer in camber, radius of curves, surface materials. For the two latter, going too fast and water on the road, though in an obvious sense variable factors, are still part of the given – it is in vehicles and road construction that *they* perceive alternative possibilities.

Before we turn to more credibly historical examples, one or two terminological matters require brief attention. One is the imperfect appropriateness of the word 'abnormal'. The contrast required seems to be between factors which, from a certain point of view, are assumed as given and others which, from that same point of view, are subject to variation. Dropping cigarette ends in wastepaper baskets is too common to be literally abnormal – the point is only that, given a body of facts about a situation, dropping a cigarette end will start a fire. The assignment of causes cannot be accounted for on the basis that 'abnormal' is taken strictly in the sense of 'unusual, statistically rare'. The recognition of this should not, however, be allowed to mislead one into supposing that the word *must* instead be taken in a sense closer to 'contrary to rule' or 'contrary to what was expected' – carelessness with cigarettes consequently attaining causal status, not because smokers are not usually careless, but because they should not be. I am not persuaded that evaluations never enter into the assignment of causes, but we have as yet no sufficient reason for supposing they always or often do.

The term 'variable' may itself have misleading implications too. Unquestionably what some of the above examples illustrate is less variability than the way in which factors may or may not fall within a person's professional competence. Road surface material is a potential cause of accidents from the point of view of the civil engineer, not so much because it is literally variable (it may be difficult or impossibly costly to vary it), as because it falls within his province. I do not suggest that the limits of professional competence usually have very great influence on the determination of the more important cause in history, but they may have some in cases where different judgements of importance are made by, say, political and social or economic historians.

Consider now some historical illustrations. Different causes will be emphasised by historians from different nations involved in the same sequence of events. The causes of the Second World War, indeed its duration, will be different for historians of Britain from what they are for those of France, Germany, America and Russia. The historian of one nation inevitably will rank as more important the acts and omissions of statesmen of that nation. They are, after all, part of his primary subject matter, connectable with and explicable by other events and situations in that subject matter, whilst those of foreign statesmen will appear either as outside influences upon or as part of the setting within which the events he is centrally concerned with take place.

Again, within a national history, the relative emphasis given to different causes will depend on the conception of the work of which the explanation of the events in question forms a part. The importance of the *entente* and the military and naval arrangements between Britain and France before the First World War will loom larger for the historian concentrating on the period starting with the so-called splendid isolation of the 1880s – in that perspective they were new departures – than for one taking a centuries-long view of British foreign policy, and who can consequently see the policy of alliances as continuous with a long tradition of resistance to any tendency for Europe to fall under the domination of a single power.

Estimates of the relative importance of causes will not only thus vary according to the length of time prior to the events in question the historian takes within his purview, but also according to the length of subsequent time he chooses to consider. (Sheer space of time is, of course, important only as a crude index of perspective, direction of interest, point of view.) An historian writing in the 1950s, say, with a second World War behind him, will have grounds for evaluating causes differently from one writing in the 1930s. The earlier writer may have been impressed by the idea that Britain had not made it clear prior to

1914 that the violation of Belgian neutrality would be treated as a cause of war, the later one will know that the second war opened with an attack on Poland despite explicit guarantees from the Western powers, and may consequently come to think that the real causal importance of the British attitude to Belgian neutrality had less to do with explaining the action of Germany than the willingness of a traditionally pacific Liberal Party to go to war. It is not that subsequent events prove earlier historians wrong in their assessment of causes – although this can happen – but rather that different assessments can be quite objectively equally correct in relation to the different ranges of comparisons and contrasts possible in the different periods considered.

There is, however, a respect in which the sort of examples I have been putting forward may lead to a false impression. It is difficult to avoid seeming to be explaining away, in the interests of preserving objectivity, the fact that historians will differ about the importance of causes – as if such differences were always unfortunate and in need of justification or excuse. In fact, as was noted above in chapter III, historians tend to be much less careful of their reputation for objectivity than are philosophers presuming to speak on their behalf, and much less anxious to be in some unchallengeable way right. I am sure that it is often felt that the value of seeing the same events and their causes in a variety of different perspectives far exceeds that of being 'right' in relation to any one of them. The sort of understanding often most valued is, so to say, something distributed among the truths discernible from a variety of points of view, or something to be collected in moving from one to another, never something confined to any one or finite set of them. The openness of history, the endlessness of the possibilities of assessment and reassessment, is a glory not a disgrace.

The dimension of variability in causal assessments so far under consideration is one related to the aims and points of view of historians. Less emphasis has been given to the presumed needs and interests of the intended reader. Historians do not simply write *about* something, but also *for* somebody. Dray gives some weight to this consideration. White, rather strangely to my mind, is unwilling to do so. He considers it in the shape of an observation he finds in J. S. Mill to the effect that 'the cause' may be used to single out a condition believed to be unknown to the readership in question (1965, pp. 160–2). The one merit seen in the view is that it is a move away from the idea that it must be in virtue of some intrinsic feature that a factor is selected for special mention as *the* cause. Otherwise it is defective as relativising causal assessments to the knowledge and ignorance of random readers, and much less illuminating than his doctrine of abnormalism from a point of view. One may easily grant that the view attributed to Mill is less than the whole story. Nevertheless it does seem to me part of that story. As emphasised in chapter III above, historians do not write in a vacuum, but with a view to what they think a reference group of fellow professionals will be interested to know.

I turn next to the question of values coming into causal assessments. I do not have in mind the sense in which exercising judgement about causes may be itself spoken of as evaluating – there is in this usage a potent source of confusion which I shall try to neutralise in the next chapter. The present concern is rather with the way in which an historian's causal judgement may be guided by his values, mainly his moral and political values, but religious – even aesthetic – ones could be important too. It is not with the role of such values in determining choice of subject matter and point of view that we are here concerned, but rather with the possibility of their having an additional influence on causal judgement within those limits.

It was noted earlier in the present chapter how evaluation of an effect as bad or good may help in practical affairs, from which there is a partial carry-over into history, to determine whether a (relatively) necessary or sufficient condition is taken as a cause. Also noted has been Dray's view that assigning causes may largely be a matter of ascribing responsibility, attributing blame (1957, p. 99; cf. the American Civil War example discussed at length in 1964, ch. 4). Indeed it seems to me virtually beyond question that causes sometimes are assigned on the basis of values, but White (1965, ch. IV sections 7 and 8) argues against the moralistic notion that a factor may be selected as a cause on account of its possessing a 'value property'. A view so formulated is certainly exceptionable, but its substance could readily be re-expressed by replacing 'value property' with 'its being judged good or bad, right or wrong, etc. from a moral or other point of view'. An example of a moralistic causal judgement would be an act's being accredited causal status on the basis of its being judged wicked (for its moral rather than its statistical abnormality). White's objection here is that there are very many cases in which factors are not selected as causal on the basis of their 'value properties'. Causal factors may be morally indifferent, or even events and states of affairs which are not proper objects for moral evaluation at all. With so much no one could disagree. The moralistic theory, if it has ever been advanced as a *general* theory, utterly fails. One can, moreover, further agree that the mere fact that a value-charged *word* is used to pick out a factor deemed causal – the Piggott *forgeries*, the *murder* of President Kennedy – is not significant. It could, so far as the mere employment of evaluative language goes, be the case that historians select causes on other grounds, and either report evaluations by contemporaries of the events in question or indulge in moral obiter dicta of their own. What does not seem, however, to follow is that historians never assign causes moralistically. Surprisingly, White in effect concedes this when, in his section 8, he admits an 'untypical' moralistic use of the expression 'is the cause of'. One may agree with him that this usage is unfortunate, that it is better not to use 'is the cause of' in the sense of 'is morally responsible for', but this does not alter the fact that usage is what it is. The ground for differing from White is largely that, as it seems, the likelihood of causal assignments being influenced by moral and other values is so great, that it makes for greater clarity to allow explicitly that it may occur, than to try to ban this employment of the word 'cause'. Such proscriptions are always in vain.

I have not, of course, covered all the ways in which values may come in. An historian's position on the radical – conservative dimension is likely to affect his judgement of what in a situation is socially possible and hence of whether a factor is variable or 'abnormal'. Radicals have the more enlarged notion of social possibility, and are thereby the more likely to identify as causally important people's failures to seize opportunities, to rise to occasions. They are correspondingly likely to discern in their more conservative colleague a tendency to explain to the point of excusing. I do not want to suggest that there can be no truth or falsity in this area, that whether or not somebody could or might have acted differently from the way he did is never decidable in the light of evidence. But questions of social possibility are not wholly determinable, and because of this there is bound to be a measure of ineliminable tension between conservatives and radicals in the assignment of causes.

I will conclude this section by recalling that the word 'cause' is often used sufficiently widely to cover reasons, i.e. what an agent would offer in explanation or justification of his actions – his intentions, his aims, his beliefs about what has to be done in order to achieve them. It is worth following up a little way the possibility that some of the problems encountered in relation to identifying the true or more important cause are matchable with regard to reasons. It will often be the case that historical agents will appear, in the light of the evidence, to have had a variety of reasons for what they did, and it will accordingly be found possible for historians to disagree over what their real or main reasons were. Certain figures – Cromwell, Robespierre, even perhaps Gladstone – may be felt to present special difficulties in this regard. This has sometimes been supposed to constitute an important ground for doubting the possibility of objectivity in *history*, though in fact it should not, since nothing is easier than to parallel with one's contemporaries the uncertainties often felt about historical personages.

As with true causes, so with real reasons. I have no wish to deny that *sometimes*, when historians disagree, one is simply right and others simply wrong in the light of actual or conceivable evidence. But it remains possible that *other times* both are right relative to different points of view. Often, to be sure, the contrast between mere reasons and real reasons is a contrast between avowed and concealed reasons – this seems to be the main possibility contemplated by Gardiner, when he suggests (1952, p. 136 note) that it is generally safe to hold that a man's real reasons are those he would avow when so to do would entail no adverse consequences to him. (Psychoanalytic conceptions of real reasons he allows to be different.) But it seems to me also to be possible for real reasons to reflect the direction of interest of an historian. Politicians, for example, operate on different levels. In a governmental system like our own they will typically be concerned with, at the least, advancing their personal political fortunes, advancing those of their party, the interests of the nation, and promoting various personal and public aims or ideals. Talk of levels is misleading if it suggests that they are clearly separated. That they are not is something naïve accusations of insincerity levelled at politicians commonly fail to take into account. It is much nearer the mark, I believe, to think of the acts of politicians as over-determined in a complex way, which affords to an historian the opportunity of emphasising one sort of reason rather than another according to his point of view. If he is concerned with foreign policy he can properly bring to the fore reasons which can be represented as continuous with persistent policy trends. If his interest is rather the fortunes of a political party another set of considerations can as properly be emphasised. The political biographer will emphasise a different set again. Superficially it may appear that the different authors disagree over their subject's reasons for acting as he did, but each may be right from his own point of view. And, as was seen in chapter III, there may be no absolute answer to the question which point of view is right, except that at certain stages in historical studies it may be more fruitful to work from one point of view than from another.

Relativism in this connection may be resisted on the ground that, whether it can be discovered from the evidence or not, the different reasons of a politician must each have had a definite weight in his deliberations. This notion gains credence from the idea that having a reason is a matter of consciously having in mind a consideration with a sensible degree of force or weight – in the sort of way, perhaps, that sensations of heat or pain may have. This picture of deliberation fails entirely to take account of the fact that there is no access to a reason, no way of estimating its strength, save on the basis of evidence. And this evidence will include, as well as any statement there may be by the subject of what his reasons were, records of persistent trends in his behaviour, variations in it as circumstances changed, interpretations by contemporaries, and the like. The subject's own testimony will always carry weight, but has no absolute privilege, and will often have to be qualified in the light of other evidence. He may well have tried to deceive others, or even deceived himself. Biographers have a hard task in attempting to determine the relative importance of their subjects' reasons, but autobiographers are not necessarily in better case. There is no escaping relativity to direction of interest and point of view.

Up to this point in the present section no question has been raised about the presupposition that there may be several causes (including reasons) for the 'same' effect. This way of looking at the matter, though natural and common, is not wholly unmisleading, and may exaggerate the extent to which judgements of relative importance among causes are relative to rather general points of view. There is in many cases the alternative possibility of relating the selection of a factor as the more important cause, not to a general point of view, but to a determinate interpretation of the question asked. Various causes are, for example, offered for the First World War – different levels of nation statehood and industrialisation among the major powers, the system of alliances worked out in the early twentieth century, the treaties concerning Belgian neutrality, the assassination. But, it may very reasonably be urged, the first two factors at most contribute to explaining why there was a tendency to armed conflict among major powers, but not to explaining which powers were on which side. In order to explain that the pattern of alliances must be taken into account, and the details of that pattern will not be explicable by reference to the large-scale, long-term factors alone. Again the Belgian guarantee may have less importance for the general question why war broke out than for the more particular question why Britain participated in the way she did. The assassination itself may bear mainly upon the question of why hostilities began precisely in August 1914.

The same sort of consideration is relevant to the discussion in the next section of different levels of causal explanation and the associated supposition that the 'same' thing admits of explanation at more or less fundamental levels. Once again there is a risk of exaggerating the extent to which explanations on different levels are even potentially competitive with one another. Before bracing oneself to choose between the methodological individualist thesis that ultimate causes are to be found in the actual individuals and the historical materialist thesis that ultimate causes are economic factors, it is worth pausing to wonder whether the truth may not rather be that *some* things are explicable one way, *other* things the other. Here, as earlier, I have no wish to suggest that there never can be intellectual confrontations; but there is a heavy deposit of cross purposes in very many of them.

5. *Levels of Causal Explanation*

(i) It was suggested at the beginning of the present chapter that there is no restriction of category upon causes in history: individual actions, reasons for them, the actions (if that is the right word) of collectives (classes, nations, churches etc.), economic, geographical, religious, cultural factors – they are none of them barred. In face of such variety it is not unnatural to think that there are different types or levels of causation, from which it is but a short step to holding one type or level more fundamental than any other. It is wholly impossible even to mention, let alone discuss, every sort of view, held in this area. I shall confine myself to two only: first the so-called *methodological individualist* thesis that the actions, beliefs, attitudes of human individuals have primacy as causes; second (collectivist) *historical materialism*, the Marx-inspired contention that in the final analysis economic factors are dominant.

At the outset it must be emphasised that there is a considerable variety of opinion within each of these very broad categories. Brief exposition is bound to appear – not only to true believers – to be vulgarisation. I can see no help for this, though I do not believe that the criticisms I shall bring forward would lose force in face of more elaborate statements of the views attacked.

The question is, of course, whether there are *philosophical* grounds for supposing views of either type true, whether generally or for history specifically. The boundaries of the philosophical are not wholly precise, but I assume do not include moral and political considerations, although these seem to weigh with some individualists and materialists.

In discussing methodological individualism I shall consider in order F. A. von Hayek's presentation of it in part I of his *Counter-Revolution of Science*, 1952 (cf. his *Economica* papers of 1942–4), Popper's more cautious doctrine, some of Popper's critics, and the question of the reducibility of social to psychological theory. There is a very extensive literature on this not unmysterious topic. On the most favourable estimate methodological individualism covers a multitude of virtues. There are influential papers by M. Ginsberg, M. Mandelbaum, M. Brodbeck, E. Gellner, and J. W. N. Watkins, and chapters in E. Nagel and A. C. Danto – to name only a few authors.

Hayek, as I understand him, wishes not only to deny ultimate causal efficacy to the 'doings' of collectives, but further denies that they are a sort of entity about which laws comparable to those of natural science could be framed. Notions like 'class' and 'capitalist system' are simply popular abstractions, but there is no substituting for them more clearly conceived entities about which laws could be made. The proper aim of history and social studies is to break through abstractions to the concepts which really influence or constitute the actions of concrete individuals. Hayek's argument thus relies upon an elaborately stated distinction between the data of natural science and those of social studies, coupled with the assumption that the aim of the latter is the rational explanation (as it was termed in chapter IV above) of human actions, though also, of course, with due account taken of their unintended consequences.

The idea is that the data of the natural sciences are (roughly) familiar objects and events – balls bouncing, metals expanding – which are explained as the resultants of the goings on of more or less mysterious particles. The complexes or collectives are given. The particles or individuals are inferred or postulated, and simply credited with whatever qualities are necessary to make possible the explanation of the complexes. In social studies, however, it is the other way round. Here the individuals (people) are given, the social complexes in which they figure are not. They have to be inferred or constructed, and may not even be observable as wholes. (I merely expound Hayek, without endorsing the absoluteness of this contrast. For other doubts, see Nagel, pp. 539–40.) 'Scientistic' conceptions of social studies, to which methodological individualism is opposed, neglect the contrast, and mistakenly suppose that complexes are given and basic in social studies as well as natural science. But in truth complexes rate mention in social studies only to the extent that they facilitate explanation of the behaviour of individuals. This sets a further limit to the role of supra-individual complexes in social studies. Whereas in natural sciences the price of obtaining exceptionless generalisations was abandonment of the classifications of common sense and common speech, in social studies it has to be recognised that it is just these classifications which, by being reflected in consciousness, are important in the genesis and understanding of behaviour. Hayek formulates this claim by contending that the data of social studies are 'subjective', not things as they are in themselves, but only as they are taken to be – not, for instance, bits of printed paper and moulded metal, but money. For natural sciences the similarities between coin and notes, and coins of different metals, are much less important than the differences (in material). Only by reclassifying on the basis of these differences can we obtain such wide-ranging generalisations as the theory of the elements, the laws of chemical combination and the like. But the sort of reclassification which has been the condition of progress in natural science would prevent the resultant theories or laws being relevant to the explanation of human behaviour in the areas of buying and selling. The study of society cannot follow the natural sciences very far down the road of abstraction and reclassification without ceasing to be of human behaviour in society. Methodological individualism is the recognition of this. It is opposition to abandoning the study and explanation of behaviour in rational terms, for the sake of pseudo-science ('scienticism'), peddling faked laws about bogus entities, capitalism, revolution and the like, in despite of more mundane concepts actually reflected in people's thinking and conduct.

In response to this it can readily be agreed that rational explanations must be in terms of concepts accessible to the agents in question. But history, let alone social science, is not restricted to the search for rational explanation; and, even when it is concerned with trends or patterns in people's rational behaviour, it is not confined to concepts those people might have framed (cf. the note on colligation appended to chapter IV). It can be further agreed that many putatively scientific generalisations about society are pseudo-laws, and that genuine laws would not help with *rational* explanations. But none of this entails that there cannot be such genuine laws. An autonomous (collectivist) sociology would not discharge the main task of the study of society as conceived by Hayek, but again it does not follow that there cannot be such a sociology. Popper, though sceptical about actual achievement in the field, allows that it is possible in principle. I cannot see that Hayek does much to show that it is not – beyond placing an arbitrary restriction on the aim of social study. He admits himself that there can be 'natural' sciences of mankind, instancing epidemiology; but it cannot be known a priori how far such studies can extend.

Popper (1945, vol. 2 chs 13–14; and 1957), although he cites Hayek with approval, seems himself to adopt a more moderate position. On the one hand he firmly repudiates an extreme form of individualism, the 'psychologism' he finds in J. S. Mill; the view, namely, that ultimate explanations are to be found in *individual* psychology (for example in instincts proper to mankind as such, or in socially invariant laws of human nature). On the other hand he professes to agree with Marx on the 'autonomy of sociology': the view that there can in principle be for social phenomena laws which are independent of anything known about individual psychology. He stops short, however, of Marx's 'methodological collectivism'. Like Hayek he thinks that it should be the aim of social study to represent the 'doings' of collectives as somehow the resultants of the doings of individuals in their social situations.

The difficulty with regard to Popper is to determine, given his concessions, the status and content of what he asserts.

Take first the term 'methodological'. In Hayek it would seem to have the force of 'having to do with method (in social studies)', although his concern is more with what is possible than what is merely desirable – i.e. he lays down constitutive rather than regulative rules. In Popper, however, the term seems intended to be understood in contradistinction to 'metaphysical'. Popper is not a metaphysical individualist. He does not deny the reality of groups, or assert that individuals enjoy a superior order of reality, whatever that could be. He would presumably think questions about the metaphysical reality of individuals and groups pointless. Groups exist and are real in the way proper to groups, individuals do and are in the way proper to them – a metaphysical platitude upon which it is difficult to improve. 'Methodological' may also be used as a contrast to 'moral', and methodological individualism thus need to be distinguished from such moral claims as that individuals count for more than do groups, even that individuals alone count morally, so that there are no morally allowable loyalties to groups which are not reducible to loyalties to individuals. The present concern is with methodological individualism alone, but it would be unrealistic to ignore the possibility of methodological, metaphysical and moral views intertwining and so mutually reinforcing one another, even in the minds of anti-metaphysicians. Here, no doubt, lies the explanation why methodological individualists continue, with more determination than argumentation, to maintain a very unclear view in the face of apparently very reasonable doubts and difficulties.

Consider next Popper's objection to Mill's psychologism. His conclusion here ought to be acceptable in view of the fact that it was agreed (in chapter IV section 3 above) that dispositional explanations were unsatisfactory from the point of view of history if they omitted reference to the social situation of the individuals in question. The problem is how to distinguish between psychologism and methodological individualism. Popper takes the former very strictly as the view that explanations must be entirely in terms of the laws of *individual* psychology, laws applying to all people everywhere, regardless of social differences among them, as do the laws of physiology. Against this Popper maintains that a good deal of what has passed for traits of human nature turns out on examination to be socially determined, adding that man was social before he was human. I take the substance of this aphorism to be that, since social influences are historically antecedent to human beings, and hence to *human* psychology, they must be logically distinct from it; and that there must therefore be some social phenomena, determined by these influences, which cannot be accounted for wholly in terms of individual psychology, entirely abstracted from all social influence. Methodological *individualism*, somewhat surprisingly, thus turns out to be the thesis that social phenomena are to be explained, not solely in terms of the actions, attitudes, expectations of individuals, but of individuals *in their situations*. It is this social reference which distinguishes Popper's position from psychologism. His insistence, also found in Hayek, that many social phenomena are the *unintended* results of human actions (for example price collapses resulting from small farmers trying to increase income by sowing larger acreages) further tends to distinguish his position from psychologism. He repudiates 'great men' and conspiracy theories and, in his *Poverty of Historicism*, even manages a good word for Tolstoy, despite the notorious collectivism of *War and Peace* (in which, for example, marching orders are represented as epiphenomenal to the movements of armies) – it is at least better than representing everything that happens in war as the intended result of the actions of commanders.

Plainly it is no easy matter to steer a middle course between psychologism and collectivism. It is not surprising, therefore, to find one of Popper's critics (Gellner, 1956) claiming that a fully worked out methodological individualism is indistinguishable from psychologism. Watkins, on the other hand, who appears to regard himself as a methodological individualist and is often sympathetic to Popper, holds that it is rather that psychologism is a 'narrow' form of methodological individualism (1957). It is instructive too to refer to two papers by Mandelbaum: 'Societal Facts' (1955) and 'Societal Laws' (1957). In the former it is held to be impossible to understand the actions of human beings as members of society without recognising 'societal' facts as ultimate, and irreducible to psychological ones. An example given is of filling in a withdrawal slip in order to get money from a bank – one has to understand the banking *system* in order to make sense of such a transaction. The behaviour of individuals is unintelligible out of relation to social status and role. There is nothing here that Popper has not allowed. Mandelbaum's second paper advances the possibly more controversial claim that there may also be irreducible 'societal' laws. It is a matter of some difficulty to assess the truth of this, but it is again a claim presumably conceded by Popper's acceptance of the autonomy of sociology. It is not easy to see what else that could involve than the recognition that social laws may be established independently of an understanding of the individual behaviour that, so to say, underlies them. Suicide rates, for example, may be found to correlate with class structure or pattern of religious affiliation quite independently of any knowledge of the individual psychology of suicide.

With regard to the question whether social laws are or are not reducible to the psychological, it is instructive to consider what such reduction would have to involve. A classic illustration here is that of the reduction of the gas laws of school physics to the kinetic theory of gases. Reduction is a matter of deriving the body of laws or the theory to be reduced (the secondary theory in Nagel's terminology) from the fundamental laws of the primary theory. For such derivations to be effected it will be necessary to make assumptions linking elements in the two theories, assumptions which may well be felt to beg the questions about primacy or ultimacy which, in the case of psychology and sociology, lead on to the question of reduction. I will not, however, strongly press this point, since it needs to be taken in the context of a much fuller treatment of the topic of reduction than is here possible. Instead I want only to emphasise that, for reduction to be contemplated, it is a prerequisite that there be *two* theories, developed initially in independence of each other, therefore *methodologically* autonomous. The first step, therefore, towards reduction of sociology to psychology would be to develop a psychological and sociological pair of theories with sufficient precision and completeness for it to be possible to determine whether, on the basis of what assumptions, the latter could be derived from the former. Reducibility makes sense only in relation to a particular pair of theories. Conceivably some theories we should be minded to call social could, on the basis of natural-seeming linking assumptions, turn out to be reducible to others we should call psychological: and/or vice versa. But the global question whether social theory as a whole (is it a whole?) is reducible to psychological theory (is that a whole?) barely makes sense. The methodological implications of this verdict are, moreover, neutral. Students of man and society should work at the sufficiently heavy task of developing theories in accordance with the evidence, without worrying whether they ought to be classed as individualistic or collectivistic, psychological or social. (Cf. Brodbeck, Nagel, and especially Danto.)

It would be wrong to conclude this criticism of methodological individualism without asking what positive reason there might be for accepting it – a question which is perhaps naturally often overlooked in the confusion and uncertainty which exists over what the theory is. For Popper the case seems to rest on a mixture (mix-up?) of a sort of no-nonsense positivism with ethical and political individualism. Explanations terminating on collectives are held to be *both* mystification, unevidenceable mumbo-jumbo *and* politically dangerous as encouraging totalitarianism. There are indeed horrific examples of views which offend on both counts, but the question is whether any methodologically collectivist view *must*. I do not think that Popper actually shows this, nor that anyone could. True, what is in question is supposed to be *methodological* individualism, but labelling a view methodological merely gives it a status; it does not remove the need to provide reasons for accepting it. Why try to ban the search for collectivist explanations when, for all that has been shown, they may be there to be found?

Controversy concerning methodological individualism has mainly been conducted with regard to social science generally rather than history specifically. In application to history it would presumably carry the implication that rational explanation, which as we have seen is quite prominent, is absolutely fundamental. But this, we have also seen, is not the case. Although historians do regularly accept human actions as causes, the factors they typically offer as long-term, fundamental causes tend neither to be human actions nor to be in any direct or obvious sense reducible to them.

(ii) I turn now to consider historical or dialectical materialism, the collectivist view that fundamental causes must be economic factors, that what some historians are content to regard as autonomous political, cultural, religious developments are to be explained in terms of conflicts between economically constituted classes. No brief characterisation could be adequate to the view, on which there is an enormous and still rapidly increasing literature. The classic summary statement is to be found in the preface to Marx's *Critique of Political Economy* (1859), although a fuller account is given in the first part of the posthumously published *German Ideology* (written 1846). There are long, relevant passages in Engels's *Anti-Dühring* (1878), and many more in other works by Marx and/or Engels, and in their correspondence. Marx's application of the theory, if theory it was for that most celebrated non-Marxist, can be studied in such occasional writings as his *Class Struggles in France* (1850) and *The Eighteenth Brumaire of Louis Bonaparte* (1852), and in more considered form in parts of the first volume of *Capital* (1867). Amongst later Marxist writings those of G. Plekhanov (1895, 1897, and 1898) are important. Recent critics writing in English include H. B. Acton (especially part II ch. I), G. Leff (1961) and J. Plamenatz (vol. II ch. v). There is a very thorough discussion in M. M. Bober (2nd edition, 1948).

I will quote a few of the familiar sentences from the preface to Marx's *Critique of Political Economy* (Feuer, pp. 84–5; my italics):

> In the social production which men carry on they enter into definite relations that are indispensable and independent of their will; these *relations of production* correspond to a definite stage of development of their material *powers of production*. The sum total of these relations of production constitutes the economic structure of society – the real foundation, on which rise legal and political *superstructures* and to which correspond definite forms of social consciousness. . . . At a certain stage of their development the material forces of production in society come into conflict with the existing relations of production,

or – which is but a legal expression for the same thing – with the property relations within which they had been at work before. . . . Then comes the period of social revolution. With the change of the economic foundation the entire immense superstructure is more or less rapidly transformed. . . . In broad outline we can designate the Asiatic, the ancient, the feudal, and the modern bourgeois methods of production as so many epochs in the economic formation of society.

In this statement there should be noted the threefold distinction between the *powers* (sometimes *forces*) of production, the *relations* of production, and the legal, political *superstructure*. The two former taken together constitute the economic foundation of society (the material conditions of life). It is on the strength of this that I think Marx and his followers are not unfairly characterised as holding economic causes to be fundamental. A distinction should be made between the theory of social change and the conclusions drawn from it about the pattern of social change up to the present day. Conceivably the theory has been misapplied, and could survive changes of view about what has happened so far and will happen in the future. A further distinction is required between materialist theory and Marxist practice (value commitments). (Cf. Aron, 1938, p. 306, who distinguishes between the Marxist *theory* of the primacy of economic factors and the Marxist *perspective*, in which the whole of the past is seen as orientated towards the present class struggle.) In principle it is possible to accept the theory and yet take up a non-Marxist socio-political attitude, i.e. not embrace the cause of the proletariat. If the theory is true and correctly applied, this would, indeed, be to support the losing side; but it is not irrational to seek to delay developments to which one is opposed, and a lifetime or so is a very long time in politics. On the other hand, acceptance of the Marxist value standpoint makes the materialist theory (supposing it true) extremely attractive. It offers assurance of ultimate victory and serves as a guide to revolutionary practice. My present aim is to outline a case against the *theory*. I do not attack the value standpoint, except to the extent of denying that it is the only possible or rational one. Notoriously theory and practice are indissolubly united in Marxist thinking, and the materialist conception of history derives much of its plausibility from this unity. Once it is fractured the theory comes to seem indistinct and uncertain.

It has to be recognised that the passage quoted, even though it comes from the pen of Marx, tells an over-simple story; and much of what

Engels, Plekhanov and Marx himself elsewhere write is devoted to the correction of misconceptions. It is, for instance, allowed that there may be reciprocal influence from the superstructure upon the foundations. Plekhanov goes to some length to deny that the development of the ideological superstructure can be predicted in full detail on an economic basis, its form is always partly the result of previous ideology (1895, p. 230). Literary and philosophical movements, although ultimately determined by material factors, still exhibit different features in different nations. He even seeks to distinguish the materialist conception of history from economic materialism or determinism (1897). All sorts of factors, economic and non-economic, interact in complex ways in concrete social reality. A history mentioning only economic (causal) factors would be as vicious an abstraction as any other one-sided history. All the same, the ultimate determining factors are the relations of production. All sophisticated Marxists allow that the development of capitalism takes different forms in different places, and serious claims to be able to predict future developments are prominent only in crude polemic.

Increase in subtlety, here as elsewhere, leads to loss of distinctiveness, and provokes uncertainty about the content of the developed theory and the nature of its claim to be believed. Can the threefold distinction, between forces and relations of production and the superstructure, be drawn in such a way that the relative influence of the different factors can be empirically determined in actual societies? If the theory cannot be established empirically, how could it be established? Derivation from a materialist metaphysic, supposing it possible, would hardly help, since the truth and significance of such a metaphysic are themselves highly questionable.

But there is no need to add to the many refutations of historical materialism considered as a metaphysical or social theory. It is more to the point to consider, first, why it continues to have an influence in history (as I think it does, and not only on historians who are for other reasons Marxists), and, second, why from the point of view of the present book it is still not acceptable.

Much of the appeal of historical materialism derives from its being opposed to superficial explanations in history. Marx, as he claimed in *The Eighteenth Brumaire* in criticism of Victor Hugo's *Napoleon the Little*, is not content to explain events by reference to the desires and intentions of a single man. He rather 'demonstrate[s] how the *class struggle* in France created circumstances and relationships that made it possible for a gross mediocrity to play a hero's part' (Feuer, p. 359) – no doubt he did not actually demonstrate this, but he persuasively suggests how it might be done. Again, in his endless (and doubtless unfair) polemic against Hegel, Marx insists that it is the clash of men and of their interests, not of socially rootless ideas, which makes history. By no means all historians would accept Marx's conception of what the fundamental forces are. Nor would they agree that men in their class groupings are alone important in history. There is the possibility of vicious abstraction here too. But Marx's emphasis on the concrete, the social fact, still seems to be a feature central to the historical consciousness.

It is further true that there goes along with Marx's materialism a very firm recognition of the way people and institutions change through time. He puts the greatest possible emphasis on the superficiality of the analogy between the class struggles of the ancient world and those of nineteenth-century Europe, on the real differences between the Civil War in England and 1789, 1830 and 1848 in France. What comes later is always different in consequence of what has gone before. Maybe these are commonplaces, though living up to them is hard enough: but they were not when Marx wrote, and he propounds them with compelling passion and conviction. Even if such insights strictly speaking do not originate with him (Hegel and the Scottish historians and economists of the eighteenth century have claims too), it is Marx who really fixed them in the intellectual consciousness of the twentieth century.

But, whilst the appeal of the materialist conception of history, taken in the broadest terms, cannot be denied, it is impossible to accept the specific claim that distinctively economic factors alone are fundamental. It may be that the class orientation (in the Marxist sense of 'class') of the groups involved in the civil struggles of nineteenth-century France offer the fundamental explanation of what there came about, and that the course and outcome of the English Civil War can be similarly explained. *Historians* have questioned the latter claim; but there can be no *philosophical* objection to explanations offered in particular situations. But there is a philosophical objection to any claim that economic factors are fundamental in all enquiries. Some Marxists would not make the claim in so many words, but it is implicit in much Marxist practice. To concede it would be to go back on the account given in this book of the relativity of objectivity in history; to deny the relativity of fact and cause to question asked; to deny that, though within some limitations, historians have great freedom in their choice of questions to ask. Of a wide variety of subject matters it is indeed possible to ask Marxist questions (questions, that is, to which the answer will ultimately be in economic terms); but these are by no means the only questions it is possible to ask – I assume no one would take seriously Plekhanov's contention that history only begins at the point where implements of labour (forces of production) exert an effective influence on the shape of social life (1895, p. 169), for this is to make the materialist conception of history tautological.

One should not, indeed, be over-generous in conceding that Marxist questions can be asked. Often they will yield uninteresting answers. Take the apparently most favourable case for Marxists, the course of events and the shifting pattern of allegiances in an apparently revolutionary situation – even if it be granted that explanation in terms of class orientation is both true and fundamental, it is still possible to be interested in matters which are not thus determined, in what, from the point of view of the materialist conception of history, are mere details. We have agreed that historians have a concern for the 'fundamental', with which the materialist conception is to an extent in line; but we have noticed, too, that they may also interest themselves in how it seemed at the time and in the minutiae of motives and actions. And such minutiae, so far from being historically trivial, may be interesting and important in the sense that they represent a gap in historical knowledge. They may also be interesting for extra-historical reasons, from an individualistic, humane value standpoint.

The materialistically unimportant detail of human action and motivation may thus be of central importance to a particular historian at a particular stage of historical study. Moreover, much of what matters in rather narrowly 'specialist' history, say, of parliament and the law courts, may similarly slip through the materialist net. There will be features of procedure which have to be explained as responses to practical difficulties encountered, or as survivals from days when the institutions served different purposes. Many of the explanations sought by the specialist historian will be internal to his narrow subject matter, which will in that sense constitute an autonomous field of study. Rigorous insistence on explanations being in economic terms would not illuminate the subject matter, but rather exclude it from history altogether. If to this it be objected that such subject matter must be unimportant, it can be replied that all that has emerged is that it is so from the value standpoint usually associated with the materialist conception of history. This nobody need deny, but the interesting question is whether there is here a necessary or sufficient criterion of *historical* importance; and the answer is that there is not.

Specialised history like that of law courts and parliament ought not to be a very difficult case for the materialist conception of history in view of the obviously close involvement of such institutions with conflicts over property. More difficult is the case of intellectual history, especially that of science and philosophy (I do not know about the history of history), in which indeed Marxist questions are asked and answered, but often without engagement with the broad outline, let alone the detail, of development in the subjects in question. From the point of view of anyone interested in these subjects *as* science or *as* philosophy, changes are much more cogently (and fundamentally) explained as developments in accordance with the logic or method of the subject from certain starting points, than in terms of the class situation of scientists or philosophers or in terms of social forces generally. (Plekhanov I have already reported as making some concessions here.) I realise that I have here made a claim, not advanced an argument: argument must take the form of a consideration of particular cases, which cannot be done at great length here. Take, however, Berkeley's idealism. If it is *philosophy* we are interested in, this has to be explained as a working out of one line of response to the representative theory of perception he found in Locke. That he took the line he did is partly to be explained by extra-philosophical considerations: his religious faith and affiliation, conceivably his class situation, even his fixation in the anal phase if the psychoanalysts are to be believed. But all this, however worthwhile it may be in its own terms, helps so little towards an understanding of his working out of the line he took, that it finds little place in the history of his philosophy. The case is similar with Kant's doctrine of the good will. I cannot say that it is simply untrue that Kant's conception of a will good in itself, irrespective of whether it achieves anything in practice, has a connection with the political impotence of the German bourgeoisie, whose 'white-washing spokesman' he is said to be in the *German Ideology*. The objection to this judgement is simply that it reveals nothing at all about Kant's *philosophical* importance. Many people, including I should have thought some of the not so impotent English bourgeoisie, have found Kant's conception of the good will attractive. But what matters philosophically is his working out of the idea, his fitting it into a conception of moral laws as rational and of moral freedom as compatible with scientific law. If this is the case with philosophy, that of science is, I am sure but cannot here begin to try to show, essentially the same. Of course, natural science has become an activity which makes significant calls upon economic resources, and its development is in this respect plainly under the direct influence of economic factors. But there remain criteria of truth internal to the natural sciences (this is presupposed by anyone who tries to show that the actual course of development has been *distorted* by extraneous factors), and with them the possibility of a type of explanation of development which is internal to the sciences. Only if the materialist conception of history maintains that this is impossible or superficial does it make a distinctive claim; but such a claim is surely false.

I do not wish to deny to Marxists the right to bring their values to history. I simply claim the equal right of everybody to do the same. There is nothing about history which makes Marxist concerns of unique historical importance. Patently, for Marxists they are; but only, it seems to me, in the sort of way such stupendous events as world wars and social revolutions have an irresistible claim on the conscience and imagination (cf. chapter III above). It remains the case that matters of the greatest human importance are not thereby important in every conceivable connection. Obviously, in a besieged city able-bodied men are not admired for fiddling about with philosophy, history, science – not unless by so doing they maintain morale or otherwise serve the purposes of the defenders. Marxists, it often seems, have developed a siege mentality. In embracing the cause of the proletariat they establish a value perspective, a conception of relevance and importance; so long as war continues they will tolerate no diversion of intellectual resources. But no one has reason to agree with them who cannot share their conviction that the emancipation of the proletariat will be the emancipation of all mankind, who cannot see that developments they favour lead in fact to that desirable if unlikely goal, who are unpersuaded that revolutionary change is invariably for the good.

6. *Necessity and Chance, Constraint and Free Will*

I will conclude the present chapter with a consideration of the questions whether history in some way presupposes necessity (or determinism), whether it requires or admits free will: whether indeed necessity and free will are compatible, so that we could have both together; or incompatible, so that a choice has to be made between them. These are large, vague, no doubt profound questions, for which simple, satisfying answers are far to seek. An account of causation in history would, however, be incomplete without some notice being taken of them.

The general problem of free will (of freedom and necessity or determinism) is in reality a tangled complex of problems. Much of its notorious intractability is the result of allowing distinguishable issues to run together. The possibility of progress correspondingly depends on sorting them out. There is, for instance, no one single conflict between determinism and freedom. There are several varieties of each, and it is more than likely that, whereas some varieties of determinism are incompatible with some conceptions of free will, other conceptions of each are wholly compatible with each other. It is by no means certain that free will, in any sense clearly required for moral accountability, is incompatible with any likely form of determinism. Indeed the dominant tradition in British empiricist philosophy is that it is not. Universal causality, as conceived by the regularity theory, unquestionably is compatible with freedom conceived as the absence of constraint, i.e. the lack of obstacles to an agent's satisfying his desires. There are, however, other traditions. Some rationalists take a more strongly necessitarian view of causality and, from a desire nevertheless to retain a sort of freedom, have been driven to identify it as the recognition of necessity – a sophism transmitted by Hegel to the Marxists. Others have taken a radically indeterminist view of freedom, holding it to involve not merely the absence of constraint (the absence, that is, of *one* sort of cause) but the absence of any sort of cause whatsoever. The empiricist thesis of the compatibility of (one sort of) causation with (one sort of) freedom, after enjoying much support in recent British philosophy, has lately tended to lose ground. It has been doubted whether freedom as absence of constraint, the hypothetical freedom to act *if* one chooses, is sufficient for moral accountability. It has been suggested that a categorical freedom, not 'can *if*' but 'can' simply, is what is required. It has been doubted, too, whether desires can properly be regarded as causes of action. For my own part, I do not see why the failure of one sort of compatibility thesis, if fail it does, need lead to the conclusion that no such thesis can succeed. I cannot help thinking that it would be very strange indeed if there were radical incompatibilities. Free will is rooted in a *practical* attitude to conduct, in which are involved notions of deliberation, decision, accountability or responsibility, and the like. Determinism, the belief that everything which happens has a cause, derives from the *theoretical* ambition to explain all happenings, including human actions. The two attitudes, the two models of thinking, are so far apart that they seem scarcely to engage with each other, far less clash. *Formulations*, of course, may very well conflict, but for that there is a remedy in reformulation. Such attempts to resolve, rather than solve, the problem of free will are sometimes condemned as superficial. This is a real, but not inescapable, hazard. Resolution is, in any event, a sort of solution. It may be wrong, but it is not an evasion. It seems that some philosophers, blinded no doubt by fear of obsolescence, forget that one cannot both solve philosophical problems and keep them.

Free will problems are, fortunately, of present concern only to the extent that they are involved with history. That they may be is evident from the fact that causal explanations are there offered, and the language of necessity, or at any rate inevitability, used along with them – especially, perhaps, in relation to long-term, fundamental causes. But are historians committed to the supposition that everything that happens has a cause? Doubtless some would think so, but the content of such a belief could not be very distinct. 'Cause', as we have seen above, is applied in history to a variety of factors. Further, it is obvious that a good deal in history never will be explained *in fact*, because of presently irremediable ignorance: lack of evidence, lost records, etc. No doubt it will be felt that there is nothing here to tell against the idea that everything is explicable *in principle*. But such claims tend to be protected, and at the same time vitiated, by a tendency to represent anything that is inexplicable as falling outside the scope of history. Conceivably the shape of Cleopatra's nose did have some influence on Mark Antony and consequently on the government of Rome. Historians cannot explain its shape, but they do not recognise it as a chance (spontaneous) beginning of a causal chain – it is just not the sort of thing they seek to explain. Instead they bend their efforts to explaining how Antony came to be in a situation which made his sexual preferences important in the history of Rome. Chance is not admitted in history – this is true, but it amounts to little more than the tautological claim that whatever is susceptible of historical explanation can be historically explained.

History then, albeit vacuously, eschews chance and proffers causation. It may to that extent be thought to pose a threat to free will. But, paradoxically, it is also often held that history is committed to free will; that it is the story of freedom (Croce), its subject matter human action, with passion and reactions, what happens to people as opposed to what they do, relegated to natural science (Collingwood, Hayek). There are as many to hold that history presupposes freedom as that it presupposes determinism. It would be agreeable if it could be found that a relevant sort of freedom were compatible with a relevant sort of determinism.

For there to be any hope of showing this it is essential to keep in mind the considerable variety we have noted in the factors recognised as causes in history. They range from an agent's reasons to, or near to, arational hopefully sufficient conditions. They do not all even appear to conflict with free will in the same degree. Reasons, indeed, are rather congenial to it. It is when it is suspected that an agent's avowed reasons are not determining his conduct (say, in cases of neurotically compulsive behaviour or of acting out post-hypnotic suggestions) that one begins to doubt whether an agent enjoys free will. 'Pressures', factors perceived as calling for, even constraining a certain response, are a different case. Unquestionably constraint may take away freedom altogether, but the undeniable possibility of constraint is not a *general* difficulty for freedom. Not all action is constrained, nor do all pressures amount to constraint. Causes in the shape of necessary conditions are no problem either. Whatever is to be understood by free will must be compatible with so obvious a truth as that human actions are subject to necessary conditions. Plainly it is causes as arational sufficient conditions – economic factors, conditions of social structure – which threaten most danger to freedom. Even here, however, the danger is easy to exaggerate for, as we have seen, the causes actually supplied in history are partial, or (to put it differently) at best sufficient relative to certain standing conditions. Causal necessity in history is always conditional. *If* certain conditions hold then, given the cause, the effect will (inevitably, necessarily) come to pass. Causal necessity is, indeed, conditional outside history too. It is always conditional. What is distinctive of history is rather the difficulty of specifying background conditions and being sure that they obtain. Even supposing that causes as arational sufficient conditions do indeed preclude free will – and this should not be taken for granted – what is actually provided in history in the way of such causes is less than formidable. Nor, as we have seen, do historians typically seem seriously concerned to push their causal explanations to the fully sufficient condition extreme.

As a way into the question of whether arational sufficient conditions would, if available, preclude free will, consider what is involved in acting from reasons. This is typically a matter of someone taking what he believes to be morally, socially or otherwise acceptable means to something he wants (his end), the wanting itself being informed by beliefs about its nature and relations to other things. A wide range of actions fit into such a schema – borrowing a lawn mower, signing a contract to purchase goods by instalment payments or taking out a mortgage, dismissing an unsatisfactory employee or applying for a job, campaigning to get somebody elected, making policy decisions – the range includes actions of sorts regularly explained in history. Acting from reasons is a matter of being led to act by one's desires as informed by one's beliefs and one's values (conceptions of what is acceptable in the way of ends and means). Desires, beliefs, values being different, actions would be different too. It is in cases where desires, beliefs, values do not serve as significant determinants of action that there is doubt about the reality of free will. Sheer physical compulsion is the clearest case in point; as when, for instance, a person is literally forced out of a room by several larger, stronger people. Here there is no action on the part of the evicted person at all. His beliefs, desires, values are irrelevant to the explanation of what occurred.

But, as we have observed, by no means every happening in which people are involved is a case of compulsion. And this remains true even if psychological compulsions are allowed as well as physical ones. Compulsion apart, however, there are other cases in which freedom is eliminated or gravely reduced – cases of duress, typified by the bank robber with his pistol, and cases of extreme pressure, for instance, to use Aristotle's example, when valuable cargo has to be jettisoned in a storm to save the ship. These cases differ from those of compulsion in that desires and beliefs – the desire for life, the belief that the gun is loaded or that the ship will sink – help to determine what occurs, although the cases are ones in which what people do goes against some of their settled desires and firm value convictions. There can be disagreement whether free will is or is not exercised in action under pressure or duress, but it does not matter for the present purpose, since it is manifest that a great deal of action is not like this at all. Even if we think there is a *continuous* graduation from the extremes of pressure and duress to simple cases of people doing what they believe they need and may do in order to get what they want, it remains the case that much human action is far removed from the extreme of unfreedom. If free will is a matter of being led to act by one's desires, beliefs, values, its possibility, indeed its actuality, is not open to doubt. A belief in free will is not the absurdly false conviction that nobody's freedom is ever reduced or eliminated, but only that some people, sometimes, act freely. The burden of proof assumed by anyone who wishes to deny this is a heavy one.

All the same freedom has been denied or doubted. One reason for this is over-assimilation of reasons and arational causes. Another, perhaps, more important, lies in the recognition that arational sufficient conditions may hold in the area marked out for free will by the present (partial) characterisation of it. I will consider these in turn.

It may appear that I have myself assimilated reasons and arational causes by permitting reasons to be referred to as causes. In fact I have no doubt that it would be better not to term reasons causes, on the same sort of grounds as were urged in support of the distinction between rational and law explanations (of which causal explanations 'proper' are a species) in chapter IV. But there is no getting away from the fact that historians often have what are better called reasons in mind when they use the word 'cause'. In their usage the distinction between reasons and causes comes out as one between two sorts of cause, the rational and the arational, the former involving mental factors – desires, values, beliefs – the latter not. In consequence it has to be held that causes are not as such incompatible with free will: some, the rational ones, are not. But this doctrine will appear paradoxical or implausible to anyone whose conception of cause is taken from the arational side of the divide. It is a real source of confusion that, on the one hand, *conceptions* of cause, as expressed in more or less formal attempts to give general definitions of 'cause', are so often founded upon such mechanical transactions as one billiard ball striking another, whilst, on the other hand, the word 'cause' is often in practice (certainly in history) applied to reasons.

Thus the former ground for doubting the possibility of free will may be rejected as a confusion. The latter, that arational causes would seem to operate in areas supposed to include free will, is less easy to dispose of. One cannot, it seems, rule out the possibility of neurological causes (sufficient conditions) in relation to actions which would ordinarily be held to be manifestations of free will. Nor does it seem that the possibility of large-scale, overlying sociological explanations can be excluded in principle either. It may, indeed, be thought that rather little, in the way of the latter at least, is presently to hand; but to emphasise this simply invites the conclusion that one's continued recognition of free will is conditional on neurological and sociological sufficient condition explanations *not* being found. Should they be found, actions hitherto held to manifest free will would not indeed thereby be shown to be unfree in the sense of compelled or constrained. (Some defences of free will largely consist in pointing this out.) But I am sure that for many people the feeling remains that freedom would still be compromised in some other way. The question is whether this feeling is well founded and deserves respect.

A line of argument that it does not starts from the contention that the (possible) neurological or sociological explanations which threaten to crowd out reason-based free will would not properly speaking be of *actions* at all. A neurological explanation would rather be of bodily movements and, whilst actions cannot generally be performed without physical movements taking place, they are not constituted by such movements alone. Similarly a sociological explanation would be of a state of society or a social change which is not to be identified with individual human actions. The essence of the argument is that arational sufficient condition explanations (neurological or sociological as the case may be) could be competitive with reason explanations, and so capable of excluding free will, only if they were of the same items as the latter explanations (namely, actions). But as they are not, they cannot be competitive. The (possible) existence of neurological and sociological explanations would not alter the fact that, if it is *actions* we want to have explained, explanations will have to be in the shape of reasons.

But this still leaves open the question why, supposing we have neurological or sociological explanations, we should continue to bother with rational ones. The thought behind the question is that, even if arational causal explanations are non-competitive (do not conflict) with rational ones, they do cover the same area, and might still supersede the latter in that we might come to transfer our interest from the latter to the former – very likely this would present itself as a matter of scientific modes of explanation superseding pre-scientific. I do not wish to deny that this sort of supersession may occur in particular cases, but would argue that rational explanations could not generally be superseded by neurological or sociological ones, on the grounds that rational explanations serve to satisfy a sort of curiosity that it is virtually incredible we shall ever give up, whatever advances there may be in neurology and sociology. I do not see how we could ever abandon our practical attitude to conduct, the procedure of deliberation, deciding what to do, judging our actions as right or wrong. I doubt whether it even makes sense to contemplate abandoning this sort of attitude towards one's own conduct, from which it follows that it will remain possible to maintain the same sort of attitude to the conduct of other people. What more could be required to provide a permanent, solid footing for rational explanations. I am not denying that arational types of explanation may be more relevant from the point of view of predicting or controlling what happens; the contention is rather that an interest in prediction and control (as opposed to deliberation and decision) is not the only interest we have, because it is not an interest we can have where our own conduct is concerned. We have and must retain a direction of interest which rational explanations alone can satisfy, and to that extent free will is secure.

The limited nature of this conclusion must be emphasised. In face of fears that historical explanations might compromise free will it has been argued that one (not the only) type of historical explanation is actually congenial to it, and that there is a permanent place for this sort of rational explanation, a place which cannot be wholly occupied by such arational explanations as might be provided within history or outside it. It is not denied that the grand, possible though as yet non-actual, sociological explanations we have been contemplating could oblige us to recognise that the scope for *effective* rational/free action was at times more limited than could have been apparent to past agents. It might well have to be recognised that actions, rationally explicable as intended, say, to maintain peace, were doomed to be ineffectual because war was already inevitable. Perfectly ordinary historical explanations, causes which are non-necessary, non-sufficient conditions, may have this sort of implication too. One of the less edifying delights of history is the consciousness of knowing, as past agents could not, that their hopes were vain, their best endeavours futile. This is fed by the familiar illusion of hindsight, which leads to exaggeration of the inevitability of past events, but by no means all is illusion and exaggeration. It does not, however, follow that what people did, what they attempted to do, was not done for the reasons they had in mind; or that it would not have been different had their reasons – desires, beliefs, values – been different. It does not follow that their actions did not manifest free will. In focusing on free will, as we have done in the present section, there is a great risk of exaggerating the extent to which historians are concerned with (free) action and rational explanation. I have tried elsewhere in this book to take due account of their concern with other matters, their interest in factors which could not have figured at all in the deliberations of past agents. All I have tried to do in the present discussion is to argue that such concerns and interests are no foundation for a general doubt about the reality of free will.

VI

Values

1. Introduction

One of the aims of this chapter is to round off the discussion of objectivity, begun with the treatment of selection in chapter III, and continued with the examination of true or real causes (more or less fundamental explanations) in chapter V. It remains to consider objectivity worries having their source in values; or rather in a prevalent *conception* of valuation, inasmuch as those who are prone to these worries seem to take it for granted that value judgements are as such subjective and arbitrary. Not least among the dire effects of this assumption is its tendency to impede the recognition of differences both among value judgements and among the ways they come into or bear upon history. It is obviously impossible to attempt here even the outlines of a comprehensive account of value judgements, but it will all the same be necessary in what follows to have regard to some of the important distinctions relating to them. In particular account will have to be taken of the distinctions: between reporting and making value judgements; between what may be termed 'life' and 'intellectual' values; and, within life values, to the distinction between the moral and the non-moral and, up to a point, distinctions within morality itself. Consideration of such broad distinctions, even at a necessarily very abstract level, will help to place valuation-based objectivity worries in their true perspective.

2. History as Factual

A common sort of doubt about the objectivity of history arises from the suspicion of a contradiction between the subject's aspiration to be factual and the indisputable occurrence of value judgements in history books. The appearance of contradiction can, however, be much reduced by making clear how narrowly limited is the sense in which history can at all plausibly be held to be purely *factual, value neutral* or *value free*. Since history cannot, on any view, have nothing at all to do with values, it is not surprising that such expressions regularly provoke misunderstanding. They appear to promise, or threaten, more than anyone has ever seriously maintained. The thesis that history can and should be purely factual may not be certainly or totally true; but it is very often attacked, perhaps excusably, for the wrong reasons. It is not my intention to attempt a complete defence even of a suitably limited formulation of the thesis. It is at best an important near truth. But, whilst over-insistence on it involves distortions somewhat similar to those attending the law theory of historical explanation, disregard of it leads to an underestimation of the possibility of objective historical knowledge.

The first distinction needful is between the occurrence of value judgements in the *subject matter* (history$_1$ in the scholastic terminology adverted to in chapter I) and their occurrence in the historian's *treatment* of it (history$_2$). Respect for this distinction should prevent a head-on collision between, on the one hand, those who want to maintain that value judgements need figure in history no differently from the way they do in physics or any other paradigmatically objective study; and, on the other, those who are persuaded that it is a distinguishing feature of history and perhaps social studies generally that they deal with values. Plainly value judgements must be admitted to the subject matter of history. Offering a rational explanation may very well involve reporting the values of historical agents. Even a law explanation may rest on assumptions about people's values – for instance, the explanation of Louis XIV's unpopularity, quoted in chapter IV above from Gardiner, presupposes that the subjects of that monarch placed a positive value on France's remaining dominant in foreign affairs. But because values are prominent in a subject matter it does not follow that they invade the treatment of it, which is what would have to happen in order to support a doubt about the objectivity of history. It is necessary in the present chapter to operate with a rough, imperfectly explained distinction between fact and value; but on any reasonable interpretation of the distinction there will have to be the possibility of facts about values. To state such facts is not, in itself, to evaluate. The value judgements come in as data, without questions about their acceptability or otherwise being raised. It can be true or false that some person *held* x or *y* to be good; but this is not at all the same as its being true or false, correct or incorrect, or whatever may be the appropriate terms for accepting and rejecting value judgements, that x or *y is* good.

Another way of putting the same point would be to contend that value judgements in history books are, as it were, in indirect speech, not asserted but reported without endorsement. It would no doubt make for greater clarity if quotation marks were more often employed, or if it was more often pedantically spelled out that what is being asserted is that somebody or other *held* something to be good or bad. That there is a real possibility of misunderstanding is evident from the following passage from Taylor's *The Origins of the Second World War* (1964, p. 7):

> I ought perhaps to have warned the reader that I do not come to history as a judge; and that when I speak of morality I refer to the moral feelings at the time I am writing about. I make no moral judgment of my own. Thus when I write . . . that 'the peace of Versailles lacked moral validity from the start', I mean only that the Germans did not regard it as a 'fair' settlement and that many people in Allied countries, soon I think most people, agreed with them.

Taylor seeks thus to defend himself from complaints that he subscribes to the sometimes startling value judgements which appear in his book, for example that the Munich settlement 'was a triumph for all that was best and most enlightened in British life' (p. 235–I think this is meant to be challenging rather than ironical). I cite him, not because I am wholly convinced that he never makes value judgements in his own person (this is not at all the flavour of his work); but only for his very firm endorsement of the distinction under consideration.

It may, of course, be asked whether it really is possible to report other people's evaluations in a perfectly neutral way. Disclaimers of personal commitment often fail to carry conviction. To quote the judgements of the wicked or insensitive without repudiation, or the making of counter-judgements, is to risk being held to share them, as reactions to Taylor's book show; omit the value judgements currently in vogue, and one will be taken to be upholding their contraries. The subject matter of history is, moreover, very often such as to evoke partisanship, and historians are not commonly deficient in keen human sympathies–if anything, the reverse. But these are practical difficulties, which consequently admit of practical solutions, or at least less or more successful attempts at such.

Unfortunately, however, they are exacerbated by theoretical (logical) uncertainty about the possibility of there being a wholly value-neutral terminology. It is far from the case that fact and value are clearly and systematically distinguishable in ordinary speech and writing. We do not, though moral philosophy would be easier if we did, typically first report what happened or was done (fact), and then separately pronounce it good or bad, right or wrong (value). Value judgements are implicit in any natural language account of the characteristic subject matter of history. Are we to say that the hostages were executed or that they were murdered? It makes an obvious difference which; and there is no easy way out in saying that they were simply killed; for this too, as well as more overtly value laden terms, will convey an attitude on the part of the speaker, as well as failing to convey how the act appeared, indeed was, at the time. With regard to a particular episode it may be possible to find, at some expense of artificiality and complication, descriptions which are neutral *relative* to the more obvious divisions among the evaluative attitudes likely to bear on their objects; but it is hardly possible to keep this up through a prolonged discussion. To repeat, this is not just a practical difficulty. A consistently value-neutral terminology is simply not available for the discussion of human affairs. Absolute value neutrality would make it impossible to engage with the subject matter of history. At the impossible extreme of purely physical description of movements in space and time, human action drops right out of the picture. If historians are to continue to treat their characteristic subject matter, they are doomed to do so in the sort of language which makes it difficult for, say, Anglicans and English Roman Catholics to agree in their accounts of the fates of the English 'martyrs'/'subversives'; or for right and left wingers to agree about what went on in Vietnam. Of course, some of the trouble in such cases can be put down to differences in point of view or question asked, as discussed in chapter III. What is here being emphasised is, however, the fact that the nature of the language available for describing human affairs is such that general differences of point of view, when they include differences of evaluative attitude, are bound to be reflected in descriptions belonging to a very detailed level.

Neutral language, then, is unavailable. This compromises another type of proposal, which is sometimes made for reducing the danger of evaluative bias – the proposal, namely, that evaluative commitments should be overt. This can indeed be attempted, and sometimes is in the prefaces to history books; but, for the reasons given, it is impossible to maintain a cards-on-the-table, take-it-or-leave-it attitude at the detailed level. The hopelessness of the attempt to do so manifests itself, I believe, in the tendency of some historians to switch evaluate subjects (change evaluative viewpoints) in the course of their narratives. A sort of value objectivity may sometimes thus be achieved; but often at the price of baffling the reader by the apparent expression of incompatible evaluative attitudes. I am, however, conscious that in writing in this way I may be too exclusively adopting the standpoint of the general reader, unacquainted with a great variety of works on any topic, and with only the haziest notions of the range of received opinions, their evidential bases, and the matters of controversy. From the point of view of the professional historian, the unavoidable evaluative directedness of historical writing may be pretty superficial, and he may have little difficulty in seeing through it the really important matters – new evidence, the discrediting of an accepted explanation, the enforcing of a new interpretation.

I have been trying to determine how far values in history may be confined to its subject matter and prevented from 'infecting', if that is the word, its treatment. The suggestion is that, whilst total value neutrality is in principle unattainable, there remains the possibility of a good measure of value-independent objectivity for professional historians. Next to be considered is another way in which values – extra-historical, moral, political, religious, in short *life* values – must exert influence in history, that is to say, in relation to choice of subject matter and the point of view from which it is studied. Brevity is possible here, since very similar ground was covered in the earlier discussion of objectivity relative to a point of view (chapter III).

Manifestly choice of topic is very often determined by extra-historical considerations. We may interest ourselves in British history out of patriotism, in the Counter Reformation because of Catholicism, in naval history from family tradition or because we think the navy is neglected nowadays and hope that reminding the public of past glories will help mend matters. Certain periods or types of history will just appeal to some people, others to others. Similarly, approach to a topic, the perspective in which it is studied, may be determined extra-historically. An atheist is unlikely to structure his account of mid-twentieth-century international relations from the point of view of their effect on the fortunes of the Catholic church, although it is a possible viewpoint from which objective history may be written.

In any case, history is not the only subject in which choice of topic may be externally determined. Even in physics, where the subject matter can hardly engage human sympathy, there are the similar possibilities of just preferring one topic to another, of following father's footsteps, of working in branches thought to be humanly useful. But a difference already noted between history and the more developed natural sciences has some importance here. These latter, as they progress in the development of laws and theories, acquire a structure, by reference to which a sharper distinction can be made between external and internal influences than is possible in history, which is innocent of systematic aspirations. There are elementary and advanced areas in physics, whereas any part of history can be treated in an elementary or advanced way. Physics has to be learnt in a certain order, whereas history can be entered at any point, and the starting point cannot but have an influence on the perspective within which a student works. Individual preferences, external values, may thus structure study. In physics, on the other hand, the external influences which bring people to the subject remain external; and thus seem not to compromise, by their subjectivity and arbitrariness, criteria of relevance within the subject or its internally determined lines of development. In history on the other hand there is no such firm internal structure; all that stand in its place are, it seems, contingent consensuses within groups of historians on what is counted as being established, what needs re-examination, what should be attempted next. In chapter III some importance was attached to such consensuses; and I do not wish to retract what was there said by conceding that they manifest as much subjectivity and arbitrariness as do the external factors which bring individuals to the study of any subject. Nor do I doubt that some diminution of the claimed difference between science and history would come from taking a wider range of sciences into account, or indeed from allowing for such things as the influence of defence expenditure on twentieth-century physics. But, all qualifications made, I cannot help believing that there is here a real difference between some of the sciences and history. Even if I have somewhat exaggerated it, the object of the present section may still be attained; for this is less to argue that history positively is purely factual than to set down what can and cannot reasonably be involved in a claim of this sort. My main concern is to suggest that any such claim must be interpreted as compatible with, first, history being about life values (having them in its subject matter) and, secondly, with individual historians' entrance to the subject and their operation within it being to an extent determined by their life values.

It has, moreover, further to be allowed that there is one way in which commitment to values is absolutely central to history. Historians must recognise such *intellectual* values as concern for truth, validity in argument and respect for evidence. These commitments are too apparent to receive much comment, and may in consequence not always be perceived as commitments to *values*. That this is what they are is, however, evident from the way they differ from mere capacity to *recognise* truth and validity and the tendency of evidence. Commitment is a matter of *caring* about these things, which a person may not do without thereby making any errors of logic or fact. Again, commitment to intellectual values is of the same character, though differently directed, as commitment to life values; intellectual and life values may be competitive with one another, just as life values may be competitive among themselves. A person may rate truth, validity, respect for evidence as more – or less – important than goodness, beauty or holiness, without necessarily making any errors of logic or fact.

Commitment to intellectual values is not indeed specific to history in the way that concern with past human actions is. But it is internal to the practice of the subject in a sense in which the values present in its subject matter and the values which bring people to it arguably are not. An historian who fails to live up to the intellectual values is the worse as an historian for it. One indifferent to beauty would only be a philistine, one who does not care about goodness or justice would only be a worse man. There is no reason in logic why a bad man should not be a good historian. (I suppose it could be the case that the capacity for human sympathy requisite in an historian tends to be associated with having, and living up to, a humane moral standpoint; but I have no idea whether this is really so.) A man who, in his writing about the past, showed little or no regard for the intellectual values would not be an historian at all.

A certain sort of evaluative concern is then essential to history. But there is nothing here to compromise its objectivity or the factual character, in any reasonable sense of the phrase, of its enquiries. Historians, as historians, cannot disagree about these values. They are no source of arbitrary or subjective variation among them. And, most importantly, there is substantially the same commitment to intellectual values over a wide range of studies – 'substantially' rather than 'absolutely' only to allow for differences among the natures of various studies. Truth, in some form, is the object of them all; but the pure mathematician is not concerned with empirical truth, and consequently does not enjoy the same opportunities as do the natural scientist and the historian for exercising the virtue of respect for evidence. I do not claim to have mentioned all the intellectual virtues, still less to have given much of an account of any of them. My sole concerns have been to acknowledge that they are involved in history, and that their being so does not in any way mark off history from other studies of which the objectivity, the purely factual character, normally goes unchallenged.

So far in the present section I have been trying to explain what might reasonably be intended, the *most* that might be meant, by the thesis that history is purely factual. (I have been at pains to claim that the thesis is not wholly true.) Next I shall consider come sources of undue scepticism concerning it. They are fed by the way in which the terms 'fact' and 'value' are used to mark other distinctions as well as the fact/value distinction we are currently concerned with. 'Fact' is as often opposed to 'opinion' as to 'value' in the sense in which I have been using the term; whilst 'value' and 'value judgement' are themselves on occasion used in very much the sense of 'opinion'. Again, matters of fact are sometimes also contrasted with matters of judgement, in a sense of the latter different from that in which I have hitherto been using 'value judgement', although that phrase is itself sometimes used in the sense in question.

Take the *fact/opinion distinction* first. Here the contrast is between what is established beyond doubt or question and what remains dubious or questionable. When the term 'fact' is used in this connection, whatever is accepted as fact is thereby accepted as true. 'It is a fact', since it expresses the conviction (makes the claim) that what is asserted is true, cannot intelligibly be followed by 'but it may not be so'. This is not, however, a feature of the usage in which 'fact' is opposed to 'value' – in this latter contrast facts or, perhaps more happily, matters of fact need not be true. The expression 'true facts', which is pleonastic relative to the fact/opinion contrast, is regularly heard in the law courts – significantly so, in that the contrast there is not with opinions (or, of course, with values) but with matters of law. Anyone for whom the dominant contrast for 'fact' is with 'opinion', and outside philosophy this may be commoner than the contrast with 'value', will be inclined to resist claims that history is a domain of fact – because, of course, much in it is entirely a matter of opinion! He will not, however, be in disagreement, only at cross purpose with anyone making the claim. There is, moreover, no difference in principle between history and the sciences, or between the social and the natural sciences, in relation to the fact/opinion distinction. In all studies there are both matters of fact and matters of opinion, i.e. matters not yet decisively settled one way or the other.

The second distinction needing to be kept apart from the fact/value distinction is that between *fact* and *judgement*. Here the contrast is between what can be established automatically or mechanically by employing established procedures or routines and that in which, as it is said, an element of judgement is involved. An example is the difference between measuring distances and estimating them. Another is that between diagnosis by physiological tests on the one hand and by clinical judgement on the other. In some cases there is the possibility of checking what may in consequence be denigrated as subjective judgement by objective procedures, for example, where finding out distances is concerned. Often, for example in medicine, there are strong practical grounds for seeking to devise mechanical procedures which can safely be entrusted to inexperienced people. But there are also cases in which there is no dispensing with judgement – applications of the mathematical theory of probability apart, the assessment of probabilities, i.e. concluding that one statement is more probable on the evidence than another, is one of them. Very obviously, a great deal of what is asserted in history is a matter of judgement; absolutely unchallengeable facts tend rather to figure as data, evidence for more dubitable claims, or matters for interpretation and explanation. Being a matter of judgement is not, however, the same as being a matter of opinion, since there can be certainty in judgements (consensus among the competent) on points which cannot be established by mechanical procedures from incontrovertible data; but this distinction will elude anyone who runs together the fact/opinion and fact/judgement distinctions. A person for whom the dominant contrast of 'fact' is with 'judgement' will, if he allows a significant role to judgement in history, tend to resist the location of history within the realm of fact. He will not, all the same, be denying anything asserted by those who insist that history is factual in the sense opposed to evaluative. It will be just another case of cross purposes.

Even if so much be granted, there might still be felt to remain an important difference of degree between history and other studies in regard to judgement. Surely, the thought might be, judgement is so prominent in history, as contrasted with the sciences, that history's aiming to be factual as opposed to evaluate does little to establish it as objective. It cannot be denied that judgement is important in history; but this objection nevertheless owes most of its plausibility to a serious underestimation of the role of judgement in the sciences. There is, in truth, no very marked contrast in this respect between history and the *applied* natural and social sciences, where the exercise of judgement is extremely conspicuous. With the pure sciences, on the other hand, there may seem to be a greater difference. But appearances are misleading. It is not that judgement is not exercised in the pure sciences; but rather that, although it is required for attaining results, the evidences of it are eliminated from the presentation of results, which are accordingly represented as having been obtained from hard data by set procedures. Even in mathematics theorems are not discovered by mechanical derivation from axioms. They have to be thought up, and those with flair and/or experience are better at thinking them up than others. Again, in finding proofs for theorems, judgement is exercised at every turn; there are conjectures, false starts, insights and inspirations – but, in the proof as finally presented, each step succeeds the previous one in accordance with definite rules. Collingwood, in one of his earlier essays, complained that people exaggerated the differences between history and science because they tended to contrast living, developing science with the finished, dead history of the textbook (1965, p. 32). I feel no confidence that I enjoy an inside view of any science, and my point is accordingly almost exactly the opposite: that we tend to underestimate the role of judgement in science, because we cannot penetrate its finished, formal surface; whereas, on the other hand, we do have some awareness of the uncertainties which attend the practice of history.

I have been considering three distinctions – fact/value, fact/opinion, fact/judgement – conflation of which tends to obstruct recognition of the intended content of the claim that history is factual, and consequently to lead to its being resisted on irrelevant grounds. These three are not, however, the sum of the contrasts in which the term 'fact' figures. Two others merit brief attention, since their unrecognised influence may lead to the factual (non-evaluative) character of history obtaining irrelevant *support*. (*a*) 'Fact' is often opposed to 'theory', and there is wide agreement, except for a minority who think history aspires to establish laws, that there is a profound difference between history and the sciences in this regard. Historians may, indeed, be said to have theories, but these are typically *either* hypotheses about matters of fact or about how they may be explained *or*, perhaps, very general theories of interpretation, which are liable to be condemned as extra-historical, and which are in any event scarcely scientific. (*b*) Otherwise 'fact' may be given the sense of 'empirical', as opposed to 'a priori' or 'necessary'. In this sense history, along with the natural and social sciences, and in distinction from the formal sciences of mathematics and logic, is factual. It is a question, one of the major questions of moral philosophy and philosophy of value generally, whether values fall within the domain of fact as thus understood. If they do, and are not even distinguishable as constituting a separate province within it, we have lost the fact/value distinction, which it has been the aim of the present section to isolate. My personal view is that values are to be distinguished from empirical facts; but, though perennially controversial, it cannot be argued for here. It cannot be denied that a different view in this area would have implications for the factual character of history. On the other side, however, it can be claimed that much of the discussion which has gone on about the factual character of history has been founded on the assumption of a distinction between fact and value. Those who insist that value judgements are essentially present in history need the distinction just as much as those who deny it. Some questions concerning values in relation to history can be discussed in advance of a successful revolution, or counter-revolution, in value theory.

3. *Moral Judgement in History*

(i) In the previous section a distinction was drawn between intellectual and life values, the latter being taken to include moral values. These and their place in history will be the topic of the present section. The position concerning them appears to be that, whilst nobody holds with Lord Acton (or for that matter Tacitus) that pronouncing moral verdicts is central to the task of history, it is rare to come across really rigorous attempts to exclude them altogether – I am referring, of course, to direct speech judgements, which an historian subscribes to himself. Moral judgements are no doubt felt to be incidental, perhaps unimportant, but keeping them out seems hardly to be a major objective. Setting out the rationale of the situation, supposing my estimate of it is correct, will therefore involve seeking reasons for denying a central place to moral judgements, but reasons which do not require their total exclusion. A general positivistic principle would not fill the bill; for total exclusion is just what it would demand. We need, moreover, reasons specific to history, ideally more deeply rooted than is the prudential counsel that historians are wise to limit their commitments in peripheral matters; and independent of the sort of moral cynicism, the feeling that morality is a patchwork of exploded pretensions, which is manifestly a temptation to some historians, as well as to other students of society.

It will appear that there are ways in which conceptions of morality and history interlock, elements in the one reinforcing elements in the other, to yield the result that moral judgements are neither central to nor wholly unacceptable in history.

(ii) Acton's position is a convenient starting point (see his letter to Mandell Creighton and his review of the latter's *History of the Papacy*, both in Acton's *Historical Essays and Studies*, 1907). Acton emerges as a moral rigorist, holding that people are to be judged by their worst not their best actions; not even, it seems, by the balance of good or evil in their lives. More important, from the present point of view, is his apparent insistence that public men are to be judged as individuals, little or no allowance being made for the pecularities of their situation and circumstances; and judged by eternal standards, little or no allowance being made for moral change through time. I write 'apparent insistence' because some qualifications are made. It is recognised that public and private standards are different, though held that they are equally definite; and allowed that morality has a history, in which change takes place – conscience, we are told, is not a very old idea, and veracity is a very new one! In another essay in the same volume Acton even permits himself to concede that Henry VIII was not dissolute by the standard of contemporary monarchy. All the same he is very ready to interpret suggestions that historical figures should be judged by the standards of their own time as treachery to that morality, which it is 'the office of historical science to maintain' (p. 437; and compare, from p. 505: 'The inflexible integrity of the moral code is, to me, the secret of the authority, the dignity, the utility of history'). Ultimately he is firm in his allegiance to a conception of moral judgement as being of individuals and by eternal standards – a conception which, it will seem, is in these very respects uncongenial to history, and not certainly adequate to morality.

Consider first the idea that moral judgement has to be of individuals. This is unquestionably true of that type of judgement, which has a good claim to be centrally moral, in which the attribution of goodness or badness, rightness or wrongness, has implications for responsibility (merit or culpability). For individuals alone can be responsible in the moral sense. This is not to deny that judgements of right and wrong, good and bad, are also passed on the 'actions' and 'characters' of collectives – nations, trade unions, political parties, churches, etc. – but they cannot be moral in the same sense as can judgements on individuals, because of the difficulty of seeing how a collective can be morally responsible. Perhaps this is possible if the responsibility of a collective can be represented as reducible to (or a construction from) the responsibility of its constituent members, otherwise the responsibility of a collective has to be regarded as a legal fiction. (Moral individualism has deeper conceptual roots than methodological.) There might be a (rare) case of the former sort, if all members of a group, having fully participated in deliberation, reached the same conclusion about what the group should do. As regards the latter (i.e. responsibility as a legal fiction), collectives frequently achieve *legal* personality, becoming capable of holding property, of suing and being sued, and are to this extent responsible for their actions. But where no individual is the author of the group act, responsibility of the moral sort remains absent. Correspondingly, it is only within limits that we can conceive of a large, organised group being punished for its wrongful acts; it can be fined, but imprisonment can be visited only upon individuals, and legal dissolution seems a rather notional form of capital punishment. Individuals can be made *legally* liable for the acts of the group but, except in very special circumstances, it is hard to see how they can be held *morally* responsible for its very acts. An individual may be morally responsible for *something* whenever there is a collective act, but not normally for that selfsame act. His own acts, which alone are imputable to him as a morally responsible agent, will not be identical with those of the collective. One of the differences between moral and legal responsibility is quite precisely that collectives can be ultimate subjects of the latter, but not of the former – post-Second World War talk of collective responsibility notwithstanding (cf. R. S. Downie, pp. 90–3).

There is, then, every reason to hold that responsibility imputing moral judgements must be of individuals. Manifestly historians are interested in individuals and their actions and, so far as this goes, there is no reason why they should not pass moral judgements upon them. But, still more obviously, historians are concerned with social matters too; notoriously the individuals to whom they pay attention have to be of social significance. Historians are always also, and often much more, interested in the social structures and contingencies in which individuals and their actions acquire social importance. Rational explanations will be of an individual's actions, but the emphasis will often fall on the background against which he acts. Historical enquiries, as we have seen, do not terminate on the actions of individuals; but go past them to longer-term, more fundamental causes, by reference to which the actions are explained. Acton fears that such enquiry is apt to degenerate into the manufacturing of excuses for tyrants and criminals (as we are all prone to feel about attempts to explain the behaviour of contemporary enemies), and the danger is as real as the opposite one of simplistic moralising. But to make the passing of moral judgements the primary office of history is of a piece with an explanatory individualism (an exaggeration of the importance of individuals and their acts), which is inappropriate even in traditional political history and largely inapplicable outside it. Political history will, indeed, continue to report the actions of individuals, upon which moral judgements could be passed. But the more socially significant the individuals in question, the more they earn their places in the story, the larger will bulk the social factors which make them important, and so the more irrelevant will seem necessarily individualistic moral judgements to the main burden of history. This is by no means an argument that moral judgements should never be admitted in history, which provides innumerable possible objects for them. It is not an objection to incidental moral judgements, which can hardly be avoided if the historian is to respond to his subjects as people, in the way that is both instrumental to the objects of history and itself one of them. But it is an objection to conceiving the historian as primarily a moral judge.

An additional limitation on the above argument is that it is specific to moral judgements of the backward-looking, responsibility-imputing type – to judgements on actions already performed. Such judgements certainly occupy a large space in morality: but there are also forward-looking, action-guiding, policy-advancing judgements concerning actions yet to be performed. Or – and this is the better formulation – it may be said that many moral judgements present both forward- and backward-looking aspects, which can be differently stressed. The argument we have been considering focused on the backward-looking aspect of moral judgements, and cannot consequently have the same force against the appropriateness in history of moral judgements in which this aspect is less prominent. It advances no reason why forward-looking judgements should not be passed on the acts of collectives. The argument against supposing moral judgements, or indeed value judgements generally, of this type to be central to history – the argument against didactic conceptions of history, according to which it is primarily a source of lessons for the future (not, nowadays, a popular view) – is the argument rehearsed in several places above that history belongs to the province of theory as opposed to practice (not, of course, theory as opposed to fact). Practical affairs, and with them the forward-looking judgements of the past, are prominent in the subject matter of history, but historians typically do not address themselves to it with a view to learning practical lessons for the future.

(iii) The argument just considered, against the notion that history is the world court of justice, relied on a lack of match between the individual nature of moral responsibility and the social concern of history. I shall next consider a line of argument, founded in a genuine if one-sided conception of morality, which leads towards the conclusion, supported also by history's horror of anachronism, that the only standards by which historical agents may be judged are their own. They are not to be judged by the standards of the historian, whether he thinks these eternal or not. Acton seems not to see how the question 'By whose standards?' can arise, except as a temptation to shirk the responsibility of pronouncing moral verdicts.

It will be necessary to give some further attention to the variety of judgements comprised within morality.

(a) First may be recognised judgements on actions by which they are, for example, condemned as damaging or applauded as beneficial. The objects of judgement are actions and their results – 'external' actions as it is sometimes said, though misleadingly; for, though motives are not taken into account, intentions have to be if the judgements are to be capable of imputing responsibility and thus counting as moral. Acts may be judged by their nature and/or results, those who perform them according as they intend acts of a certain sort and/or leading to certain results. A difficulty in excluding all reference to motives is that there are few terms of commendation or condemnation from which reference to them is entirely absent. 'Courageous' and 'cruel' import actions which are both *of* a certain nature and/or tendency and *from* certain motives. The distinctions here being attended to are not built into unstudied moral speech.

(b) Next are judgements of actions on the basis of motives, results not being regarded in the judgement, though action and expected result must be encompassed in an intention for an action to be imputable at all; and there has to be a relation between motive and intention – for instance, the motive of benevolence cannot as a matter of logic lead to the performance of actions which are intentionally damaging on the whole, nor can avarice lead a person into expenditure which promise no over-compensating gains. From the present point of view a person may be praised for a courageous act (an act motivated by courage) in circumstances in which an uncontroversially better result would have come about if he had been cowardly. On any view it must be allowed that actions commendable in sense (*a*) may not be so in sense (*b*), and vice versa; but there may be differences of opinion over how the two sorts of judgements are related to each other. A tidy, perhaps over-simple view is that judgements on motives are secondary to judgements on actions; a good motive being one which tends to lead to good actions, though in particular cases it may not. Other views are that judgements on motives are at least independent, or even primary from the moral point of view; but it is rare for it to be held that judgements on actions are wholly derivative from judgements on motives.

Some eighteenth-century writers termed judgements of the former sort judgements of *natural* goodness and badness, those of the latter having a stronger claim to be judgements of *moral* goodness and badness. There is some justice in the idea that movement from (*a*) to (*b*) is towards the centre of morality, but there is still further to go in that direction.

(*c*) Sometimes an action is held to be morally good, not in the sense of being from a good motive such as courage; but as being performed from the pre-eminently moral motive of obligation or duty, i.e. as being done, in the face of difficulty or temptation to the contrary, because it was thought by the agent to be right, to be required by his own standards. Judgements of types (*a*) and (*b*) may be by standards other than the agent's, those of type (*c*) are necessarily by his own. Kant thought this the moral judgement par excellence – an exaggeration which nevertheless evokes a response in the (Protestant/bourgeois) moral consciousness, a response manifested in the respect widely accorded to conscientious action even, indeed especially, in cases where the action conscientiously performed or omitted is thought from points of view other than that of the agent to be bad or wrong.

For myself I neither maintain that, nor can see how, judgements of this third sort can be the *only* ones with a claim to be moral – there must be retained the possibility of morally questioning the standards by conforming to which agents earn moral worth in the narrow sense of the phrase. (It is not, in spite of Kant, clearly of no moral consequence from which motive other than the sense of duty a person acts, nor indeed is it morally indifferent whether what is done is intentionally or in fact beneficial or harmful.) But it is a type of judgement with an important place in our conception of morality, and one which probably obtains greater prominence in times of moral uncertainty – people who are doubtful what is right may yet be sure that people ought to do what they think right. Strictly speaking, it is not a judgement entirely by the agent's own standards; but rather one in accordance with the second order standard that conformity to the agent's own standards, whatever they might be, is a major or at least distinctive form of moral goodness. The second order standard is formal in the sense that it accommodates any first order or substantive standard an agent may have. The only substantive standards in the case will be the agent's own. Emphasis on this type of judgement as especially moral is thus congenial to the view that, *morally* speaking, only an historical agent's own standards are admissible, which carries the consequence that the historian's personal substantive standards should not enter the picture.

The argument sketched for this conclusion depends on an authentic, if partial, conception of *morality*. In the present book, however, the concern ought rather to be with arguments drawn from the nature of *history*. In fact it is apparent that a thoroughgoing historical approach to substantive standards, a recognition of how they change through time, will both reinforce and be reinforced by a morality-based view that the historian's own substantive standards should be kept out of history. The need to accord independent, even if not supreme, value to an agent's acting on his own standards (to his conscientiousness) is most likely to become evident in cases where one thinks his substantive standards wrong or misguided. A somewhat sophisticated moral attitude is here required, involving stepping aside from one's own standards, in recognising that the agent has and is guided by his own. It is the harder to achieve such moral self-abnegation in proportion as the agent's standards are felt to be wrong, bad or bizarre. Conscientious objection to military service emerges in precisely the circumstances in which it is most likely to be dismissed as cowardly or subversive: conscientious objection to blood transfusions and vaccination seems ridiculous. It is hard to respect standards as moral when one cannot fit them into a context in which they make sense. The historically ignorant or inexperienced consequently have difficulty in allowing that historical personages had, and felt obliged by, standards of their own – difficulty, that is, in seeing them as moral agents like themselves. Correspondingly, however, it is a central feature of historical activity that it should tend to remedy such purblindness by filling in the sort of context that enables the people of the past to be seen as exercising moral agency. The historian, operating in a characteristic manner, may thus enable past people to be seen as moral agents; but not in a way which involves his passing moral judgements of his own on them. Moral and historical sophistication, the feeling that it is as morally inappropriate to judge people by standards not their own as it is historically preposterous to attribute to them standards they did not have, combine to discourage the passing of substantive moral judgements on historical personages, and altogether to prevent the historian from regarding it as his main business so to do.

I have tried to isolate a conception of moral judgement which, however small its claim to be the whole truth about morality, is congenial to history. Reference to it contributes to the explanation of the common doctrine that moral judgements in history should be by the standards of the time referred to, a doctrine which seems otherwise undetermined and arbitrary – if moral judgements are admissible at all in history, why restrict them in this way? But it is now possible to see how a conception of morality can reinforce a distaste for anachronism, and how these can readily combine with the doctrine, discussed in the previous section, that moral judgements should appear in its history only in inverted commas, in the subject matter not the treatment. It can be seen too how this conception of moral judgement undermines simplistic notions of moral progress (of which, in fairness it should be said, Acton is not guilty), which are themselves an abundant source of dismissive moral judgements on historical agents, and consequently an important part of what is objected to as moral judgement in history. According to the view we have been considering, moral merit is manifested in an agent's living up to his *own* standards. Moral progress is possible in an individual, but just because some later period has standards which *we* think superior it will not follow that there has been progress from the earlier to the later period. Everybody, regardless of time or place, has the same opportunity of attaining, or falling short of, moral excellence. (Collingwood reaches a similar result about the possibility of moral progress in a rather different way. It depends on an individual's success or unsuccess in coping with the particular problems confronting him. See his *Essays in the Philosophy of History*, published in

1965 but in fact written in the 1920s; however, section VII of part V of the later *Idea of History* does recognise a sense in which there may be progress in moral institutions.)

(iv) The first section of this chapter considered the notion that history might be purely factual, concluding that the most which could plausibly be maintained was that the life values of the historian should be excluded, although not supporting much optimism about the prospects of total success. In the present section, the topic so far has been moral judgements; and the aim to set out the rationale of the view that, whilst they cannot be excluded altogether, the pronouncing of them should not be considered a major task of history, and that they should be by the standards of the time studied. The moral are, however, only one species of life values; and some attention must be given to at any rate aesthetic and religious values as well. In so far as such values are, like the moral, capable of being perceived as in some way absolute or of eternal validity, they raise the same sort of problem. Political values, on the other hand, except to the extent to which they are included in the moral, are much more readily allowed to be relative to time and place.

How far does the case of aesthetics parallel that of morality? I am not here concerned with histories of art, for which the principles of selection are bound to be determined by the historian's own aesthetic preferences or those of his day, with the result that a great deal of space may quite properly be given to works which were quite insignificant in their time –judgements of relative importance in all specialist history are relative to the specialist point of view. My question is rather whether aesthetic concerns may be congenial or uncongenial to history in the way moral concerns have been found to be.

The answer obviously will depend on conceptions of the aesthetic, which are at least as variable and controversial as those of the moral. A further difficulty is that the moral and the aesthetic tend to be conceived in contradistinction to one another, so that the boundary between them is capable of shifting. Judgements on people's characters and qualities (their virtues), which at times have been held to be centrally moral, have at other times (including now) been regarded as aesthetic. For present purposes, however, it will suffice to take as typically aesthetic those value judgements of which the objects are works of art. This is not to deny that notions of art and the aesthetic have themselves a history; or to assert that what *we* think of as the art of prehistoric cave-dwellers, ancient Greeks, medieval Christians, West African tribesmen, had the same place in their societies as art in ours.

If the aesthetic is thus delimited as having to do with the appraisal of works of art, one difference between it and the moral becomes at once apparent. In morals we are all practitioners, whereas in aesthetics most of us are spectators only. This is partly a conceptual, partly a sociological point. It is of the essence of morality that all should be participants; but that there should be a few producers and many consumers of art, though very much the way it is in our society, is most certainly not logically necessary, and perhaps not sociologically inevitable. The moralist considers conduct as an agent, recognising that what he says about that of others has implications for his own, and vice versa. The maker of aesthetic judgements, on the other hand, approaches art as a consumer, concerned with what he and others can find in it or get out of it. (I am not denying that practitioners in the arts make value judgements too.) This is why the value put on catholicity of taste is greater in aesthetics than in morality. It is true that there are still, as there always have been, 'moralists in criticism' (to use S. Hampshire's phrase, 1954, x); and there are too, perhaps increasingly, aestheticians in morality, who place high positive value on 'experiments in living' (Mill, 1859, ch. III) and diversity in individual life styles (P. F. Strawson, 1961). It is, however, widely felt that the rigid exclusions of the former tend perversely to restrict the range of possible aesthetic responses; and I, if no one else, sometimes fear that there is a risk of the practical essence of morality being eroded by fashionable moral aestheticism. In any event, even when allowance is made for the above qualification, the tendency of the account I have been giving of the difference between aesthetic and moral attitudes is to suggest that the former are less uncongenial to history than the latter were found in a certain respect to be. The moralist, as a moralist, is prone to judge people of the past by his own standards; yet history requires that, without ceasing to regard them as moral agents, he should refrain from applying his substantive standards to them – a requirement which finds support in a certain conception of morality ((c) above), but a difficult feat none the less. The aesthetician (if the term may be misused as shorthand for anyone with strong aesthetic interests), on the other hand, conceives his task less as that of judging the art works of the ages by his own supposedly eternal standards – comparative evaluations, a single order of merit, will often seem to him to be impossible – than as trying to see and point out the different sorts of value in them, thus facilitating the appreciation of the widest possible range of works.

Whereas moralistic zeal is an obstacle to discharging the historical duty of seeing the past in its own terms, aesthetic concern if anything smoothes the way for it. There is not, indeed, any guarantee that we shall succeed in appreciating the art of the past in exactly the same way as contemporaries did – often we cannot; but the more we understand about the way it was produced, the purposes it served, the more we become able to appreciate it in *our* terms. It is true that we can hardly hope to understand the paintings of cave-dwellers in their terms, yet we still think we can appreciate them aesthetically; but there is little doubt that we should welcome any information that might become available about the way of life in which they were produced as tending to extend and deepen our appreciation. Against this there is a strain in philosophical aesthetics and critical theory according to which all 'background' information, cultural or biographical, is irrelevant. *Aesthetic* appreciation, some hold, must be founded exclusively on features of the works themselves. Such a view is intelligible as the outcome of attempts to isolate the essence of the aesthetic, or as a reaction against moralistic excesses in criticism; but it is contradicted by the virtually universal practice of those interested in art, who surely find themselves unable to resist making use of any background information they can find.

I will conclude this section with a glance at religion as a possible further source of life values. It differs from the cases of morals and aesthetics in that a personal religion is not nowadays to be taken for granted as an essential part of the equipment of an historian. He cannot fail to have a morality, since this is an aspect of being human and living in society, nor will he want to be, or to be thought to be, a philistine; but he may well have no religion whatever. It was claimed in chapter III above that religious partisanship is no longer felt to be an obstacle to objectivity in history. The present question is how far an unbelieving historian is competent to deal with the religious values which are bound sometimes to crop up in his subject matter. It might be thought difficult for him to assess their influence on those who held them. There is a danger of underestimating it, and a complementary danger of exaggerating it by over-compensation. Roman religion, according to Collingwood (1946, p. 329), is too remote from our own experience for us to be able to reconstruct in our minds what it meant to the Romans. It is even a matter of difficulty to think oneself into seventeenth-century religious attitudes – that of Hobbes, for instance, a reputed atheist, who fills the latter two books of *Leviathan* with arguments from Scripture and produces in all apparent seriousness one of the standard arguments for the existence of God. In the next century Hume's infidelity is easier to understand; the difficulty is rather to grasp the inwardness of the sufficiently wordly Boswell's horror and incredulity at Hume's equanimity in the face of death. Hypotheses of insincerity are often cloaks for want of understanding.

The question is whether there is a problem of principle over the possibility of understanding the religion of the past; or only a difficulty which, with more or less labour, different people will overcome with differing degrees of success. It is not easy to give a simple answer. My inclination is to say *both* that there is no general problem of principle *and* that our present conception of religion may incline us to ask questions which for some periods cannot be answered. As regards the former point, the notion that there is a problem of principle derives, I suspect, from forgetting the necessary truth that history is dependent on evidence, that it is (as we have noted Collingwood insisting) an inferential not an intuitive study. Reconstructing attitudes involves more than putting oneself in another person's place. Hypotheses have to be framed, and verified or falsified by turning up new evidence or rearranging old. Lack of imagination, including lack of religious awareness deriving from personal inexperience of religion, may make it difficult or impossible to think up hypotheses; but, once a start has been made, descriptive and explanatory claims have to be assessed in the light of evidence, in ways open to non-religious and religious historians alike. Certain sorts of religious activity may remain opaque to some contemporary historians. But it may be questioned whether the problem is peculiar to religion. It is rather a facet of the platitudinous general truth that no one person can be equally at home in all departments of human activity.

With regard to the second point, however, it must be re-emphasised that the boundaries between different domains of life values are not fixed. The religious frontier has varied a great deal. The word 'religion', as applied over time, refers to a greater variety of activities than do 'morality' and 'aesthetics', activities which have been integrated with others in different ways and in different degrees in different times and places. It is a feature of our own secular society that religion presents itself as a distinct activity, a socially optional extra. Manifestly it has not always done so, and it will be impossible to understand religion as a distinct activity when it was not one. The categories in terms of which philosophical questions are framed themselves change through time; with the result that we may, when there is gross mismatch between now and then, be led to ask questions which cannot be answered.

4. Progress

So far the present chapter has been concerned with questions about the propriety of historians' passing value judgements on particular individuals, institutions, episodes, events within history. I shall conclude it, and the book, with a discussion of the feasibility of passing judgement on the course of history generally. It has been maintained sometimes that the course of history is generally for the good, a progress; other times that it is generally for the bad, a regress or deterioration. Notoriously the former, optimistic evaluation was common in the nineteenth century; the latter, pessimistic one in the ancient world. Hegelians and Marxists see history as progressive; for Plato it was retrogressive. Cyclical views too have frequently been maintained, both in antiquity and later. Vico took this sort of line, as does Toynbee in so far as he holds that civilisations, even if they do not exactly have a fixed life span, nevertheless exhibit a common pattern of development and decay.

Progress is by definition change from worse to better; decay from better to worse. At a superficial level, at least, there ought to be no difficulty in making sense of these notions. Surely we are entitled to speak of progress whenever we are prepared to judge a change to have been for the better, of regress when we suppose it to have been for the worse. But difficulties concerning both knowledge and evaluation (of which the latter are the more serious) crowd in as soon as any attempt is made to apply the notions outside narrow fields and short periods of time.

To take the knowledge difficulties first: there must be considerable doubt about the justifiability of claims to know that historical developments over wide areas and long periods of time have been in a certain direction or in accordance with a certain pattern. Intellectually delightful though they may be, such purported synopses look more like patterns it has been decided to impose upon history than anything that might be read off from what happened there, the detail of which for all periods no one person can command. There is, as was emphasised above, the possibility of insecurely founded generalisations serving historical purposes by structuring argument and research; but it is very doubtful whether generalisations wide-ranging enough to support notions of general progress or decay are often very useful in this way. (The materialist conception of history may be an exception, at least up to a point.) Generalisations about the whole of the past are as unlikely to be useful as they are unlikely to be true – their prospects are worse, not better, if they are supposed to cover the whole of the future too. H. A. L. Fisher was wholly right, in the well-known preface to his *History of Europe* (1936), to repudiate the idea that progress might be a law of nature. It will appear much less certain that he was right in conceding that the 'fact of progress' could be read 'plain and large on the page of history' – an alleged fact of regress would be in no better case. Valuations with the objectivity, immutability and scope of application necessary to give substance to such supposed 'facts' are by no means certainly available.

Judgements of progress and regress which do no more than reflect an individual's purely personal preferences or value judgements need be of no interest to anyone else. Any 'facts' of progress or regress it may make sense to talk about must reflect value judgements which individuals cannot arbitrarily set aside. The implication of this is that notions of progress and regress are most clearly applicable in narrow fields, with integral standards of value, which are both determinate and invariant over time. Elsewhere serious problems arise in the shape of clashes between and changes of standards, and of incommensurabilities between values of different kinds.

The least dubious applications for the notions of progress and regress are, accordingly, certain academic subjects, with built-in standards of relevance and attainment, and a correspondingly high degree of professional solidarity among practitioners. (The present concern is less with the question of where progress/regress has occurred than with the question of where they apply; but, of course, where it is clear that the notions do apply, it will often also be very clear whether progress has or has not taken place.) Mathematics, despite the length of its history, presents itself as a subject with firm and clear internal standards. No doubt detailed acquaintance with this history would reveal that there had been some change in them; there have certainly been periods of innovation and others of consolidation, and there may well not be perfect unanimity among present-day practitioners. On the other hand, still firmer and clearer standards would be found, and with them a correspondingly sounder basis for judgements of progress and regress, by considering particular branches of the subject rather than mathematics generally. None of this entails that progress in mathematics has been continuous, that it is entirely independent of general social circumstances, or that it is certain to go on. The sole claim is that the subject is one to which ideas of progress and regress, 'objective' progress and regress, have application.

Some of the natural sciences would normally be held to be others. I earlier characterised a developed science as one to which principles of selection are internal, as they are not to anything like the same degree in history. To this extent there is a flavour of tautology about the doctrine that progress and regress are intelligible in relation to the sciences. They would not be sciences if this were not so. But it is not tautological to observe that studies of some aspects of natural phenomena have achieved this scientific status; and doubts about whether we enjoy clear conceptions of what to count as progress in social science are tantamount to doubts whether any genuine science of society has yet been constructed.

It may be suspected that in expressing the above admittedly very conventional opinion, a simplistic, external view is being taken of natural science and its history. Justice, it may be held, is not done to Popper's contention, more than once adverted to above, that science is not just a matter of piling up stocks of highly confirmed generalisations, but more one in which audacity and imagination in hypothesis is followed by strenuous attempts at refutation. Nor has any account been taken of the distinction emphasised by T. S. Kuhn (1962; 2nd edition 1970) between periods of 'normal science', during which there is incremental progress by accepted standards, and revolutionary changes of 'paradigms' (i.e., roughly, methodological orientations) in which a scientific community, in ways necessarily not governed by antecedently accepted standards, comes to accept new paradigms. Kuhn's account of scientific revolutions may suggest that the distinction, drawn principally in chapter III above, between standards internal to science and contingent consensus on principles of selection within schools of historians, is less than absolute. (It is interesting that Kuhn's conclusions result from his attempting to improve upon a prevalent 'Whiggism' – to adopt Butterfield's expression – in the history of science, i.e. from his opposition to the practice of ignoring or disparaging those 'reactionaries' who opposed or did not contribute to developments directly reflected in present-day science.) Some have read Kuhn as making a case for relativism, as representing paradigm change as an arational process in which a scientific community comes arbitrarily to adopt a new paradigm, which is then imposed by essentially authoritarian procedures – control of education, entry, publication outlets – on would-be members. Passages in Kuhn's writings no doubt lend credence to such interpretations, and his apparent suggestion that observations are somehow determined by the theories they are supposed to verify or falsify at the very least needs careful handling; but I do not myself see him as radically relativist. *Scientific* communities have for him a special character, a commitment to rationality and a standing interest in opening up new dimensions of soluble problems (i.e. inaugurating new periods of normal science), in the light of which paradigm changes can intelligibly be held to be progressive or, no doubt, regressive. Kuhn recognises, as Whig historians of science tend to forget, that scientific revolutions, like other sorts, may bring losses as well as gains. He questions the significance of holding science to be progressive in the sense of getting ever nearer to the whole truth about reality, because he is not persuaded that reality can be characterised independently of particular scientific findings. But science may be, and conspicuously has been, progressive in so far as scientific communities have notions of scientific merit such that paradigm changes can meaningfully be judged to be for the good.

If the conditions for the intelligibility of judgements of progress and regress are at all like those I have been attempting to illustrate, it is clear that they are not fully met in subjects like history and philosophy, which nevertheless aspire to truth and rationality. Here relevance and objectivity are conspicuously relative to points of view not internal to the subjects. The most it has been possible to argue for on the other side is that there may be schools, within which there are conceptions of what matters and what needs to be done, which will present themselves to members as objective. There have for a long time been writers who interpret the existence of different schools of thought as an aspect of the pre-scientific condition of history and philosophy. There is truth in this, in so far as it appears that a pre-history of competing schools of thought has often preceded the establishment of a branch of natural science. But, according to the viewpoint of the present book, it would be wrong to proceed to the inference that the present 'pre-scientific' state of affairs in history and philosophy might terminate in their finding the sure path of science and ceasing to exist as they are now known. New sciences might grow out of history as they have from philosophy, sciences which develop their own techniques and concepts, grow away from ordinary patterns of thinking, develop internal standards, and thus admit the notions of progress and regress. But, whether this happens or not, I have suggested that there will always remain a need for history much as it now is, a response to a form of curiosity which can be satisfied in no other way; and, though it has not really been argued here, the same is true of philosophy. The sciences which grow out of it cannot replace it, if only because no one of them can deal with philosophical questions concerning their relations to one another and to human concerns generally.

Another clear field for the application of ideas of progress and regress is the development of utensils, tools, instruments, apparatus, techniques – technical matters generally, it may be said. Here again is a narrowness of concern and, in the relatively constant purposes served by technical devices and procedures, a source of relatively determinate standards of value capable of enduring through time. Sometimes, it is true, claims that there has been technical progress are resisted on account of the costs which have been involved, for example in the consumption of scarce resources or the pollution of the environment; but such objections are often misconceived, in that the object of representing a development as a case of *technical* progress may be quite precisely to exclude such wider considerations, and the uncertainties about and conflicts between standards which come with them. Technical progress may, from wider points of view, be for the bad, without ceasing to be *technical* progress. Economic progress, which has to do with the better or worse allocation of resources among a variety of different ends, and with striking a balance between shorter- and longer-term considerations, is consequently harder to assess. Those who pay the costs find it hard to agree with those who reap the benefits that progress has unequivocally taken place. Typically, in fact, economic progress tends to be assessed from a point of view more confined than that of the whole of mankind (usually from that of a class or nation), and when thus restricted in scope judgements of economic progress or regress lose much of their indeterminacy. The economic is a wider area of concern than the technical; but the term 'economic' is often used with restrictive intent, to confine attention to changes in the material wealth of a group, excluding the possibility of increases or decreases in wealth being held to be offset by opposite changes in relation to other values. Compared with the undecidabilities attending the notion of progress on the whole, economic progress (or regress) is a pretty straightforward affair.

We may turn next to the question of progress in art, where Collingwood, who discusses it in several places, is strikingly ambivalent. On the one hand, he seems inclined to hold that there are no periods of bad or good art, only periods worse or better understood (1965 and 1946). On the other hand, in his *Autobiography* (1939, ch. 11), he is insistent that, in comparison with the art of both the pre-Roman period and the Celtic revival, Romano-British art was bad. I interpret this inconsistency as a matter of his failing to maintain the paradoxical position, to which he is strongly inclined, that the possibility of progress in art is excluded, because the art of any period has to be good by the standards of that period. Such plausibility as this position has derives from the way in which art is far removed from the situations of mathematics, science and matters technical. In those cases sense can be made of the notions of long-term progress and regress because there are standards relatively fixed and stable through time. In art, on the other hand, it is tempting to suppose that substantive standards change in step with the works produced contemporaneously with them. (The thought that our only access to the standards is via the works makes the temptation logically irresistible.) If this were really so, there could be no progress or regress in art; but it is impossible to accept it as anything like the whole truth, and Collingwood himself did not consistently do so. If it be allowed, as it is by Collingwood, that it makes sense for a practitioner to think of his own works as better or worse, and as capable of improvement, then it is surely possible for there to be judgements of better or worse between works of different contemporary artists; and, if that, then surely also among works of non-contemporaries not too widely separated in time. Unless it is to be held that nobody other than the artist himself is entitled to judge a work, and I do not think Collingwood intended this, I do not see how the possibility of discerning progress or regress within artistic traditions over moderate periods of time can be ruled out. This does not, of course, establish the possibility of meaningful comparative judgements between works which are culturally and temporally very far apart.

My argument for the possibility of modest judgements of progress or regress in art, about which people with confidence in their aesthetic standards may not feel very doubtful, is governed by two thoughts expressed in the previous section. One is that a generous responsiveness to a variety of standards is characteristic of the aesthetic attitude as we at present understand it. The other is a fair measure of scepticism about the possibility of firm, culturally invariant, purely aesthetic standards.

Art is surely much harder to wrench from its cultural setting than are mathematics, natural science, technical affairs; and long-term, trans-cultural conceptions of artistic progress and deterioration are correspondingly harder to make sense of.

With regard to moral progress, some attention has already been paid to a conception of morality, which is such that the principal concern is the extent to which an individual lives up to his own standards of right and wrong, good and bad. So far as this goes, moral progress is entirely an individual matter. Beyond this (and I have maintained that it can hardly be the whole truth about morality) the fundamental obstacle to making sense of moral progress is the way that substantive moral standards change. There is, indeed, a practical side to morality, which makes it easier to relate the content of a group's standards to its social circumstances than is the case with aesthetic standards. Moral variation has a good deal of rhyme and reason to it; but even so we mostly do not think that transportation to Rome would oblige us to adopt Roman standards of what we ought to do. There are conflicts as well as explicable differences between the moral standards of different times and places. Relative to the standards of a time and a place there might be progress in the extent to which they are accepted and acted upon. But why should *we* count that as progress if our standards are different? Again, by *our* standards, we may discern progress in periods which were increasingly discontented with themselves, and regress in complacent ones; but why should anyone with different standards be impressed by this? Some moral changes cannot in any objective way be held to be progressive or regressive. There is, however, one sense in which there is some possibility of a widely recognisable progress or regress in morality, compatibly with considerable variation in and/or disagreement about substantive standards. Our conception of morality has certain 'formal' features (i.e. features relatively stable through substantive variation), which make it possible to regard certain general changes in attitudes to conduct in a society as progressive or, for that matter, regressive – progressive or regressive in the sense of becoming more or less close to the authentically moral. A change in the direction of universality, extending moral status (the capacity for rights and duties) to wider and wider groups, and ideally to all people as such, would generally be regarded as progressive. So would a tendency towards internalising rules or ideals of conduct; they are, at least arguably, not properly moral for people who feel entitled not to observe them if only there is no one to see. (This feature would, for instance, tend to distinguish moral rules from rules of etiquette, which it would be senseless to suppose people ought to obey when on their own.) Even this conception of morality, of which I have attempted only the sketchiest indication, although characteristic of 'developed' modern societies, can be called into question. It has a history and reflects social conditions, and changes in the direction of it – from closed to open societies, in Popper's terms – can be evaluated by intelligent men not as progress but as deterioration.

It may be asked whether it is possible to recognise progress or regress in institutions of moral significance, for example property or marriage, which even Collingwood allowed. There can be no doubt that existing arrangements may come to be felt defective in relation to existing notions, say, of fairness as between the sexes; and a change in them accordingly recognised, by the same standards, as progressive. Judgements that such changes increase welfare are, however, of much more dubious significance, since notions of welfare are to a very high degree internal to the institutions supposedly judged by reference to them. People opposed to divorce, for instance, will not see the liberalisation of the divorce laws as increasing welfare. Much supposed utilitarian argument is circular for this reason.

The tendency of the above survey of the prospects of finding application for the ideas of progress and regress is plainly to call into question the intelligibility of any claim that there has been progress or regress over a period, let alone any more extravagant claim that there always must be – progress or regress on the whole, that is, in the conditions of human life generally, not in a particular department of them, nor as they are assessed from a partial, non-inevitable point of view. In any change from one time to another, even in a nation, still more in the world, there will be alterations which are (judged to be) for the better, and others which are for the worse. There will be *both* progress and deterioration, and no doubt neutral changes too. But what rule could be set up for balancing the pluses against the minuses, for cancelling out? There is no way of obtaining an over-all, resultant valuation of the total change. Values are not always commensurable, so that it can be worked out to what extent decline in respect of one may be offset by increase in another. To *choose* to regard all values as commensurable, for example by adopting the hedonist position that all value changes are to be interpreted as changes in the pleasures and pains (happiness) of those involved, apart from its inherent difficulties, will not make the objective assessment of over-all value changes possible, because hedonism is a partial viewpoint which not everybody shares. (It may be doubted whether any other commensurability-entailing value theory is in any better case.) There is, finally, very little in the apparently attractive idea that a period may sometimes be objectively worse or better than another, in the sense that in the former basic human disvalues (things which *nobody* thinks good in themselves) – slaughter, disease, famine – are more or less prevalent than in the latter. It cannot be taken for granted that such disvalues will, always and everywhere, be regarded as having overriding importance. States of affairs, characterised by these disvalues in high degrees, may be perceived as the inevitable and therefore acceptable consequences of the service of other ruling values, say, in a warrior society.

In particular areas and from particular points of view we can be confident in judging that there has been progress or its opposite – such, and such alone, are the 'facts' of progress and regress. With regard to progress and regress on the whole, however, there is only the subjective choice between optimism and pessimism.

Works Cited in the Text

Abbreviations

ASP: *Aristotelian Society – Proceedings*.
ASS: *Aristotelian Society – Supplementary Volume*.

ACTON, H. B. (1955), *The Illusion of the Epoch* (London).

ACTON, Lord (1907), *Historical Essays and Studies* (London).

ARON, R. (1938, 1948), *Introduction to the Philosophy of History*; English translation of the 1948 revision (London, 1961).

ASHLEY, M. (1968), *Churchill as Historian* (London).

ATKINSON, R. F. (1972), 'Explanation in History', *ASP*, LXXII.

AYER, A. J. (1936, 1946), *Language, Truth and Logic* (2nd edition, London, 1946).

—— (1952), 'Statements about the Past', *ASP*, LII.

—— (1956), *The Problem of Knowledge* (London).

BEARD, C. A. (1935), 'The Case for Historical Relativism'; reprinted in Nash (1969); originally called 'That Noble Dream'.

BECKER, C. L. (1955), 'What Are Historical Facts?'; reprinted in Nash (1969).

BLAKE, C. (1955), 'Can History Be Objective?', *Mind*, LXIV; reprinted in Gardiner (1959).

BLOCH, M. (1941), *The Historian's Craft*; English translation (Manchester, 1954).

BOBER, M. M. (1927, 1948), *Karl Marx's Interpretation of History* (2nd, enlarged, edition, Cambridge, Mass., 1948).

BRADLEY, F. H. (1874), 'The Presuppositions of Critical History'; reprinted in *Collected Essays of F. H. Bradley*, vol. I (Oxford, 1935).

BRODBECK, M. (1958), 'Methodological Individualisms: Definition and Reduction'; reprinted in Dray (1966).

BUTLER, R. J. (1959), 'Other Dates', *Mind*, LXVIII.

BUTTERFIELD, H. (1931), *The Whig Interpretation of History* (London).
—— (1955), *Man on His Past* (Cambridge).
CARR, E. H. (1961), *What Is History?* (London; paperback edition, Harmondsworth, 1964).
CHATEAUBRIAND, F.-R. de (1802), *Le Génie du Christianisme* (Paris).
COLLINGWOOD, R. G. (1938), 'On the So-called Idea of Causation', *ASP*, XXXVIII.
—— (1939), *Autobiography* (Oxford).
—— (1940), *Essay on Metaphysics* (Oxford).
—— (1946), *The Idea of History* (Oxford).
—— (1965), *Essays in the Philosophy of History* (Austin, Texas).
CROCE, B. (1938), *History as the Story of Liberty*; English translation (London, 1941).
DANTO, A. C. (1965), *Analytical Philosophy of History* (Cambridge).
DOWNIE, R. S. (1971), *Roles and Values* (London).
DRAY, W. (1957), *Laws and Explanation in History* (Oxford).
—— (1963), 'The Historical Explanation of Actions Reconsidered'; reprinted in Gardiner (1974).
—— (1964), *Philosophy of History* (Englewood Cliffs, New Jersey).
—— (1966, ed.), *Philosophical Analysis and History* (New York).
ELTON, G. R. (1967), *The Practice of History* (Sydney; paperback edition, London, 1969).
—— (1970), *Political History* (New York and London).
ENGELS, F. (1878), *Anti-Dühring*; English translation (Moscow, 1954).
FAIN, H. (1970), *Between Philosophy and History* (Princeton, New Jersey).
FEUER, L. S. (1969, ed.), *Marx and Engels: Basic Writings in Philosophy and Politics* (London, 1969).
FISHER, H. A. L. (1936), *History of Europe* (London).
GALLIE, W. B. (1964), *Philosophy and the Historical Understanding* (London).
GARDINER, P. (1952), *The Nature of Historical Explanation* (Oxford).
—— (1959, ed.), *Theories of History* (Urbana, Illinois).
—— (1974, ed.), *The Philosophy of History* (Oxford).
GELLNER, E. (1956), 'Holism vs Understanding in History and Sociology'; reprinted in Gardiner (1959).
—— (1959), *Words and Things* (London).
GEYL, P. (1955), *Use and Abuse of History* (New Haven, Connecticut).
GINSBERG, M. (1954), 'The Individual and Society'; reprinted in his *The Diversity of Morals* (London, 1956).
GOLDSTEIN, L. J. (1976), *Historical Knowing* (Austin, Texas).

GOSSE, E. (1907), *Father and Son*; reprint (Oxford, 1974).

GREEN, J. R. (1878–80), *A History of the English People* (London).

HALE, J. R. (1967, ed.), *The Evolution of British Historiography* (London).

HAMPSHIRE, S. (1954), 'Logic and Appreciation', in W. Elton (ed.), *Aesthetics and Language* (Oxford, 1954).

HART, H. L. A. and HONORÉ, A. M. (1959), *Causation in the Law* (Oxford).

HAYEK, F. A. von (1942–4), *The Counter-Revolution of Science*; reprinted (Urbana, Illinois, 1952).

HEMPEL, C. J. (1942), 'The Function of General Laws in History'; reprinted in Gardiner (1959) and in other collections.

—— (1963), 'Reasons and Covering Laws in Historical Explanations'; reprinted in Gardiner (1974).

HOSPERS, J. (1956, 1967), *An Introduction to Philosophical Analysis*, 2nd edition, 1967 (London).

HUME, D. (1739–40), *A Treatise of Human Nature*, 1888 edition (Oxford).

KUHN, T. S. (1962, 1970), *The Structure of Scientific Revolutions*, 2nd edition, 1970 (Chicago).

LEFF, G. (1961), *The Tyranny of Concepts* (London).

—— (1969), *History and Social Theory* (London).

LUCAS, P. G. (1956), 'Explanation in History', *ASS*, xxx.

McCULLAGH, C. B. (1969), 'Narrative and Explanation in History', *Mind*, LXXVIII.

MACKIE, J. L. (1974), *The Cement of the Universe* (Oxford).

MANDELBAUM, M. (1938), *The Problem of Historical Knowledge* (New York).

—— (1955), 'Societal Facts'; reprinted in Gardiner (1959).

—— (1957), 'Societal Laws'; reprinted in Dray (1966).

MARROU, H.-I. (1954, 1962), *De la Connaissance Historique*, 4th edition, 1962 (Paris).

MARWICK, A. (1970), *The Nature of History* (London).

MARX, K. (1850), *Class Struggles in France*; English translation (London, 1937).

—— (1852) *The Eighteenth Brumaire of Louis Bonaparte*; English translation (New York, 1926).

—— (1859), Preface to *A Critique of Political Economy*; English translation (London, 1971).

—— (1867), *Capital*, vol. I; English translation (Moscow, 1954).

MARX, K. and ENGELS, F. (1846), *The German Ideology*; English translation (Moscow, 1964).

        Relevant excerpts from these works are to be found in Feuer (1969) – see above. Page references to these works in the text are to this collection.

MEILAND, J. W. (1965), *Skepticism and Historical Knowledge* (New York, 1965).

MILL, J. S. (1859), *On Liberty*; reprinted in *Utilitarianism etc.* (London, 1910); paperback edition, ed. G. Himmelfarb (Harmondsworth, 1974).

NAGEL, E. (1961), *The Structure of Science* (London).

NASH, R. H. (1969, ed.), *Ideas of History* (New York).

NOWELL-SMITH, P. H. (1957), 'Are Historical Events Unique?', *ASP*, LVII.

—— (1971), *What Actually Happened* (Lawrence, Kansas).

OAKESHOTT, M. (1933), *Experience and its Modes* (Cambridge).

—— (1962), 'The Activity of Being an Historian', in his *Rationalism and Politics* (London).

PEARS, D. (1956), 'Time, Truth and Inference', *ASP*, LVI.

PLAMENATZ, J. (1961), *Man and Society*, vol. II (London).

PLEKHANOV, G. (1895), *The Development of the Monist View of History*; English translation (Moscow, 1956).

—— (1897), *The Materialist Conception of History*; English translation (New York, 1940).

—— (1898), *The Role of the Individual in History*; English translation (New York, 1940).

PLUMB, J. H. (1969), *The Death of the Past* (London).

POPPER, K. R. (1934), *The Logic of Scientific Discovery*; English translation (London, 1959).

—— (1944–5, 1957), *The Poverty of Historicism*; articles in *Economica* subsequently published in book form (London, 1957; 2nd edition, 1961).

—— (1945), *The Open Society and Its Enemies*, vol. II (London, with subsequent editions).

RANKE, L. von (1824), *History of the Latin and Teutonic Nations*; English translation (London, 1915).

RENIER, G. J. (1950), *History: Its Purpose and Method* (London).

RUSSELL, B. (1921), *The Analysis of Mind* (London).

RYLE, G. (1949), *The Concept of Mind* (London).

SCRIVEN, M. (1966), 'Causes, Connections, and Conditions in History', in Dray (1966).

STRAWSON, P. F. (1961), 'Social Morality and Individual Ideal', *Philosophy*, XXXVI.

TAYLOR, A. J. P. (1961), *The Origins of the Second World War* (London; paperback edition, Harmondsworth, 1964).

—— (1965), *English History, 1914–1945* (Oxford).

THOMSON, D. (1950), *England in the Nineteenth Century* (London).

—— (1969), *The Aims of History* (London).

THUCYDIDES, *The Peloponnesian War*; English translation (Harmondsworth, 1972).

TOYNBEE, A. (1934–54), *A Study of History*, 10 vols (Oxford); abridgement of vols I–VI and VII–X by D. C. Somervell (Oxford, 1946, 1957).

TREVELYAN, G. M. (1930), *Clio: A Muse* (London).

WALSH, W. H. (1951, 1967), *An Introduction to the Philosophy of History* (London; 3rd edition, revised, 1967).

—— (1967) 'Colligatory Concepts in History'; reprinted in Gardiner (1974).

WATKINS, J. W. N. (1957), 'Historical Explanation in the Social Sciences'; reprinted in Gardiner (1959).

WHITE, M. (1943), 'Historical Explanation'; reprinted in Gardiner (1959).

—— (1965), *Foundations of Historical Knowledge* (New York and London).

WISDOM, J. (1952), 'Metaphysics', in *Other Minds* (Oxford).

WISDOM, J. O. (1953), *The Unconscious Origins of Berkeley's Philosophy* (London).

WRIGHT, G. H. von (1971), *Explanation and Understanding* (Ithaca, N.Y.).

Index